BEHAVING DECENTLY

Kurt Vonnegut's Humanism

© 2022 Humanist Press LLC
1821 Jefferson Place NW
Washington, DC 20036
www.humanistpress.com

Wayne Laufert
Behaving Decently: Kurt Vonnegut's Humanism

All rights reserved. No part of this book may be reproduced in whole or in part without written permission from the publisher, except in the case of brief quotations embodied in critical articles and reviews; nor may any part of this book be reprinted or reproduced or utilized in any form or by any electronic, mechanical, or other means, now known or hereafter invented, including photocopying and recording, or in any information storage or retrieval system, without written permission from Humanist Press, LLC.

Cover and interior design by Sharon McGill.
Cover image of Vonnegut used by permission of The Wylie Agency LLC. Comic art adaptation from *Cat's Cradle* on pages 32–33 by Wayne Laufert and Sharon McGill.

Published by: Humanist Press LLC. Sections of this book have previously appeared in the *Humanist* magazine. Full copyright and permissions listings appear on pages 252–254.

Print ISBN: 978-0-931779-86-2
Ebook ISBN: 978-0-931779-87-9
Library of Congress Control Number: 2022935500

BEHAVING DECENTLY

Kurt Vonnegut's Humanism

WAYNE LAUFERT

HUMANISTPRESS.COM • WASHINGTON, DC

To Jean
and to Jane

Time, have mercy upon us;
Elements, have mercy upon us.
Rest eternal grant them, O Cosmos,
and let not light disturb their sleep.

Kurt Vonnegut, "Mass Promulgated by Me in 1985"

Don't be a fool! Close this book at once!
It is nothing but foma!*

Kurt Vonnegut, *Cat's Cradle*
*Harmless untruths

Contents

Foreword: A Note from Kurt Vonnegut 1

Introduction: Who is Kurt Vonnegut? 2

Chapter 1: He's Up in Heaven Now 9

Chapter 2: About Five Dollars for Each Corpse 16

Interlude | A Reading from the First Book of Bokonon 32

Chapter 3: Comforting Lies 34

Chapter 4: Thanks a Lot, Big Brain 49

Interlude | Life: Half Full or Half Empty? 57

Chapter 5: A Great Time for Comedians 58

Chapter 6: A Man Within a Country 75

Chapter 7: Science Certainly Tried 83

Chapter 8: Good for the Common Man 100

Interlude | The Sermon on the Mount 120

Chapter 9: Christ Worshiper 121

Chapter 10: The Eyes and Ears and Conscience
of the Creator of the Universe 142

Chapter 11: Becoming 161

Chapter 12: Dignity 174

Conclusion: Balderdash 182

Appendix A: Timeline 188

Appendix B: Behaving Decently in an Indecent Society 194

Appendix C: Humanism and Its Aspirations:
Humanist Manifesto III (2003) 201

Notes 204

Bibliography 246

Copyrights 252

Acknowledgments 255

About the Author 258

Foreword

A Note from Kurt Vonnegut

At the time this note was written (and drawn), Kurt Vonnegut was the American Humanist Association's honorary president. Fred Edwords was the AHA's director of communications and editor of its national magazine, the *Humanist*.

Introduction

Who is Kurt Vonnegut?

I myself am a work of fiction.

Kurt Vonnegut, Wampeters, Foma & Granfalloons

If you have bought, borrowed, rented, or stolen this book intending to read it, you probably know at least a little about the deceased American writer named Kurt Vonnegut (Jr.). Maybe you know a little about humanism too. You might hope to supplement what you know about one of these subjects with more information about the other.

Vonnegut and humanism go hand in hand. Still, some explaining is called for.

Defining an *ism* is one thing. I'll try to provide adequate background about humanism as we begin and a little more as we move along. A good reference point, a public document called "Humanism and Its Aspirations," is in the back of this book.

Defining a human being, however, is a fool's enterprise. A biographical timeline can start you off, and you'll find a summary of major points in Vonnegut's life among the appendixes. Refer to it if you need it. I hope the main text provides a decent albeit incomplete portrait of the man and a useful analysis of his work.

What about separating Kurt Vonnegut the person from his writings? How do we weigh his published words against his deeds and against the things he said when interviewed and when addressing an audience? What of the character who appears in some of the writer's fiction as an unnamed "I" that we are led to believe is a version of the writer himself?

What's more, Vonnegut's introductions to a few of his novels describe incidents that, mostly, really happened, as far as we know. They reveal feelings and attitudes that mimic what we think are the real Vonnegut's.

Educated readers are suspicious about all of that. They do not assume that "I" is the writer even if "I" has the writer's name. It's part of the art of fiction, we are told. I'm supposed to agree with my college professors about that because I have a bachelor's degree in English.

Yes, but...

When it makes sense to do so, I will treat Kurt Vonnegut the man (1922–2007) and Kurt Vonnegut the man at the typewriter and "I" the embedded author about the same. They are different voices from the same mouth—not all the time, of course. But as his career advanced and he gave more speeches and interviews, Vonnegut often quoted himself and his characters interchangeably.

This book was proposed as a compilation of Vonnegut's numerous quotes concerning humanistic themes, with a short biography added. I wanted to do more, though, wanted to wade deeper into the *ideas* that Vonnegut favored and the worldview that connects them.

His characters, including himself, frequently served those ideas. Vonnegut the writer included some of his real self in his fiction, and some of his imagined self in his nonfiction. Whether it's Eliot Rosewater in *God Bless You, Mr. Rosewater*, Horlick Minton in *Cat's Cradle*, or many other examples, his characters can be mouthpieces for his more urgent messages about life.

This practice can be disorienting. The all-powerful Creator in *Breakfast of Champions* and the author/narrator in *Timequake* and the afterlife-visiting interviewer in *God Bless You, Dr. Kevorkian* all converse with Kilgore Trout, Vonnegut's most famous (and entirely fictional) character, who himself is a Vonnegut alter ego.

Both Vonnegut's real and imagined selves were incorporated into Kurt Vonnegut the public speaker in the late 1960s and early 1970s. Then he stopped pretending to be a modern Mark Twain, a white-suited "glib Philosopher of the Prairie" who was the darling of hippies, draft dodgers, and other nonconformists.

After all, he wrote, "I myself am a work of fiction."

Although I will bounce around between various versions of Kurt Vonnegut, we will not get lost. The versions can be contradictory, but they also can overlap, making it easier to figure out how he (apparently) feels about something.

Take his writings about a certain American holiday. Vonnegut was born on November 11, 1922. Now on November 11 we commemorate Veterans Day, but from 1919 to 1954 it was known as Armistice Day. Vonnegut, a veteran of World War II, much preferred the holiday's original name, a point he first got across through one of his best characters, Howard W. Campbell Jr., in the 1961 novel *Mother Night*.

The book's conceit is that *Mother Night* is Campbell's memoir edited by Vonnegut, so it's the fictitious Campbell and not Vonnegut the "editor" or Vonnegut the author who has written the following:

> "Oh, it's just so damn cheap, so damn typical," I said. "This used to be a day in honor of the dead of World War One, but the living couldn't keep their grubby hands off of it, wanted the glory of the dead for themselves. So typical, so typical. Any time something of real dignity appears in this country, it's torn to shreds and thrown to the mob."

Twelve years later, Vonnegut elaborated on that sentiment in *Breakfast of Champions*. It is Indianapolis-born Kurt Vonnegut Jr. himself who in that novel's preface writes about advice columnist Phoebe Hurty, briefly mentions his mother and father, laments the state of American culture, and comments on November 11.

"When I was a boy," Vonnegut writes,

> all the people of all the nations which had fought in the First World War were silent during the eleventh minute of the eleventh hour of Armistice Day, which was the eleventh day of the eleventh month.
>
> It was during that minute in nineteen hundred and eighteen, that millions upon millions of human beings stopped butchering one another. I have talked to old men who were on battlefields during that minute. They have told me in one way or another that the sudden silence was the Voice of God. So we still have among us some men who can remember when God spoke clearly to mankind.
>
> Armistice Day has become Veterans' Day. Armistice Day was sacred. Veterans' Day is not.

Adding another layer of identity, he self-deprecatingly signs the preface with a nickname from one of his editors, who used it to characterize a hypothetical writer of turgid prose: Philboyd Studge.

Eighteen years after *that*, Vonnegut made the same point entirely as himself in one of his nonfiction books, *Fates Worse Than Death*.

> On Armistice Day, children used to be told how horrible war was, how shameful and heartbreaking, which was right...[But] Armistice Day became Veterans Day, and by the time I was preaching

in St. John's [in 1983], the message of November 11 was that there were going to be lots more wars.

In the *Breakfast of Champions* excerpt above, Vonnegut refers to "the Voice" of a god he did not believe in. This happens repeatedly in his work, and the freethinking Vonnegut directs even more genuine admiration toward Jesus Christ.

Why would someone skeptical about the Bible's supernatural claims do this? How does this fit into humanism? We'll figure it out.

The fictional and real Vonneguts overlap again during the final third of *Breakfast of Champions*: Although the Creator sitting at the cocktail bar cannot literally be the author, in some ways he might as well be. Like the real Vonnegut, he frets that he will kill himself, as his mother did, and wonders whether he is schizophrenic.

At the end he frees the failed science fiction writer Trout, apparently honoring the "I" of the novel's preface who pledges he is "not going to put on any more puppet shows." The "I"/Creator sure sounds like the Kurt Vonnegut who complains about Veterans Day and other facets of America in the preface written by "Philboyd Studge."

Guess what? Trout later returned to Vonnegut's novels, and there were more puppet shows.

So Vonnegut the writer and speaker did not fulfill all his promises. Likewise, Vonnegut the person did not always live up to his moralistic aphorisms.

That is, I *assume* he did not always live up to them, because no one does. I never met Vonnegut, and I cannot presume to know for certain whether he exemplified humanistic convictions from day to day. Plenty of people have commented about his often good-natured demeanor, puncuated with coughs and laughter. Others—or sometimes the *same* people—have said he could be hell to get along with, especially when he was trying to write.

"I loved him, and I was afraid of him," said by movie and TV script writer Steve Adams, one of the nephews Vonnegut and his first wife raised as their own, echoes remarks made by several others who best knew the private Kurt Vonnegut.

My focus will be on the writing and speaking, the public parts of Vonnegut that will survive through the ages, long after the world has forgotten whether he was always a good husband or father or client.

You can't write about Vonnegut without getting into the major events of his life. But this book is not a complete biography. Charles J. Shields wrote one called *And So It Goes: Kurt Vonnegut, A Life*, which was received pretty well by critics and not so well by several of Vonnegut's relatives and friends.

Shields aired some of Vonnegut's dirty laundry: a short temper; treatment of his literary mentors that sometimes was better in print than in person; occasionally disengaged parenting; marital affairs; a late-life descent, periodically, into petty bitterness.

And supposedly there were questionable investments, including ownership of stock in napalm manufacturer Dow Chemical. (This was disputed by his oldest child, son Mark Vonnegut, who insisted that his father "had next to no interest in investments or expensive things and never bought Dow stock.")

These faults, it seems to me, are not the sorts of things that condemn a person.

Members of the Vonnegut book club I run (yes, there is such a thing—in Baltimore, Maryland, of all places) learned about some of these flaws while reading Shields's biography. A few regulars were disappointed enough to stop reading Vonnegut. Most proceeded undeterred.

Vonnegut could be inconsistent both in print and public speech. This can make studying him problematic, which is another way of saying "more interesting." We will spend some time, for example, trying to figure out whether Vonnegut was an optimist or a pessimist—and which he *considered* himself to be.

(The answer, by the way, is that he was both. Please read chapter 5 anyway.)

Strangers like us can know only so much about someone through their writing, even someone who writes as autobiographically as Kurt Vonnegut did. He's been dead since 2007, so the only way we can experience him now is through his books, interviews, and speeches, and to some extent through adaptations in other media.

All of which are worth a look or a listen if you think you might like Vonnegut and you have a passing interest in humanism.

Why pay attention to Kurt Vonnegut?

Do you read Vonnegut because so many other people have read and liked him, and you're wondering what the fuss is about? Because Modern Library deemed his *Slaughterhouse-Five* to be the eighteenth-best English-language novel of the twentieth century? Because he was named Humanist of the Year in 1992 and served as honorary president of the American Humanist Association for the last fifteen years of his life?

He wasn't a humanitarian whose writing allows us to gain insight to marvelous, selfless deeds. No, Vonnegut just wrote books and spoke to crowds and answered questions. He didn't claim to be anything more than a man who was funnier than most. Were he not a writer, there would be no need to discuss his version of humanism.

But there are those books. There is the desperate message within them that we simply must treat our fellow human beings better than we do: "*God damn it, you've got to be kind.*" Vonnegut embraced kindness and community and dignity and art and "farting around" as reasons to go on with our lives.

His message comes in easily digestible portions, mostly, in simple sentences and at times ridiculously brief chapters. It is conveyed by memorable, funny characters, including Kurt Vonnegut himself.

The message resonates today because the things Vonnegut complained about and cared about are the same things we complain about and care about:

- What's wrong with America?
- What's wrong with *people*?
- What's *right* with people?
- Why do so many people need religion?
- Why isn't religion enough for some people?
- Is humor useful?
- What is life for?

And so on.

People have been asking those questions, of course, in many ways for a long time. The resulting lessons—not *answers*, but *lessons*—can outlast the antiquated means by which they're delivered. Confucius lived several centuries before even woodblock printing was invented, but he is still quoted every day. Charles Chaplin instructs and entertains us now even though only a few of his movies used a technique as basic as recorded dialogue.

Given that Vonnegut was born back in 1922, few people can think of him as a contemporary anymore. He could be a man of his time. His depictions of female and minority characters, for example, occasionally seem to be stuck in the 1950s.

But such characters grew in importance over the decades. In two of Vonnegut's later novels, *Galápagos* and *Bluebeard*, both from the mid-1980s, women play crucial, transformative roles.

Time is relative anyway, Vonnegut reminds us. Most famously, his *Slaughterhouse-Five* protagonist, Billy Pilgrim, bounces around randomly from one moment of life to another. And Vonnegut put time in perspective for Syracuse University graduates in 1994, albeit with tongue in cheek.

I apologize because of the terrible mess the planet is in. But it has always been a mess. There have never been any "Good Old Days," there have just been days. And as I say to my grandchildren, "Don't look at me. I just got here myself."

People are newly turned onto Vonnegut all the time. The Baltimore book club still attracts thirtysomethings (and their elders) who show up having read one or two Vonnegut books. Some of them stay with it as we make our way through his fourteen novels and other writings, and then circle back to the beginning and do it all over again. He connects with readers today much as he did when he was alive.

Vonnegut has informed, sustained, and embellished the way I look at the world since I was about fifteen years old. He isn't just funny or perpetually topical, although those are important qualities. He conveys a highly *moral* way of seeing things. Writer/publisher Dave Eggers declared that Vonnegut's "body of work reveals one of the most consistent and principled points of view of any twentieth-century artist."

I am a white, male humanist who reads Vonnegut because Vonnegut knows what's wrong with life but tries to make things a little better through humor and clear prose with sound moral thinking. He reminds me to take small steps along hopeful paths.

Once again, those steps are: kindness and community and dignity and art and farting around.

As we watch Vonnegut take those steps, get ready for a lot of quotes, from him and from others. This book has my name on it, but much of it is the work of people who write better than I do.

While you're reading, think about how the inhabitants of the far-off planet Tralfamadore perceive reality as occurring all at once. It will help you forget about the pitiless advancement of time.

Take a break and watch Chaplin's speech at the end of his 1940 movie, *The Great Dictator*. It's a plea for peace that briefly and wisely quotes from the Bible. It will help you prepare for glimpses of the New Testament as we proceed.

And listen to jazz. It will make you feel good.

Chapter 1

He's Up in Heaven Now

I am a humanist, which means, in part, that I have tried to behave decently without any expectation of rewards or punishments after I'm dead.

Kurt Vonnegut, God Bless You, Dr. Kevorkian

The well-circulated quote featured above is extracted from Kurt Vonnegut's introduction to a slim 1999 collection of his short radio scripts. Once those words are presented, it's tempting to move on. *Humanist* is defined, somewhat. Vonnegut's approach to life is summed up. Why continue at all, let alone at book length?

Well, that quote is typically forthright and simple, but it goes only so far. There's more to humanism than being good without believing in an afterlife. Vonnegut acknowledges as much with the qualifier *in part*. He knows that a full explanation cannot be achieved in just a few words.

Beyond that sentence, once we delve into Vonnegut's output we find that, for all of his inborn freethinking—even atheism—he had values in common with many believers. Without expecting eternal rewards or punishments, he nevertheless was enchanted by a selective characterization of an earthly Jesus Christ: "that greatest and most humane of human beings," he called Jesus, a moral instructor whose love for all of humanity is worth emulating.

Vonnegut's published writing provides easy entrée into humanism, with characters and subjects evaluated morally. He provides antagonists rather than real villains, but he does give us plenty of flawed individuals, including himself, and people who are at the mercy of forces beyond their control.

Vonnegut was an industrious manufacturer of memorable quotes. In his lifetime, his pithy judgments about kindness and trashing the planet and being careful what we pretend to be and so on were spread worldwide in books and on refrigerator magnets. Now they're in memes. You might've seen a few.

Mostly these snappy excerpts are about the human condition and how we can improve it. That subject is the business of humanism.

Former American Humanist Association executive director Fred Edwords identifies eight varieties of humanism. Two broad categories are secular and religious, the latter referring to belief not in the supernatural but in the satisfaction of personal and social needs that otherwise are typically filled by churches. So even "religious" humanism is not religious in the sense that many people understand that word.

All types of humanists value science, reason, and art. They seek to treat others "as having inherent worth and dignity," states the aforementioned "Humanism and Its Aspirations" (see Appendix C), which was endorsed by Vonnegut and more than a hundred other signatories in 2003.

In his essay "What is Humanism?," Edwords includes a category called Christian humanism, a philosophy he identifies as "largely a product of the Renaissance." Arthur G. Broadhurst, a Unitarian Universalist minister who writes and edits the website christianhumanist.net, offers the definition "religionless Christianity that begins and ends with the teachings of Jesus as a guide to ethical behavior."

Philosopher Chris Sunami and others would object to the descriptor *religionless* when applied to the slippery term *Christian humanism*, but Broadhurst's take does seem to fit Vonnegut's outlook.

Labels, though, tend to work imperfectly with Vonnegut. He did not want to be considered a science fiction writer, for instance, but much of his best work relies on aliens, spaceships, time travel, and something called a chrono-synclastic infundibulum. He disagreed with another term applied to him—black humorist—even though he treated comically such dark topics as death, war, and something called Richard Nixon.

Humanist, though, was a label that "charmed" him.

Many others who have accepted the label find it expansive enough to contain their beliefs about humankind's rights and responsibilities.

"We are talking about a society in which there will be no roles other than those chosen, or those earned. We are really talking about humanism," said feminist icon Gloria Steinem, who was named Humanist of the Year in 2012. Vonnegut was no feminist icon, but he deplored inequality caused by the abuse of power, and he realized that women and racial minorities are among the most frequently abused.

Zora Neale Hurston, a libertarian author and part of the Harlem Renaissance, put an empowering, cosmic spin on her humanism.

> I have made my peace with the universe as I find it, and bow to its laws...The stuff of my being is matter, ever changing, ever moving, but never lost; so what need of denominations and creeds to deny myself the comfort of all my fellow men?...I am one with the infinite and need no other assurance.

Hurston's thoughts about religion's effects on others were similar to what Vonnegut later expressed, as we'll see. "It seems to me," she wrote,

> that organized creeds are collections of words around a wish...I would not, by word or deed, attempt to deprive another of the consolation it affords. It is simply not for me.

Once in a while, that kind of tolerance goes in the other direction and an influential religious figure seems to give humanism its due. Martin Luther King Jr. wrote this:

> I would be the last to condemn the thousands of sincere and dedicated people outside the churches who have labored unselfishly through various humanitarian movements to cure the world of social evils, for I would rather a man be a committed humanist than an uncommitted Christian.

Sounds good.

On the other hand, immediately before that passage, King had expressed substantial reservations about nonreligious goodwill.

> Man by his own power can never cast evil from the world. The humanist's hope is an illusion, based on too great an optimism concerning the inherent goodness of human nature.

Only by placing faith in the divinity of Jesus, King asserted, can evil be eradicated. Humanists believe that no such faith is necessary. They contend that evil is not a force in the universe but rather is something that Earthlings are responsible for, so we're the only ones who can cast it from the world.

King might be correct that humans on their own never will entirely overcome their proclivity for bad behavior. But for many humanists, his notion that they necessarily possess "optimism concerning the inherent goodness of human nature" is a misconception.

Potential to achieve, rather than *inherent goodness*, might be more like it. As expressed in "Humanism and Its Aspirations," the humanistic hope that King called "an illusion" is actually "the informed conviction that humanity has the ability to progress toward its highest ideals."

Ability, not *inevitability*. *Progress toward*, not necessarily *achieve*.

King was killed years before even the second iteration of what is called the Humanist Manifesto was published, let alone before "Humanism and Its Aspirations," the third and most recent version, saw the light of day. (That version is the one in the appendix.)

He could have been familiar with only the original 1933 document, which also did not mention anything like "inherent goodness" but declared that "man at last is becoming aware that he alone is responsible for the realization of the world of his dreams, that he has within himself the power for its achievement."

(By the way, the patriarchal language was gone by the manifesto's 1973 sequel, showing that humanist leaders are both fallible and willing to make amends and that the affirmations are subject to change.)

King got so much right in his remarkable, inspiring life. And his and others' faith, after all, provided significant impetus to the societal improvements he helped achieve. So King's erring in his appraisal of humanism is no reason to think less of him, all things considered, but it does leave one to seek a more straightforward defense by a cleric.

That comes from John Shelby Spong, a retired Episcopal bishop of Newark, New Jersey: "To be anti-humanist is to be inhumane." Here's more from Spong:

> The task of the Christian church is to free every person in this world to live more fully, to love more wastefully, and to have the courage to be all that they can be in the infinite variety of our humanity. I submit, my brothers and sisters, that that is not far removed from the ideals and the goals of the American Humanist Association.

To be fair, many clergypersons and moralists would disagree with Spong because they consider themselves humane and yet oppose humanism—and they go far beyond King's "the humanist's hope is an illusion" remark. They consider humanism dangerous and evil.

"The idolatry of Western man is humanism, materialism, and sex," wrote Billy Graham, the most famous evangelist of the twentieth century.

"Humanism is satanic in origin," says an analysis by writer Bob Sutton. "It is the spirit of self-exaltation and self-determination." Sutton's justification comes exclusively from the Bible, with emphasis on the story of Adam and Eve, which of course is about pride leading to the Fall of Man.

Christian apologists like Sutton have no use for Vonnegut's view of Jesus as an extremely kind and influential person who was not the embodiment of God. Sutton's diagnosis for the failure of the "Jesus Movement": "Young people accepted 'Jesus,' but in reality, Jesus was just another 'trip,' no different from a drug experience or Eastern meditation."

Setting aside criticism by humanism's avowed enemies, countless other perceptions of this worldview or philosophy or lifestance or religion, when put together, might suggest someone can be a humanist without ever acknowledging it.

There's something to that. The lack of sacred doctrine and ultimate clerical leadership is liberating and welcoming. Being a humanist or not "isn't an either-or proposition," Edwords says in his essay. "Humanism is yours—to adopt or to simply draw from. You may take a little or a lot, sip from the cup or drink it to the dregs."

Did Vonnegut sip from that cup or drain it?

Tremendously interested in human beings

If nothing else, Vonnegut took frequent swigs from the cup and made humanism appear nourishing to those with a taste for it. He was less of a boozer and more of a social drinker.

Shortly before *Slaughterhouse-Five* made him rich and famous, Vonnegut used the subject to set up a quip.

"You have called me a humanist," he told a gathering of scientists in February 1969, "and I have looked into humanism some, and I have found that a humanist is a person who is tremendously interested in human beings. My dog is a humanist."

Even though a dog is not a person—as pleasant as it might be to think it is—we get from that incomplete definition a statement of humanism's essential quality: simple interest in fellow people. That's a swig from the cup.

A few paragraphs later in the same speech, Vonnegut made the case for humanism being nearly universal. He said he tells beginning writers that "readers are human beings, mostly interested in human beings. People are humanists. *Most* of them are humanists, that is." The connection Vonnegut longed to have with other human beings is central to his appeals to behave well toward them. That's another swig.

When elaborating, the inveterate humorist could not resist telling another joke. Here again is the 1999 quote that leads off this chapter, this time surrounded by context:

> About belief or lack of belief in an afterlife: Some of you may know that I am neither Christian nor Jewish nor Buddhist, nor a conventionally religious person of any sort.
>
> I am a humanist, which means, in part, that I have tried to behave decently without any expectation of rewards or punishments after I'm dead. My German-American ancestors, the earliest of whom settled in our Middle West about the time of our Civil War, called themselves "Freethinkers," which is the same sort of thing. My great grandfather Clemens Vonnegut wrote, for example, "If what Jesus said was good, what can it matter whether he was God or not?"
>
> I myself have written, "If it weren't for the message of mercy and pity in Jesus' Sermon on the Mount, I wouldn't want to be a human being. I would just as soon be a rattlesnake."
>
> I am honorary president of the American Humanist Association, having succeeded the late, great, spectacularly prolific writer and scientist, Dr. Isaac Asimov, in that essentially functionless capacity. At an AHA. memorial service for my predecessor I said, "Isaac is up in Heaven now." That was the funniest thing I could have said to an audience of humanists....
>
> So when my own time comes to join the choir invisible or whatever, God forbid, I hope someone will say, "He's up in Heaven now." Who really knows? I could have dreamed all this.

A bit later in the same passage, Vonnegut, as Hurston did, acknowledges the position that people of faith also take in defending religion. For many individuals—probably including several of those working for the radio station that aired Vonnegut's "Reports from the Afterlife"—belief in a higher power has benefits.

> Whereas formal religions surely comfort many members of the WNYC staff, that staff's collective effect on its community is humanism—an idea so Earthbound and majestic that I never capitalize it. As I have used it here, "humanism" is nothing more supernatural than a handy synonym for "good citizenship and common decency."

Vonnegut has toasted both believers and nonbelievers. He takes a gulp there and sets down the cup.

Humanism is not the same as atheism. Nonbelief in the supernatural is an important component, but humanism goes beyond ignoring or denying the existence of God. It tries to figure out how human beings can live well together while relying only on themselves.

There is an official definition on the American Humanist Association's website: "Humanism is a progressive lifestance that, without theism or other supernatural beliefs, affirms our ability and responsibility to lead meaningful, ethical lives capable of adding to the greater good of humanity."

No matter how it's defined, humanism is concerned with improving life on Earth, the only life we can be sure to have.

Here's how the 2006 Humanist of the Year, the Canadian-American psychologist and author Steven Pinker, put it: "The goal of maximizing human flourishing—life, health, happiness, freedom, knowledge, love, richness of experience—may be called humanism." Pinker quotes from "Humanism and Its Aspirations" and concludes that with humanism "acts and policies are morally evaluated by their consequences."

> The consequences needn't be restricted to happiness in the narrow sense of having a smile on one's face, but can embrace a broader sense of flourishing, which includes childrearing, self-expression, education, rich experience, and the creation of works of lasting value.

Not only is *flourishing* rather than *happiness* the more frequently accepted translation of the Greek word *eudaimonia* among scholars, it seems better suited to our understanding of human well-being. *Happiness* tends to make us think of smiling and being carefree, and that often is not a realistic goal.

Vonnegut did not directly address the difference between *happiness* and *flourishing*, but he advised college graduates and others to experience at least momentary pleasantness by acting upon some simple Hoosier wisdom he learned from his uncle Alex Vonnegut: "I urge you to please notice when you are happy, and exclaim or murmur or think at some point, 'If this isn't nice, I don't know what is.'"

Do that often enough and, who knows, you might be happy.

For humanity to achieve happiness and to flourish, Vonnegut advocated the same behaviors that humanism embraces. He took many sips from the cup. It's a big cup, and he offered us a few drinks.

So "tried to behave decently without any expectation of rewards or punishments after I'm dead" doesn't cover everything, or even try to. But it's a good start. A sip.

And surely Kurt Vonnegut (1922–2007) is up in heaven now.

Chapter 2

About Five Dollars for Each Corpse

It was the largest massacre in European history, by the way. And so what?

Kurt Vonnegut, *Mother Night*

Kurt Vonnegut, age twenty-two, was in a meat locker deep underground with several dozen fellow American prisoners and "our six guards and ranks and ranks of dressed cadavers of cattle, pigs, horses, and sheep." Above, a beautiful German city was destroyed in a spectacular firestorm caused by explosives and incendiaries dropped from British and American aircraft.

First, more than seven hundred Royal Air Force planes in two nighttime waves unloaded some fourteen hundred tons of high-explosive bombs and eleven hundred incendiary devices on Dresden. Hundreds more US bombers targeted the city's infrastructure over the next two days.

In between, on February 14, 1945, the captors and their malnourished captives rose from the depths to find that most of the buildings had been leveled and that many thousands of inhabitants had been incinerated.

"We heard the bombs walking around up there," Vonnegut wrote of the experience twenty-one years later.

> Now and then there would be a gentle shower of calcimine. If we had gone above to take a look, we would have been turned into artifacts characteristic of the fire storm: seeming pieces of charred

firewood two or three feet long—ridiculously small human beings, or jumbo fried grasshoppers, if you will.

"But not me," Vonnegut wrote in a letter home three and a half months after the bombing, matter-of-factly remarking upon his good fortune. He and the others had been spared. However, they had been forced into weeks of gruesome corpse recovery, until finally the bodies—too numerous to collect, let alone properly bury—were burned with flamethrowers.

For many people, surviving such a cataclysm would be a life-altering milestone, if not an epiphany. *It was not my time*, they might think. *Something more is expected of me.*

And nearly a quarter century after it happened, Vonnegut used his Dresden experience as the moral center of *Slaughterhouse-Five*, the novel that brought him wealth and celebrity and his greatest critical acclaim. A reader might assume that Vonnegut regarded Dresden as a crucial turning point, an occurrence that triggered significant change in his life and his outlook.

But even after he'd had a few years to contemplate the money and renown that followed *Slaughterhouse-Five*, Vonnegut said the bombing had *not* changed him.

> The importance of Dresden in my life has been considerably exaggerated because my book about it became a best seller. If the book hadn't been a best seller, it would seem like a very minor experience in my life. And I don't think people's lives are changed by short-term events like that. Dresden was astonishing, but experiences can be astonishing without changing you.

"A very minor experience in my life"? It sounds defensive, as if Vonnegut wants to remind everyone that he created *Slaughterhouse-Five*, and Dresden did not create him. But his point goes beyond justifying the book's literary merit. If surviving the deadly attack did not change him in any important way, then he must have felt much the same about life before the bombing as he did afterward.

In 1991 he recalled commenting about the subject.

> During the question-and-answer period following my speech at the National Air and Space Museum, I was asked what being bombed strategically had done to my personality. I replied that the war had been a great adventure for me, which I wouldn't have missed for anything, and that the principle shapers of my personality were probably neighborhood dogs when I was growing

up. (Some were nice, some were mean. Some looked nice but were mean. Some looked mean but were nice.) This is true.

As it turns out, by the time he was fighting in the war, something much more relevant than the neighborhood dogs' behavior had already shaped Vonnegut's makeup. It was a personal blow with long-lasting effects.

Early on Mother's Day 1944, while Vonnegut was home on a three-day leave shortly before his unit headed overseas, his mother overdosed on sleeping pills and died.

Five months later, he was on a passenger ship with the 106th Infantry Division bound for Europe and what came to be known as the Battle of the Bulge. Under heavy fire in the Ardennes Forest at the Germany-Belgium border in mid-December, Vonnegut and a handful of scouts surrendered to the Germans. They were among thousands of US troops captured in the battle. About a hundred of them eventually were put to work in the slaughterhouse.

Only nine months after his mother's death, Vonnegut was surviving underground while Dresden was perishing above.

We can begin to understand why Vonnegut would minimize the impact of Dresden on his psyche when we realize that the more private tragedy was still fresh. And there was another severe blow thirteen years later when his sister died of cancer.

Those two deaths are certainly crucial factors in his life. How could they not be? They affected his writing too. I will have some more words about those deaths later, but going much beyond that is outside the scope of this book.

Dresden is not. Although Vonnegut called it "a very minor experience" for him, the annihilation of Dresden provides a lot for humanists to consider.

Justifiable homicide?

Even without taking his mother's death into account, Vonnegut's relationship with "the Dresden atrocity" was complicated. When discussing it publicly over the years, he claimed no tears should be shed over that city's fate, that it was just one of the countless examples of humankind's self-destructive tendencies, that it was no revelation to him.

At the same time, *something* had begun to change in Vonnegut. Dresden and the global conflict surrounding it affected how he felt about his government despite his belief that "World War II was a good one."

First, there was uncertainty about the need to level a cultural center that many contend was not a suitable military target. Dresden, sometimes called "Florence on the Elbe," was renowned for its baroque

About Five Dollars for Each Corpse

architecture and world-class museums. It also was the site of a rail hub and more than a hundred factories, some of which produced poison gas and other warfaring materials.

Dresden was one of Germany's last significant centers of industry and transportation. Still, the nation had been crippled, Hitler was hiding in a bunker, Russian troops were advancing from the east, countless refugees had flooded the city, and Vonnegut felt Dresden was "about as sinister as a wedding cake."

The inner part of the city was virtually wiped out in the mid-February air raids. Most of the roughly twenty thousand people who were killed—that death toll is the generally accepted estimate now, although Vonnegut relied on an earlier, since discredited figure of 135,000—were women and children, or males too young or old for military service.

You can hear the failed attempt at resolution in a quote that in 1971 writer Richard Todd attributed to Vonnegut.

> How the hell do I feel about burning down that city? I don't know. The burning of the cities was in response to the savagery of the Nazis, and fair really was fair, except that it gets confusing when you see the victims. That sort of arithmetic is disturbing... How do you balance off Dresden against Auschwitz? Do you balance it off; or is it all so absurd that it's silly to talk about?

That is something less than a classic humanistic response. Staunch advocates of strategic aerial bombing will disagree, but can "fair really was fair" even be a consideration if, in both Dresden and Auschwitz, many innocents were killed? Does the concept of fairness get "confusing when you see the victims"—or should seeing a city full of dead noncombatants actually clarify one's moral judgment?

In this instance, Vonnegut does not exhibit the certainty of, say, the British Humanist Association (now called Humanists UK). The concept of "just" wars goes back to Greek and Roman ideas about avenging the deaths of innocents—*without* providing that further such killings were permissible as a response, University of Kent philosophy professor and BHA member Richard Norman wrote in a statement about war.

> If it's always wrong intentionally to kill the innocent, aren't all wars fought with modern weapons going to be wrong? Most modern conflicts, for example, involve the bombing of cities, in which innocent civilians are bound to be killed.
>
> More fundamentally, can we really make this distinction between those who are "innocent" and those who are not? Most soldiers have not chosen to go to war; they are forced to fight.

Aren't their deaths just as terrible as those of most civilians (some of whom may have supported aggressive actions of their state)?

Although the distinction between the innocent and the less innocent can be a difficult one to make, many people would say that there is something especially wrong with the deliberate targetting of civilians in war. Modern weapons of mass destruction such as nuclear bombs and chemical and biological weapons, whose use would kill thousands, and maybe millions, of ordinary people, seem to be impossible to justify.

That statement seems to place humanists unequivocally against the slaughter of many thousands of Germans even during wartime, even during a "just" war, regardless of what Nazis—not all or most Germans—perpetrated. Still, lacking a sacred text that commands belief or disbelief in "just" wars, different humanists may arrive at different answers to the questions raised in the last few paragraphs.

Although Vonnegut condemned some of the actions taken by Allies in World War II, he consistently stated that he felt American involvement in that war was warranted. By the time he successfully volunteered to serve in March 1943 (following an attempt that had failed two months earlier because of lingering pneumonia), Vonnegut seemed to have overcome the isolationist views he'd held even months after the United States entered the war. His willingness to enlist also might have developed for more practical reasons.

"I was flunking everything by the middle of my junior year" at Cornell University, he wrote in a 1977 "self-interview." "I was delighted to join the Army and go to war."

"World War II made war reputable because it was a just war," he told *Rolling Stone* the year before he died. "You know how many other just wars there have been? Not many."

Americans of Vonnegut's generation "thought it was not only a duty but a privilege for a young man to kill or be killed in time of war," he wrote. "I believed that, and was not mistaken to believe that during World War II."

His enthusiasm could have been stirred by the possibility of adventure, but there was a mission too: "near-Holy motives" in trying to defeat Nazis and the nation that had bombed Pearl Harbor.

"Especially from the point of view of the Western allies, the second world war comes the closest that any war ever has done in history to being a just war," said philosopher A. C. Grayling, a British Humanist Association vice president, in a 2008 interview. "It makes more poignant the fact that, in the course of fighting a just and justified war, we did things that are deeply questionable, deliberately choosing civilians as a target of a sustained attack."

Humanists abhor violence as a way to solve problems, so war is to be avoided at all costs—or *almost* all costs, according to former American Humanist Association executive director Roy Speckhardt:

> This isn't to say that peaceful solutions to political and personal conflicts are always possible. In rare circumstances, such as full-blown genocides, diplomacy may be insufficient, necessitating the use of force.

And not all force is created equal. There is no way to, in Vonnegut's words, "balance off Dresden against Auschwitz" morally, many humanists would say. One atrocity cannot justify another.

Vonnegut's fellow Dresden survivor and author Victor Gregg, another Brit, explicitly called the Allied bombing of that city "a war crime at the highest level, a stain upon the name Englishman."

"Is it all so absurd that it's silly to talk about?" That's one way to look at it. Calling the comparison of deadly acts of war "absurd" suggests that such acts lie beyond the bounds of logical comprehension, that reason cannot apply. As Vonnegut writes in the first chapter of *Slaughterhouse-Five*, "there is nothing intelligent to say about a massacre."

A military man in Vonnegut's play *Happy Birthday, Wanda June*, which had 96 performances in its initial 1970–1971 Broadway run, struggles when asked "to say something about killing." Colonel Looseleaf Harper, who had "dropped an atom bomb on Nagasaki during the Second World War," sheepishly replies, "Jesus—I dunno. You know. What the heck. Who knows?"

His final declaration is also inadequate: "It was a bitch."

That sort of bumbling response comes from a struggle to believe in a cause worth dying for while knowing that morally dubious or even indefensible acts are committed in the name of that cause.

Even a just war has unintended negative consequences, a young Vonnegut realized.

> Certainly enemy military installations should have been blown flat, and woe unto those foolish enough to seek shelter near them. But the "Get Tough America'"policy, the spirit of revenge, the approbation of all destruction and killing, has earned us a name for obscene brutality.

Later in his life, Vonnegut wrote that leveling Dresden was "pure nonsense, pointless destruction," but that it was not the fault of the United States.

> The whole city was burned down, and it was a British atrocity, not ours. They sent in night bombers, and they came in and set the whole town on fire with a new kind of incendiary bomb. And so everything organic, except my little POW group, was consumed by fire. It was a military experiment to find out if you could burn down a whole city by scattering incendiaries all over it.

Before Dresden, he said, "American civilians and ground troops didn't know that American bombers were engaged in saturation bombing. It was kept a secret until very close to the end of the war." The monumental triumph over the Axis powers overwhelmed the queasiness that some Americans might have felt about how victory had been achieved. Increasingly horrific revelations about the concentration camps helped further reduce misgivings about the more problematic of the Allies' tactics.

But realizing what American bombers had done contributed to Vonnegut's growing disenchantment with his country's leadership, a disillusionment that worsened later.

Another factor: Vonnegut and his fellow American soldiers could have been killed by Allied bombs.

> It wasn't as though the bombardiers knew where I was and were careful not to hurt me. They didn't know or care who was what or where...Same scheme as Hiroshima, but with primitive technology, and with white people down below.

Sheer revenge, then as now, can seem reasonable to the victors. It can be cathartic. Dresden's firebombing "was a work of art," Vonnegut told an audience in May 1990. "It was a tower of smoke and flame to commemorate the rage and heartbreak of so many who had had their lives warped or ruined by the indescribable greed and vanity and cruelty of Germany."

Noting that "two more such towers would be built by Americans alone in Japan," referring to the atomic bombs dropped by US planes on Hiroshima and Nagasaki, Vonnegut admitted that at the time he "regarded those twin towers as works of art. Beautiful!"

"That was how crazy I had become," he said. "That is how crazy we had all become."

Poo-tee-weet?

The birdsong that appears a few times in *Slaughterhouse-Five* is a question that follows a massacre. It is the last word of the novel. But what does it mean?

"*Poo-tee-weet?*" is a question without an adequate answer, perhaps the only sane conclusion that's possible after Vonnegut has spent a couple hundred pages telling us about war. He has not spun thrilling combat tales. He has not tried to justify World War II or wept over concentration camps and Pearl Harbor or condemned evil Nazis or praised heroic Allies.

The bombing of Dresden was largely unfamiliar to the American public upon the book's release in 1969. Instead of describing the event in detail, Vonnegut describes the effects the Allied attack had on Dresden, and the effects that war had on him and his fellow soldiers.

We are told about hungry and sick prisoners, a ruined metropolis, charred corpses by the thousand, a good man who survives the firestorm but is shot to death for stealing a teapot. We get ridiculous-looking extraterrestrials, plot summaries of novels by an obscure science fiction writer, and a protagonist so listless that he finds "no important differences...between walking and standing still."

More than a hundred times throughout the novel, Vonnegut's famous detached refrain, "So it goes," follows whenever the death of someone or something is mentioned, whether on an individual or a mass scale. It acknowledges that death is the most common thing imaginable.

"So it goes."

"*Poo-tee-weet?*"

One is resignation, the other bewilderment.

They are humanistic responses because the novel leaves no room for help from God—or for that matter from patriotic fervor or cold scientific progress. Rather than lose himself and his readers in existential dread, though, Vonnegut builds upon the elements of fantasy that were in two of his previous novels, *The Sirens of Titan* and *Cat's Cradle*. He indulges his absurdist streak, leavening his moralizing with ludicrous science fiction that carries an intriguing message or two along with comic relief.

Slaughterhouse-Five protagonist Billy Pilgrim is "unstuck in time," having been abducted by little green plumber's-helper-shaped travelers from the planet Tralfamadore who can see in four dimensions. These aliens have taught Billy how to perceive time as they do, to "look at all the different moments just the way [humans] can look at a stretch of the Rocky Mountains."

An example of their philosophy: "Well, here we are, Mr. Pilgrim, trapped in the amber of this moment. There is no *why*."

Death is not final to a Tralfamadorian, to whom a dead person "is just fine in plenty of other moments." So, when Tralfamadorians along with Billy and the author/narrator respond to death with "So it goes," that phrase seems a little less glum than it might. Even so, it surrenders to fate.

The novel takes Billy far afield, such as when he and porn actress Montana Wildhack are captured and kept naked in a zoo on Tralfamadore. There, when she asks him to tell her a story, he talks about Dresden.

Billy repeatedly jumps through time and space, finding himself back in Dresden, or in a Vermont hospital, or in a doctor's waiting room when he was sixteen, or at his eighteenth wedding anniversary party, or in a Chicago ballpark telling tens of thousands of people about Tralfamadore on the night of his death.

Billy's fantastic flights read like dreams or hallucinations caused by wartime trauma—what we now would identify as post-traumatic stress disorder. *Slaughterhouse-Five* is "not about time travel and flying saucers," William Deresiewicz wrote in *The Nation*, "it's about PTSD."

The trauma is where Billy is stuck. His memory and imagination free him from the horrors he has witnessed—and from his fear of death—but they also reinforce his belief that he has no control over what happens to him.

Experiencing life out of sequence is a trick that Vonnegut uses to describe the night in 1967 when Billy is abducted by the aliens. Billy knows the flying saucer is coming, knows he can't do anything about it. Tralfamadorians find the human concept of free will incomprehensible, and Billy sees things their way. He even knows when he is going to die, and he is comfortable with the inevitable.

Unable to sleep, he wanders downstairs to his living room, turns on the TV, and sees "a movie about American bombers in the Second World War and the gallant men who flew them" playing backward and then forward.

Running in reverse, the movie shows American planes flying back from an English airfield, being met over France by German planes that inhale bullets and shrapnel, joined by wrecked American bombers that miraculously rise from the ground.

> The formation flew backwards over a German city that was in flames. The bombers opened their bomb bay doors, exerted a miraculous magnetism which shrunk the fires, gathered them into cylindrical steel containers, and lifted the containers into the bellies of the planes. The Germans below had miraculous devices of their own, which were long steel tubes. They used them to suck more fragments from the crewmen and planes. But there were still a few wounded Americans, though, and some of the bombers

were in bad repair. Over France, though, German fighters came up again, made everything and everybody as good as new.

The American bombers return to their bases, and the "cylinders" are taken to factories in the United States, where they are dismantled and broken down into components that are converted into minerals. ("Touchingly, it was mainly women who did this work.") Then, "specialists in remote areas...put them into the ground, to hide them cleverly, so they would never hurt anybody ever again."

Another vision has spared Billy from real-world savagery, at least in his mind.

Viewed more positively, the vision is a pacifist's—a humanist's—dream.

Children's Crusade

Slaughterhouse-Five, Vonnegut's sixth novel, was not the first published piece he wrote about Dresden. It's the flowering of seeds he'd been planting for more than twenty years.

Most of the earlier attempts were short stories Vonnegut submitted to general-interest weekly magazines that were popular after the war. He made enough money selling to the "slicks" that he quit his job as a General Electric publicist and lived fairly well on his writing income until the nation's attention and advertising dollars switched to television.

Avoiding combat thrillers, Vonnegut produced domestic dramas, some science fiction, and occasional forays into army life reflecting his own background and observations, such as the German-speaking American in "*Der Arme Dolmetscher*," the aimless veteran in "The Cruise of *The Jolly Roger*," the purveyors of pillaged relics in "Souvenir" and "Spoils," and the suspected fink in "Just You and Me, Sammy."

As US-Soviet relations soured and the Korean War raged, Vonnegut had better luck selling Cold War-influenced stories like "All the King's Horses"—with its tense standoff played out using human beings in a chess game—than World War II-inspired tales. In either case, Vonnegut's message is that ordinary people are pawns.

Several of his war-related stories from this period were rejected. Some of these—"Spoils," "Just You and Me, Sammy," and others—were published after his death in the 2008 collection *Armageddon in Retrospect*. A few concern males, one a mere boy, who long for combat action, envisioning perhaps the kind of adventure that PFC Vonnegut imagined he was entering.

Other early, posthumously published stories concern prisoners of war in or near Germany. One of these, the undated "Guns Before Butter," actually focuses on three American POWs who are guarded by a German corporal "amid the smashed masonry and timbers of Dresden"—but a competition over recipes and the demotion of the guard after he seizes the Yanks' notebooks is workmanlike material a long way from the more vivid perspectives on war that Vonnegut produced later.

"Brighten Up," a slight comic tale about an opportunistic American POW in Dresden, describes how bombers demolished cigarette factories and "a number of human beings got blown up as well—something like 200,000."

That exceedingly high casualty count probably was derived from German government propaganda, but it shows how accurate information about Dresden was lacking for years afterward. The letter Vonnegut wrote home on May 29, 1945, had put the figure at 250,000, so at least the estimate seemed to be headed in the right direction.

By the time Vonnegut wrote an essay titled "Wailing Shall Be in All Streets," he claimed that "over one hundred thousand" had died. "Wailing" was written while Vonnegut attended classes at the University of Chicago on the GI Bill. The piece was turned down repeatedly by the likes of *Harper's*, *The Atlantic*, and *Time*.

The essay is a heartfelt recording of Vonnegut's growing disgust with wildly imprecise air attacks. "It is with some regret that I here besmirch the nobility of our airmen," he writes, "but boys, you killed an appalling lot of women and children." He compares the killing of innocents at Dresden to one of the Nazis' infamous death camps, claiming that "we surely created a Belsen of our own."

In the essay, Vonnegut's most pointed early condemnation of American culpability, he directs his outrage toward the specific types of airborne acts he witnessed while maintaining that US participation in the war was well-reasoned.

> The death of Dresden was a bitter tragedy, needlessly and willfully executed. The killing of children—"Jerry" children or "Jap" children or whatever enemies the future may hold for us—can never be justified....
>
> There can be no doubt that the Allies fought on the side of right and the Germans and Japanese on the side of wrong. World War II was fought for near-Holy motives. But I stand convinced that the brand of justice in which we dealt, wholesale bombings of civilian populations, was blasphemous. That the enemy did it first has nothing to do with the moral problem.

The Americans accepted congratulations from Russian troops who marveled over the utter devastation of Dresden, "but I felt then as I feel now, that I would have given my life to save Dresden for the World's generations to come," Vonnegut concluded. "That is how everyone should feel about every city on Earth."

Whatever his convictions, putting his experience into sellable fiction proved more difficult than Vonnegut expected.

> I thought it would be easy for me to write about the destruction of Dresden, since all I would have to do would be to report what I had seen. And I thought, too, that it would be a masterpiece or at least make me a lot of money, since the subject was so big.
>
> But not many words about Dresden came from my mind then—not enough of them to make a book, anyway. And not many words come now, either, when I have become an old fart with his memories and his Pall Malls, with his sons full grown.

Between the short stories and *Slaughterhouse-Five*, Vonnegut worked Dresden into two of his 1960s novels. These passages work better than anything of his on the subject since "Wailing Shall Be in All Streets" because they're more focused and personal than his short fiction of that time.

First came a brief but telling mention in Vonnegut's 1965 novel, *God Bless You, Mr. Rosewater*. Eliot Rosewater, an ultrarich, war-damaged philanthropist accused of being insane, is on a bus leaving his namesake hometown for good. Approaching Indianapolis, Eliot has a vision: "He was astonished to see that the entire city was being consumed by a fire-storm."

Eliot remembers reading about such a thing in *The Bombing of Germany* by Hans Rumpf (an actual book published in 1963). He has hidden the book in his office, fixated on a passage that clinically describes how Dresden was incinerated. He can't shake the vision.

> Eliot, rising from his seat in the bus, beheld the fire-storm of Indianapolis. He was awed by the majesty of the column of fire, which was at least eight miles in diameter and fifty miles high. The boundaries of the column seemed absolutely sharp and unwavering, as though made of glass. Within the boundaries, helixes of dull red embers turned in stately harmony about an inner core of white. The white seemed holy.

In the next chapter, Eliot awakens on the rim of an outdoor fountain to a bird singing *"Poo-tee-weet?"*

This resembles autobiography. Vonnegut had left his hometown of Indianapolis while still a young man, fighting in the war, moving to Chicago, then Schenectady, New York, then Cape Cod. Visions of a firestorm were consuming him too.

One year after *God Bless You, Mr. Rosewater* was published, Vonnegut expanded upon the sentiments of his "Wailing" essay in an introduction he wrote for a new edition of his 1961 novel, *Mother Night*. The book purports to be the memoir of an American who broadcast Nazi propaganda by radio in Germany while also delivering secret messages to the Allies.

The story of narrator Howard W. Campbell Jr. does not involve Dresden, but Vonnegut's introduction is his first published description of what happened there. It is unsentimental, containing the graphic images mentioned earlier in this chapter, the "six guards and ranks and ranks of dressed cadavers" and the "jumbo fried grasshoppers" and so forth.

The attack on Dresden, he writes, "was the largest massacre in European history, by the way. And so what?" And he offers a startling conclusion about evil's insidious nature.

> If I'd been born in Germany, I suppose I would have *been* a Nazi, bopping Jews and gypsies and Poles around, leaving boots sticking out of snowbanks, warming myself with my secretly virtuous insides. So it goes.

Vonnegut was much closer to the candidly bleak tone he needed. He'd even found his signature catch phrase.

The type of characters and situations he required to write a whole book about Dresden, however, were eluding him. He took side trips to Iowa City, where he taught a writing course for two years, and to Dresden, which he and his wartime buddy and fellow firebombing survivor Bernard V. O'Hare visited on a Guggenheim grant that had been awarded to the author. Then Vonnegut, as he told it, was shamed into a eureka moment back in Bernard and Mary O'Hare's kitchen in Pennsylvania.

Vonnegut's youngest daughter and a friend were upstairs playing with the O'Hare children. Mary had left Vonnegut and her husband alone to talk. The men, though, were failing again in their attempt to come up with suitable war stories. Mary was making noise, moving about the house, obviously agitated about something.

Then she spoke up: "You were just babies in the war—like the ones upstairs!"

> "But you're not going to write it that way, are you," [Mary] said. "You'll pretend you were men instead of babies, and you'll be played in the movies by Frank Sinatra and John Wayne or some of those glamorous, war-loving, dirty old men. And war will look just wonderful, so we'll have a lot more of them. And they'll be fought by babies like the babies upstairs."

So Vonnegut promised that, if he managed to actually finish the book, "there won't be a part for Frank Sinatra or John Wayne."

"I tell you what," he told her, "I'll call it 'The Children's Crusade.' "

By the way, Vonnegut really did use "The Children's Crusade," albeit as the first part of *Slaughterhouse-Five*'s lengthy subtitle. The next part is "A Duty-Dance with Death." There, Vonnegut paraphrases the French writer Céline to emphasize fate over free will, as do the Tralfamadorians.

The exchange between Vonnegut and Mary O'Hare is the principled heart of *Slaughterhouse-Five*'s opening chapter, which is another introduction, really, like *Mother Night*'s but with even more assurance despite Vonnegut's claim that he's written a "lousy little book."

To properly represent his experiences in the war, Vonnegut realized, he had to forget about scenes portraying soldiers as something other than hapless victims of circumstance. And by including Mary O'Hare's admonition, he had chosen to include himself in the portrayal.

That decision affected even the fictitious passages, of which he wrote, "The war parts, anyway, are pretty much true."

Vonnegut himself, unnamed, makes a few brief appearances in *Slaughterhouse-Five*. He points out his presence when describing, for instance, a procession of prisoners being loaded into boxcars or arriving in Dresden, "the loveliest city that most of the Americans had ever seen."

He is one of the men suffering ingloriously in a latrine, sickened by a feast that had been prepared for them by English prisoners.

"That was I. That was me," Vonnegut writes. "That was the author of this book."

Some of *Slaughterhouse-Five*'s other characters also were based on real people.

Poor Edgar Derby, who also makes it through the firestorm but is shot to death for stealing a teapot, is modeled after American POW Michael Palaia. Vonnegut and three fellow soldiers had to dig a grave for Palaia, who was executed for stealing a jar of pickled string beans from a basement.

Derby is the closest thing to a hero in the novel, a truly decent man who believes deeply in American values. His death is a Tralfamadorian anticlimax, telegraphed from the novel's first paragraph. The meaningless carnage happening all around Derby is so vast that his tragic fate is barely noticeable.

Billy Pilgrim himself is an imaginative extension of Rochester, NY, native Edward R. "Joe" Crone Jr. (October 26, 1923, to April 11, 1945), who survived Dresden but died "on a hospital cart of starvation and despair" two months later.

"Joe was deeply religious and kind and childlike," Vonnegut told Crone's hometown newspaper in 1995. "The war was utterly incomprehensible to him, as it should have been."

In Billy Pilgrim, Crone lives on. It's a dubious immortality.

> Billy wouldn't do anything to save himself. Billy wanted to quit. He was cold, hungry, embarrassed, incompetent. He could scarcely distinguish between sleep and wakefulness now, on the third day, found no important differences, either, between walking and standing still.
>
> He wished everyone would leave him alone. "You guys go on without me," he said again and again.

The war that was incomprehensible to Crone is the one that ended in 1945, but by the time *Slaughterhouse-Five* was published in March 1969 America had already lost well over thirty thousand soldiers in Vietnam and was being wracked by protests.

The book found an enthusiastic audience. *Slaughterhouse-Five* was on best-seller lists for months, peaking at number four. It was a National Book Award finalist and was nominated for Hugo and Nebula awards, high honors in the field of science fiction. It routinely appears on lists of the best novels of the twentieth century.

Vonnegut for a couple years had been "doing quite well" as a writer—"living in easy circumstances on Cape Cod," he called it—but *Slaughterhouse-Five* made him a star.

So how badly can Vonnegut feel about Dresden? After all, he might be a hypocrite if he complained too much.

> Being present at the destruction of Dresden has affected my character far less than the death of my mother, the adopting of my sister's children, the sudden realization that those children and my own were no longer dependent on me, the breakup of my marriage, and on and on. And I have not been encouraged to go on mourning Dresden—even by Germans. Even Germans seem to think it is not worth mentioning anymore.

He then quotes from his introduction to the Franklin Library's 1978 edition of *Slaughterhouse-Five*.

> I...learned only that people can become so enraged in war that they will burn great cities to the ground, and slay the inhabitants thereof.
>
> That was nothing new....

About Five Dollars for Each Corpse

The Dresden atrocity, tremendously expensive and meticulously planned, was so meaningless, finally, that only one person on the entire planet got any benefit from it. I was that person. I wrote this book, which earned a lot of money for me and made my reputation, such as it is.

One way or another, I got two or three dollars for every person killed. Some business I'm in.

By the time Vonnegut gave his National Air and Space Museum speech in 1990, that figure had risen to "about five dollars for each corpse," he said, "counting my fee tonight."

A Reading from the First Book of Bokonon

A Reading from the First Book of Bokonon

Chapter 3

Comforting Lies

Live by the foma* that make you brave and kind and healthy and happy.

The Books of Bokonon, I:5
*Harmless untruths

As a student of anthropology, Kurt Vonnegut was interested in the cultural impact of religion more than its theological soundness. He wondered what religion *does* for people.

The invented belief systems that Vonnegut placed in a handful of his novels show that the purpose of religion is to enhance the culture that creates it. Religion provides reassuring explanations for humanity's place in the universe, and it offers hope.

Whether it's *true* or not is beside the point.

"Only in superstition is there hope," Vonnegut said during a commencement address at Bennington College in 1970.

> If you want to become a friend of civilization, then become an enemy of truth and a fanatic for harmless balderdash...I beg you to believe in the most ridiculous superstition of all: that humanity is at the center of the universe, the fulfiller or the frustrator of the grandest dreams of God Almighty.
>
> If you can believe that, and make others believe it, then there might be hope for us. Human beings might stop treating each other like garbage, might begin to treasure and protect each other instead. Then it might be all right to have babies again.

You could argue that the majority of humanity already believes it's "the fulfiller or the frustrator of the grandest dreams of God Almighty." But humanity does not *act* like it is, Vonnegut seems to be saying. True belief would result in better actions, even if that belief is based on "harmless balderdash."

Vonnegut is advocating for better outcomes. He contends that, for religion to lead to such outcomes, truth is not necessary.

His most enduring contribution to religious studies is his fourth novel, *Cat's Cradle*, from 1963. In fact, it also ended up being his greatest academic achievement. Eight years after *Cat's Cradle* was published—and two years after Vonnegut had become famous—the book earned him a master's degree in anthropology from the University of Chicago. Vonnegut submitted it for consideration in 1971 because he needed a college degree to teach at Harvard.

Back in 1947, the midwestern institution had rejected graduate student Vonnegut's first thesis, on "similarities between the Cubist painters in Paris in 1907 and the leaders of Native American, or Injun, uprisings late in the nineteenth century." That summer, he worked on a narrower subject that the departmental committee found more promising: "Mythologies of North American Nativistic Movements."

Vonnegut abandoned his studies, however, and later that year took a job in the publicity department at General Electric in Schenectady, New York. Eventually he left GE to become a full-time fiction writer.

He did not abandon the exploration of myths, whether Native American or from another culture. Having already regarded God as a human construct, Vonnegut found that studying anthropology helped further shape his thoughts about myth and cultural relativism.

> It confirmed my atheism, which was the faith of my fathers anyway. Religions were exhibited and studied as the Rube Goldberg inventions I'd always thought they were. We weren't allowed to find one culture superior to any other. We caught hell if we mentioned races much. It was highly idealistic.

He had made use of his research into Indian myths in his first novel, *Player Piano* (1952). A rebellious faction in the novel named the Ghost Shirt Society is inspired by the actual historical group of Lakotans who believed that sacred clothing would protect them even from the bullets of white conquerers. In December 1890, the US Army opened fire on captive ghost-shirt-wearing warriors at Wounded Knee, South Dakota, resulting in some three hundred Sioux deaths, including dozens of women and children.

So the Ghost Shirts of *Player Piano* were based on a relatively new, entirely real religion. For his second novel, *The Sirens of Titan* (1959), Vonnegut created the Church of God the Utterly Indifferent. It's as provocative and amusing as it sounds. Later, in *Slapstick* (1976), there's the Church of Jesus Christ the Kidnapped. I'll take a closer look at these original productions later in this chapter.

But first, the self-described pack of lies called Bokononism, from *Cat's Cradle*.

A useful religion

Bokononism is Vonnegut's most fully formed made-up religion, complete with several sample verses, a unique vocabulary, and a biography of its prophet. And beneath the satirical surface is a philosophical foundation: The universe is senseless, so we lie to ourselves in our quest for meaning.

Lie might seem to be a harsh word for religion, revealing a rudely dim view of faith. A lie in this case is defined as a claim its utterer does not know to be objectively true or proveable, with or without good intentions, with or without knowing for sure the claim is false. I will use *lie* in this way.

The intent of the deception could be to hurt a perceived enemy, to avoid embarrassment or punishment, to gain or keep status or power, to impose order—or to provide hope, which helps retain power and preserve order. There's self-deception in the pursuit of a fulfilling, even spiritual, life through harmless untruths, called *foma* in the sacred text of Bokononism.

Religion ought to make people happy but too often does not, Vonnegut told *Playboy* magazine in 1973. Preachers, he complained, "don't say anything to make anybody any happier, when there are all these neat lies you can tell.

> And everything is a lie, because our brains are two-bit computers, and we can't get very high-grade truths out of them. But as far as improving the human condition goes, our minds are certainly up to that. That's what they were designed to do. And we do have the freedom to make up comforting lies. But we don't do enough of it.

What sort of lies should preachers tell? "'Thou shalt not kill.' That's a good lie," Vonnegut said. "Whether God said it or not, it's still a perfectly good lie. And if it gives it more force to say that God said it, well, fine."

Here Vonnegut is speaking about the lack of objective truth out there somewhere and saying that the comforting lies we agree upon *become* truth.

A lie can be quite useful, Vonnegut reasoned. It can soothe the populace. Many a despot has realized the same thing. From Vonnegut's perspective, though, answering some of life's difficult questions could help people find meaning and give them a reason for living, not simply make them docile and obedient.

That's what he was getting at, anyway, in a 1970 *60 Minutes* segment in which interviewer Harry Reasoner asked the author whether he was providing young readers "the information that they need, a philosophy that will be good for them."

> Well, I'm giving them information that will make them kinder. You know, you can give them certain kinds of information that would make them extremely tough, you know, about what God wants and all that, so you just make up somethhing that would tend to make people gentle. It's all made up anyway, you know, we really don't know anything about that stuff.

Vonnegut provided the information through fiction, an acceptable way of lying that tries to establish, if not truth, then at least meaning. So why not make up a religion that acknowledges doing the same thing? "It's all made up anyway."

In that spirit, his *Cat's Cradle* narrator says, "Anyone unable to understand how a useful religion can be founded on lies will not understand this book either."

A *useful* religion need not be demonstrably true.

Vonnegut provides the genesis of his demonstrably untrue religion, supplying a condensed biography of its creator, as he does with many of his major and minor characters.

Bokononism's prophet, Lionel Boyd Johnson, is a black British subject who was born on the island of Tobago. Johnson and a US Marine deserter were on a schooner that crashed into San Lorenzo in 1922. They learned that the little island's impoverished population was controlled entirely by a sugar manufacturing company's plantation bosses.

The two castaways declared they were setting up an actual government, and Castle Sugar withdrew without a fight, finally giving up on San Lorenzo's worthless topography of clay and gravel. In the duo's attempt to create a Utopia, they applied the muscle-building system developed by Charles Atlas, of comic book ad fame, to governance. It was called Dynamic Tension.

San Lorenzo's experiment relied on the push and pull of good and evil. Johnson, called "Bokonon" in the island's dialect, "cynically and playfully" established a religion. He explained in his tract,

> I wanted all things
> To seem to make some sense,
> So we all could be happy, yes,
> Instead of tense.
> And I made up lies
> So that they all fit nice,
> And I made this sad world
> A par-a-dise.

Despite legal and economic reforms, San Lorenzans were miserable. They, like many dispirited people today, turned to religion. Bokononism "became the one real instrument of hope," according to Dr. Julian Castle, who witnessed much of the island's history after using his portion of the family fortune to build a hospital in the jungle. "Truth was the enemy of the people, because the truth was so terrible, so Bokonon made it his business to provide the people with better and better lies."

Applying the principle of Dynamic Tension, Johnson/Bokonon took on a role.

> So I said good-bye to government,
> And I gave my reason:
> That a really good religion
> Is a form of treason.

An elaborate but empty series of actions followed. Bokonon retreated to comfortable exile in the jungle, well fed by disciples. Government leader Earl McCabe, the erstwhile Marine who had accompanied Johnson on the wrecked schooner, directed half-hearted efforts to find and execute Bokonon the traitor. For most San Lorenzans, the law was bad and the outlaw was good.

Castle, the island's chronicler, described the result of these performances.

> "The truth was that life was as short and brutish and mean as ever.
>
> "But people didn't have to pay as much attention to the awful truth. As the living legend of the cruel tyrant in the city and the gentle holy man in the jungle grew, so, too, did the happiness of the people grow. They were all employed full time as actors in a play they understood, that any human being anywhere could understand and applaud."

Virtually everyone in San Lorenzo, including the narrator of *Cat's Cradle*, becomes a Bokononist even though the religion is banned upon penalty of excruciating death by "the hook." The people are content, but Castle says McCabe and Bokonon "both became, for all practical purposes, insane."

Keeping the populace content can be maddening. At their own expense, Johnson and McCabe conspire on a fiction that works as intended. Accepting a set of lies that Bokonon acknowledges are lies helps the islanders see through even bigger lies, such as the ones created to explain a senseless universe or to justify war.

Even someone who is not a Bokononist can think and talk like one. Bokononism has that quality in common with humanism. At their best, both try to cut through self-deception and fabricated excuses to discern the real roots of human behavior.

In *Cat's Cradle*, the American ambassador to San Lorenzo has a moment of clarity. Horlick Minton addresses a small gathering of San Lorenzans on the solemn day that memorializes the Hundred Martyrs to Democracy, known by the islanders as *lo Hoon-yera Mora-toorz tut Zamoo-cratz-ya*. The occasion honors the crew of men who, after San Lorenzo declared war on Germany and Japan immediately following the bombing of Pearl Harbor, were headed for training in the United States on a ship that almost immediately was sunk by a German submarine.

Ambassador Minton flatters the nation's president with "a whopping lie[:] 'There is not an American schoolchild who does not know the story of San Lorenzo's noble sacrifice in World War Two.' " In his "strikingly Bokononist speech" the next day, however, Minton does what he calls "a very un-ambassadorial thing...I am about to tell you what I really feel.

"We are gathered here, friends," he said, "to honor lo Hoon-yera Mora-toorz tut Zamoo-cratz-ya, children dead, all dead, all murdered in war. It is customary on days like this to call such lost children men. I am unable to call them men for this simple reason: that in the same war in which lo Hoon-yera Mora-toorz tut Zamoo-cratz-ya died, my own son died.

"My soul insists that I mourn not a man but a child.

"I do not say that children at war do not die like men, if they have to die. To their everlasting honor and our everlasting shame, they do die like men, thus making possible the manly jubilation of patriotic holidays....

"But if today is really in honor of a hundred children murdered in war," he said, "is today a day for a thrilling show?

"The answer is yes, on one condition: that we, the celebrants, are working consciously and tirelessly to reduce the stupidity and viciousness of ourselves and of all mankind."

That sounds much like Vonnegut's feelings toward Veterans Day that we saw a few chapters ago. He considered its antecedent, Armistice Day, to be sacred. In commemorating the end of a war, Armistice Day acknowledged a moment of peace so profound that it might as well have come from the Creator of the Universe.

Minton's simple, humane appeal to "reduce the stupidity and viciousness of ourselves and of all mankind" is both Bokononist and humanistic.

John, the formerly Christian narrator of *Cat's Cradle*'s, discusses his new religion with Frank Hoenikker, a Major General and Minister of Science and Progress in the Republic of San Lorenzo. John asks whether Bokononism considers anything sacred, and Frank attempts an answer.

"Not even God, as near as I can tell."
"Nothing?"
"Just one thing."
I made some guesses. "The ocean? The sun?"
"Man," said Frank. "That's all. Just man."

Plausible new religions

Bokononism is the most complete of Vonnegut's invented religions, but there are others. They function much like his science fiction, as satirical supporting devices.

A comprehensive list of these inventions would include the one that is briefly mentioned in the first Vonnegut fiction to appear as his writing career began in earnest. Published in *Collier's* in February 1950, the short story "Report on the Barnhouse Effect" concerns an ultrapowerful professor who causes mass destruction using only his mind. The one detail we get about the First Church of Barnhouse in Los Angeles is that it "has a congregation numbering in the thousands."

Being at the mercy of a man with pacifistic intentions but godlike abilities, it's no wonder humanity constructs a religion by which to worship, appease, and fear him.

More calculated, and thus more like Bokononism, is the religion that appears in Vonnegut's second novel, *The Sirens of Titan*. Millionaire Winston Niles Rumford creates the Church of God the Utterly Indifferent after steering his private spaceship into the middle of a chrono-synclastic infundibulum, a point in the solar system at which "all the different kinds of truth fit together."

Rumfoord and his traveling companion, a dog named Kazak, are transformed into spiraling waves that materialize on Earth once every 59 days. As one consequence, Rumfoord gains the ability to travel through time, and thus he can see the future. He finances and directs a Martian invasion of Earth that he knows will fail.

The invasion of Earth is carried out by ill-equipped, unprepared former Earthlings. Rumfoord has this message in mind for the suicide mission's aftermath: "That Earth's glorious victory over Mars had been a tawdry butchery of virtually unarmed saints, saints who had waged feeble war on Earth in order to weld the peoples of that planet into a monolithic Brotherhood of Man."

Unity will be achieved through an outsized event that, it is hoped, will bring humans together. Rumfoord will orchestrate a senseless massacre that will be followed by regret.

In his *Pocket History of Mars*, he explains:

> Any man who would change the World in a significant way must have showmanship, a genial willingness to shed other people's blood, and a plausible new religion to introduce during the brief period of repentance and horror that usually follows bloodshed.

That religion, which history professor and Vonnegut admirer Gregory D. Sumner calls "Rumfoord's humanistic anti-faith," has two tenets: "Puny man can do nothing at all to help or please God Almighty, and Luck is not the hand of God." Its blue-and-gold flag is inscribed "Take Care of the People, and God Almighty Will Take Care of Himself."

> "Why should you believe in this religion, rather than any other?" said Rumfoord. "You should believe in it because I, as head of this religion, can work miracles, and the head of no other religion can. What miracles can I work? I can work the miracle of predicting, with absolute accuracy, the things that the future will bring."

Thanks to his time-traveling ability, Rumfoord does just that. He predicts fifty events, every one of which comes true. This distinguishes him from all other prophets known to humankind.

Bokonon, had he gained such powers by way of the chrono-synclastic infundibulum, would have told everyone exactly how he predicted the future. The idea of miracles would have been deemed laughable. And the future nevertheless would have been seen as inevitable.

(About that inevitability: "As it happened" is a phrase a Bokononist always follows with "as it was *supposed* to happen." Believing that every occurrence is part of God's plan is a reassuring lie found in many faiths. It also resembles the Tralfamadorian fatalism that results from the ability to see the past, present, and future all at once.)

Bokononism is enforced, albeit sparingly, by the torture device called "the hook." In *The Sirens of Titan*, the Church of God the Utterly Indifferent's billions of followers are kept in line through other means. Like the citizens of a futuristic America in Vonnegut's 1961 story "Harrison Bergeron," they gladly agree to wear weights and other physical handicaps so that "the weakest and the meekest were bound to admit, at last, that the race of life was fair."

Rumfoord also implies that an all-powerful deity relies on human cruelty for its accomplishments on Earth.

> "During my next visit with you, fellow-believers," he said, "I shall tell you a parable about people who do things that they think God Almighty wants done. In the meanwhile, you would do well, for background on this parable, to read everything that you can lay your hands on about the Spanish Inquisition."

Implicit threats from God, not humans, help popularize the religion that Vonnegut devised for his 1976 novel, *Slapstick, or Lonesome No More!* The Church of Jesus Christ the Kidnapped gets only a few pages of description about three-quarters of the way into the book, and Vonnegut does not do much with it.

Like Bokonon's and Rumfoord's contrivances, though, the Church of Jesus Christ the Kidnapped serves a need. In a nation wracked by bankruptcy and deadly epidemics, it becomes "the most popular American religion of all time."

It too has a contemporary founder, the Right Reverend William Uranium-8 Wainwright of Chicago, who claims that Jesus is alive but has been abducted by "the Forces of Evil." In a leaflet, Wainwright has one exhortation:

> We must drop whatever we are doing, and spend every waking hour in trying to find Him. If we do not, God will exercise His Option[:]...
> He can destroy Mankind so easily, any time he chooses to.

Christians could be guided by essentially the same instructions, but Wainwright's followers are constantly, absurdly vigilant. The novel's narrator watches one of the church's leaflet distributors at dinner.

I marvelled that he could jerk his head around and still eat without spilling a drop. He even looked under his plate and water glass for Jesus not once, but over and over again.

I had to laugh.

Vonnegut is poking fun at religion once more, but he's also explaining again why people believe in it: Because they feel they must have faith in *something*.

We have seen that other humanists share the gentle idea that, whatever else you can say about it, religion fills a basic human need. It's one reason why Joyce Carol Oates expressed hesitancy in a response she gave shortly after receiving the Humanist of the Year award in 2007. An appeal to decency worthy of Vonnegut's runs throughout Oates's reply to a question about her atheism.

> I'm not averse to acknowledging it, but as a novelist and a writer, I really don't want to confront and be antagonistic toward people. As soon as you declare that you are an atheist, it's like somebody declaring that he is the son of God; it arouses a lot of antagonism. I'm wondering whether it might be better to avoid arousing this antagonism in order to find—not compromise—some common ground...
>
> Basically, I have characters who present different points of view. Some of them are extremely atheistic and irreverent, and mock religion, which seems very easy to do given the sort of cartoon or caricature aspect of people who have blind faith. [Christopher] Hitchens points out this comic aspect very well, and he is very funny about it. But if you do that, you demonize people and turn them into ridiculous objects. Again, I'm not sure that's a really good idea, because though you can say religion poisons everything, the fact is that religion seems to be hardwired in our species.

Pretend to be good always

Even outside religion, human beings cannot resist the lure of untruthfulness in their search for meaning, or at least for a means by which to survive. That search can be internal. Sometimes the greatest lies we tell ourselves are *about* ourselves.

Mother Night, Vonnegut's fictitious account of an American spy who faces trial for broadcasting Nazi propaganda in wartime Germany, is concerned more with lying to oneself than lying on a broader scale. The invective spewed by first-person narrator Howard W. Campbell Jr., perhaps Vonnegut's most complicated character, is rooted in his duplicity.

A successful playwright who marries a beautiful German actress and parties gracefully with Nazi elite, Campbell is comfortable acting like a Nazi. He futilely hopes his performances reading government-supplied screeds against Jews on the radio will be perceived as "merely ludicrous."

Instead, he recalls, "so many people *wanted* to believe me!"

Still, Campbell is unconcerned about the effects of his lies. He does not even necessarily perceive them as lies. Then, given the opportunity to slip coded messages into his scripts—with imposed coughs, pauses, and other verbal cues that are meaningful to Allied agents but incomprehensible to the man broadcasting them—he agrees because it's all the same to him. It's an acting job.

> I would fool everyone with my brilliant interpretation of a Nazi, inside and out.
>
> And I did fool everybody. I began to strut like Hitler's right-hand man, and nobody saw the honest me I hid so deep inside.

Campbell justifies his behavior at the time as a means of existing in a world he did not make. He can temporarily escape that world in idyllic bliss with his wife.

> No matter what I was really, no matter what I really meant, uncritical love was what I needed—and my Helga was the angel who gave it to me....
>
> We didn't listen to each other's words. We heard only the melodies in our voices....
>
> If we had listened for more, had thought about what we heard, what a nauseated couple we would have been! Away from the sovereignty of our nation of two, we talked like the patriotic lunatics all around us.
>
> But it did not count.
>
> Only one thing counted—
>
> The nation of two.

That romantic ideal is based on the faith, the false hope, that reality can be ignored. The US government official who asks Campbell to consider spying warns the playwright that "this war isn't going to let anybody stay in a peaceful trade." He might have added "or in a nation of two."

Once that nation is destroyed when Helga disappears and is presumed dead, Campbell realizes he's lost his refuge for good: "I became what I am today and what I always will be, a stateless person."

Campbell's behavior, however much an act it might be, brands him as complicit with the Nazi state because his role as a spy is known to very few and cannot be revealed publicly. For years after the war, he lives quietly in New York until being discovered and captured. Writing his memoir, he awaits trial in Israel as what the world thinks he is: not a stateless person, but a war criminal.

Other characters in *Mother Night* have their own layers of identity.

One of Campbell's prison guards is a Hungarian Jew who obtained fake papers, joined the ranks of the S.S., and was placed in a special detachment that sought to root out an internal leak who was tipping off the Jews. The Hungarian himself was that leak, and fourteen S.S. men were shot based on information the special unit collected.

He says to Campbell, without regret, "Tell them the things a man does to stay alive!"

Early in his introduction to *Mother Night*'s second edition, Vonnegut says this is the novel's moral: "We are what we pretend to be, so we must be careful about what we pretend to be."

He does not say "we must not pretend" but that "we must be careful" about it.

The Hungarian guard, who pretended to an extreme degree but was sufficiently careful, survived. Campbell, who was not careful enough, cannot avoid the consequences of being, as he puts it, "a man who served evil too openly and good too secretly, the crime of his times."

And yes, Campbell comprehends evil. He does not consider himself capable of it. There's a showdown with Bernard B. O'Hare (the near namesake of Vonnegut's wartime buddy), who had captured him at the war's end fifteen years earlier and according to Campbell is "the man who perceived his noblest aspect in his loathing and hounding of me." O'Hare calls Campbell "absolutely pure evil."

Campbell rejects the charge and fires back at O'Hare with contempt.

> "There are plenty of good reasons for fighting," I said, "but no good reason ever to hate without reservation, to imagine that God Almighty Himself hates with you, too. Where's evil? It's that large part of every man that wants to hate without limit, that wants to hate with God on its side. It's that part of every man that finds all kinds of ugliness so attractive."

Humanist or otherwise, most people can appreciate the dilemma facing Campbell, the Hungarian Jew, and anyone else who is a pawn in a war game: The only way to survive an immoral situation when you are powerless might be to act in ways that otherwise could be considered immoral.

An accompanying ethical lesson to be derived from all of this can be found two novels and four years after *Mother Night*, in Vonnegut's *God Bless You, Mr. Rosewater*. It is etched into the rim of a fountain on the grounds of a mental hospital:

> "Pretend to be good always, and even God will be fooled."

Bokonon teaches his followers that, if you're going to believe lies, then believe lies that make you happy. Vonnegut tells us to be careful when pretending. The fountain inscription advises that we should pretend to be good.

Rabo Karabekian, the artist who narrates Vonnegut's 1987 novel, *Bluebeard*, sums it up: "Belief is nearly the whole of the Universe, whether based on truth or not."

Different kinds of truth

Although the words of Rabo Karabekian and the hospital fountain and Bokonon are found in Vonnegut's novels, by now we know his fictional statements often matched his real thoughts.

That's the case with his claim that he truly believed in the cosmic phenomenon that is the source of Winston Niles Rumfoord's miraculous powers in *The Sirens of Titan*. Twelve years after creating that phenomenon, Vonnegut declared the idea behind it—the "intolerable balancing of characters and arguments"—to be a reflection of his "true feelings."

> I felt and I still feel that everybody is right, no matter what he says...I gave a name in that book to a mathematical point where all opinions, no matter how contradictory, harmonized. I called it a *chrono-synclastic infundibulum*.
> I live in one.

The passage is from Vonnegut's 1971 preface to *Happy Birthday, Wanda June*. It is part of his explanation of why his stories lack true villains and how he feels the flatness of his characters doomed an earlier version of that play. The rest of the preface explores normal thoughts about the play's production.

When first inspected, Vonnegut's claim to exist in "a mathematical point where all opinions [are] harmonized"—even considering that he sometimes employed hyperbole to make a point—is curious, to put it mildly.

There is plenty to find wrong with the notion that all opinions can be harmonized. For one thing, how can racism, misogyny, and other types of mean-spirited prejudice—that is, noxious opinions—be right?

How can they be harmonized with tolerant, respectful viewpoints? Why *should* they?

Well, imagine a place where human differences don't matter. A haven that exists now, not in an afterlife, and is somehow accessible. Where there are no heroes and no villains. Where contradictory opinions don't lead to conflict.

Where nevertheless, because of our very differences, we remain human.

By embracing the chrono-synclastic infundibulum, a bit of fiction in a typically confessional piece of writing, Vonnegut was being careful about his pretending. He had chosen, he said, to live by that particular foma.

This is the man who the year before, as we saw early in this chapter, was asking freshly minted college graduates to "become an enemy of truth and a fanatic for harmless balderdash"—for example, that human beings are instruments of God's plan—because "if you can believe that and make others believe it, then there might be hope for us."

He was aware, he later wrote, that "many people find my speeches, and probably my books, too, hopelessly ambiguous." Part of the ambiguity is because his approach to characters and situations, learned from his study of anthropology, is relative.

Back where the chrono-synclastic infundibulum is originally described, in *The Sirens of Titan*, the wondrous galactic portal is a merging point "where all the different kinds of truths fit together."

Those are not Rumfoord's words. We're told they are from "the fourteenth edition of *A Child's Cyclopedia of Wonders and Things to Do*," which instructs its young readers that "there is room enough for an awful lot of people to be right about things and still not agree" because "there are so many different ways of being right."

The *Cyclopedia* asks its young reader to imagine that his or her Daddy knows everything there is to know and that he meets another man just as smart and just as right from another planet far away: "They would get into a terrible argument, because they wouldn't agree on anything."

There's hope, however. The *Cyclopedia* teaches that infundibula are places "where each Daddy could finally catch on to what the other Daddy was talking about."

Places where we can truly *understand*, in other words. Where prejudice doesn't matter—the only kind of place where harmony is possible.

This is also what Vonnegut felt about the merits of various cultures. He believed all cultures on Earth made valuable contributions, so why couldn't all the planets in all the universe do the same?

Vonnegut wished he'd learned about cultures long before attending the University of Chicago after the war, but once he learned he never forgot.

> A first-grader should understand that his culture isn't a rational invention; that there are thousands of other cultures and they all work pretty well; that all cultures function on faith rather than truth; that there are lots of alternatives to our own society.

That notion had become fashionable, he realized, "but it's more than fashionable—it's defensible, attractive. It's also a source of hope. It means we don't have to continue this way if we don't like it."

The chrono-synclastic infundibulum's visions of harmony and possibility provided the kind of hope that some people get from religion.

> People will believe anything, which means I will believe anything. I learned that in anthropology. I want to start believing in things that have shapeliness and harmony.

What should humanists think about this? As it turns out, "Humanism and Its Aspirations" does not address chrono-synclastic infundibula. It does say we "accept our life as all and enough, distinguishing things as they are from things as we might wish or imagine them to be."

Such distinguishing does not mean we should stop wishing and working for things to be better than they are. Humanists value civic and planetary duty and "the rich heritage of human culture." That heritage, surely, includes our imagination.

Taken word for word, Vonnegut's conviction "that everybody is right, no matter what he says" is nonsensical. Assuming Vonnegut did not literally believe that, it becomes a work of imagination, an invitation to join him in his comforting lie or to concoct one of your own.

A humanistic lie might be: Human beings ought to be treated with kindness.

Maybe that's what Vonnegut meant by his odd sentiment, and maybe it isn't. We can grant that he wished opinions could harmonize. They cause so much trouble when they don't.

Of course, nothing was quite that simple for the often ambiguous Vonnegut, not even comforting lies. He realized that unfounded notions also can be harmful. In *Galápagos*, opinions are "hobgoblins," and they help lead to the demise of humankind as we know it.

Chapter 4

Thanks a Lot, Big Brain

Nothing ever happens around here anymore that I haven't seen or heard so many times before. Nobody, surely, is going to write Beethoven's Ninth Symphony—or tell a lie, or start a Third World War.

Leon Trout, Galápagos

Any writer can tell us that life is an absurdity in which human beings find meaning in religion and art and national identity and so on, but I know of only one author who used a one-million-year-old headless ghost to describe how we escape the mess we're in.

The solution Kurt Vonnegut offered is fraught with side effects that we of the Holocene Epoch might consider deal breakers. Do we want to give up art and romance and imagination in favor of evolving to a contented but less intelligent state? Is that an acceptable way to continue existing, even if it saves the planet from us?

As usual, in his 1985 novel, *Galápagos*, Vonnegut examines more than one side of the argument. He asks us to think about which qualities make us human—including those that lead us toward destruction—and questions whether those qualities are worth preserving.

A confluence of events in *Galápagos* appears to be pushing Homo sapiens to extinction. Women across the Earth—although no one knows it yet—are being rendered sterile because of a "bacterium which eats human eggs." Worldwide financial ruin is contributing to global famine and increased acts of war. In Guayaquil, Ecuador, just east of the archipelago that Charles Darwin made famous, the upcoming Nature Cruise of the Century seems doomed to failure.

BEHAVING DECENTLY

In fact, the ship runs aground near the (fictional) island of Santa Rosalia, and one of its intended passengers, a widowed schoolteacher named Mary Hepburn, becomes the savior of the human race.

The novel is narrated far in the future by obscure science fiction writer Kilgore Trout's son, who has seen people evolve into seal-like creatures that we would not recognize as human. Shortly after being decapitated in a shipyard accident in 1986, Leon Trotsky Trout takes on spectral form in which he can inhabit minds and travel anywhere at will. He observes as a few key moments set in motion a course of nature, nudged by happenstance, that takes humankind on a journey of survival and change.

Along the way, people lose the feature that Vonnegut identifies as our most distinctive and most troublesome.

"Human beings had much bigger brains back then than they do today," Leon Trout reports a million years from now, "and so they could be beguiled by mysteries."

Art and romance and imagination are some of those beguiling mysteries. Art and romance *are* imagination, mixed in with the opinions that come from our big brains, which also lead us to war, to greed, to behaving badly toward fellow humans.

The big brain of con artist James Wait, a passenger on the Nature Cruise of the Century, works overtime to invent identities and biographies with which to ensnare rich widows. And it isn't just Wait, it's the entire species, Trout says: "Nobody believed anybody anymore, since there was so much lying going on."

Because of oversized brains, we convince ourselves to act against our own interests, as the narrator admits about himself:

> When I was alive, I often received advice from my own big brain which, in terms of my own survival, or the survival of the human race, for that matter, can be charitably described as questionable. Example: It had me join the United States Marines and go fight in Vietnam.
> Thanks a lot, big brain.

In *Galápagos*, evolution streamlines our brains and eliminates "the hobgoblins of opinions." This is a big success, if you define success as surviving regardless of what is lost and whether anyone is capable of *realizing* it has been lost.

And you have to wonder whether the next stage of evolution is even human; that is, Homo sapien. Do furry, fish-eating swimmers with flippers instead of arms and legs qualify as human beings? Maybe so. Trout still calls them "people."

Success comes at an enormous cost: People lose art and romance. On the other hand, they don't seek distractions to make life worthwhile. They just need to find stuff to eat, and to avoid being eaten.

"Take it from somebody who has been around for a million years," Leon says. "When you get right down to it, food is practically the whole story every time."

Ethics and morality are gone too, a million years from now. People's brains are too small to conceive of anything so fancy.

In mixing outcomes with accidents, *Galápagos* might give the impression that the willful acts of humans have little to do with the fate of the species. And yet, there's postmenopausal Mary Hepburn secretly trying to artificially inseminate the few young women remaining from a nearly extinct Ecuadorian tribe.

Mary intends to continue the lineage of the handful of humans who are stranded on Santa Rosalia. Unwittingly, her ultimately successful project helps to continue the lineage of *all* humans.

For most humanists, the combination of accident and adaptation will sound about right. Whether the evolutionary gain is worth the loss is another matter.

Galápagos might be another Vonnegut masterpiece, joining, say, *Cat's Cradle* and *Slaughterhouse-Five* in the author's pantheon, where he seems most confident and at the top of his novel-writing talent.

Vonnegut liked *Galápagos* very much. "The best book I ever wrote," he called it in 1991. Back in 1986, the year after *Galápagos* was published, he told radio show host Terry Gross it was one of his favorite books of his, along with *The Sirens of Titan* and *Deadeye Dick*. (He had previously given grades of A or A-plus to *Mother Night*; *Cat's Cradle*; *God Bless You, Mr. Rosewater*; *Slaughterhouse-Five*; and *Jailbird*, generally following critical opinion.)

On his sixty-ninth birthday—during an interview conducted, incidentally, inside a Lincoln, Nebraska, strip club—Vonnegut awarded *Galápagos* the highest grade.

> That's an A+, I think, because it's gotten a very good response from the scientific community and it caused no comment elsewhere...I think it was a whizbang of a scientific essay on the chanciness of evolution.

"I'm not very grateful for Darwin"

Vonnegut thought better of his novel about evolution than about evolution itself. That is, he deplored how Darwin's theory was often appropriated as justification for contemptible behavior by creatures who, besides harming and killing themselves, were destroying the environment.

Darwin's 1859 book, *On the Origin of Species by Means of Natural Selection, or the Preservation of Favoured Races in the Struggle for Life,* is described in *Galápagos* by ghost narrator Leon as "the most broadly influential scientific volume produced during the entire era of great big brains," a publication that "did more to stabilize people's volatile opinions of how to identify success or failure than any other tome."

That second point is what bothered Vonnegut. Talking to *Playboy* twelve years before *Galápagos* was published, he was prepared to cast aside Darwin, or at least Darwinism as it's often understood in modern times: an interpretation of natural selection that benefits the powerful and the cunning, who imagine themselves to be "the fittest" and therefore the best suited for survival.

"I'm not very grateful for Darwin," Vonnegut said,

> although I suspect he was right. His ideas make people crueler. Darwinism says to them that people who get sick deserve to be sick, that people who are in trouble must deserve to be in trouble. When anybody dies, cruel Darwinists imagine we're obviously improving ourselves in some way. And any man who's on top is there because he's a superior animal. That's the social Darwinism of the past century, and it continues to boom. But forget Darwin.

Heartless people, in other words, use Darwin's scientific conclusions to justify their ruthlessness, as if natural selection is all about pouncing on weakness and has nothing to do with chance.

Blaming the famed naturalist for such entitlement—if that was Vonnegut's intent—unfairly assigns guilt to Darwin by association, it seems to me. Darwin Day (February 12) is celebrated by humanists for scientific, not social, Darwinism. It reaffirms that we should learn through discovery rather than believe through superstition.

Certain theories derived from Darwin's discoveries made Vonnegut queasy about the man. That's too bad. Most humanists, although they don't have to revere Darwin—or anyone else—*are* grateful for him.

Vonnegut did realize that evolution is more than the "survival of the fittest." In *Galápagos,* luck is a significant factor in pushing humanity to the next stage of its development.

The fortuitous wreck on Santa Rosalia isolates the ship's few passengers from the biological calamity taking place everywhere else on Earth. Mary's actions are crucial, and they're possible only because, in a low moment, she decides not to commit suicide and because a crazed Ecuadorian soldier on a rampage inadvertently provides a means to sustain the lives of six starving girls who "would become the mothers of all humankind."

Reviewing the novel, author Lorrie Moore concludes that Vonnegut wants to tell us, among other things, "It is not the fittest who survive—it is merely those who happen to survive who survive."

Later in his life, while not abandoning his suspicion that Darwin was right, Vonnegut further lamented that humans ended up with dominion over the planet. "Evolution," he wrote, "can go to hell as far as I am concerned. What a mistake we are."

Such misanthropy can be traced to more than Vonnegut's longstanding penchant for making provocative statements, although it's certainly another one of those. And it's not just the bitterness of an old man two years from death.

Vonnegut gets to "What a mistake we are" as an anthropologist would. What else could be deduced from the self-destructive human habits he complained about? Over the decades, his public comments grew increasingly alarmed about the ecological threats that people create.

His interest in the health of the environment goes back to his childhood. *Galápagos* is dedicated to the man who led a memorable high school excursion:

> In memory of Hillis L. Howie,
> (1903—1982) amateur naturalist—
> A good man who
> took me and my best friend Ben Hitz
> and some other boys
> out to the American Wild West
> from Indianapolis, Indiana,
> in the summer of 1938.

On that trip to the Four Corners of New Mexico, Howie taught the boys how to sleep outdoors,

> and he told us the names of many plants
>   and animals,
> and what they needed to do
> in order to stay alive
> and reproduce themselves.

Many years later, in 1982, Vonnegut and his second wife, Jill Krementz, visited the Galápagos Islands. There, unlike on his trips to Biafra and Mozambique (which we'll review later), he saw life on the planet at its wondrous best: harmless creatures in their own communities, oblivious to the activities of the earth's smarter inhabitants.

"I have seen those birds, by the way—up close," he told an audience at the Cathedral of St. John two months after the trip, referring to the islands' blue-footed boobies. "I could have unscrewed their heads, if I had wanted to."

It's like the ghost narrating *Galápagos* says: "This was a very innocent planet, except for those great big brains."

Vonnegut's fatalism about humanity's treatment of its home did not dissipate just because his novel found a way to prevent our descendants from harming the Earth the way we have. His grim outlook persisted in a 1988 magazine article that, ironically, primarily concerns how things were much *better* in America than they used to be.

> There is no stopping us. We will continue to breed like rabbits. We will continue to engage in technological nincompoopery with hideous side effects unseen. We will make only token repairs on our cities now collapsing. We will not clean up much of the poisonous mess that we ourselves have made.

In that article, Vonnegut conceded he has become in at least one significant way like a James Thurber creation called the Royal Astronomer, an aging medieval court adviser who reported that the stars were going out—because he himself was going blind.

Vonnegut for the most part did not feel like that Thurber character, "a sort of old poop who imagined that life was ending not merely for himself but for the whole universe." In his lifetime Vonnegut had seen improvements: no more lynchings, for example, far less overt racism and anti-Semitism, better opportunities for women.

Moreover, he felt, many revered figures of the past were unworthy of the unconditional respect accorded them. "Almost none of the ancient wise men believed in real equality," he pointed out, "but we believe in it."

Vonnegut admitted to being a Royal Astronomer, however, when it came to the prospect of Earth remaining habitable. His contention that the planet has been doomed by human excess and neglect is summed up in a quote that he tried out in the 1988 article, which was reprinted in the nonfiction collection *Fates Worse Than Death* (1991). He used a shorter version in the novel *Hocus Pocus* (1990).

Then, in *A Man Without a Country* (2005), he devised an epitaph for the planet with wording closest to what still appears on social media:

> "The good Earth—we could have saved it, but we were too damn cheap and lazy."

The document "Humanism and Its Aspirations" states that we have "a planetary duty to protect nature's integrity, diversity, and beauty in a secure, sustainable manner." Vonnegut was convinced it's too late to make up for our having failed miserably in that duty.

Hope for humankind

And yet *Galápagos*—written in the mid-1980s, when his glum vision was fully formed—is one of Vonnegut's most optimistic books. From the epigraph quoting Anne Frank ("In spite of everything, I still believe people are really good at heart.") to the last sentence ("You'll learn, you'll learn."), Vonnegut seems buoyed by the clever way he has found for people, in spite of everything, to be content with life.

Leon Trout sure sounds content as he prepares to enter the "blue tunnel to the Afterlife." He could have joined his late father on the tunnel's other side back in 1986. That's when curmudgeonly Kilgore Trout tells Leon that, like his mother, also deceased, Leon is an optimist.

"You believe that human beings are good animals," Kilgore says, "who will eventually solve all their problems and make earth into a Garden of Eden again."

Leon's curiosity about the fate of humanity cost him the chance to reunite with his parents. He had hesitated at the tunnel's entrance upon hearing Mary Hepburn, the schoolteacher and ultimate savior of her species, cry out.

Mary happened to be shouting "Land ho!" as Santa Rosalia came into view, and when Leon "looked back at the tunnel, the tunnel was gone." He remains a ghostly presence on Earth for a million years, long enough to see how things turn out and to narrate the proceedings that he assumes no one ever will or ever can read.

With that chronicle nearly finished, Leon Trout reflects. He is satisfied.

> I have now completed that sentence of one thousand millennia. I have paid in full my debt to society or whatever. I can expect to see the blue tunnel again at any time. I will of course skip into its mouth most gladly. Nothing ever happens around here anymore that I haven't seen or heard so many times before. Nobody, surely, is going to write Beethoven's Ninth Symphony—or tell a lie, or start a Third World War.
>
> Mother was right: Even in the darkest times, there really was still hope for humankind.

That rosy belief underpins the book's idea that we will evolve out of our miseries, albeit into something we might not recognize as human.

I find the ending of *Galápagos* similarly upbeat: "You'll learn, you'll learn," a Swedish doctor tells the narrator, who at the time is a still-living, syphilitic Marine and not yet a headless ghost. The doctor is assuring the Marine: You will figure it out if you seek political asylum in Sweden even though you do not speak the language there.

That is: You will *adapt*. That's what living things do.

Given enough time and luck, maybe evolution will prove beneficial to both us *and* the planet.

The novel leaves unstated but open an intriguing possibility. What if we spend the next few million years catching fish and lying in the sun, hurting nothing except a constantly replenishing food supply while natural selection continues to work in the background?

Slowly but surely, perhaps we'll again regain the abiity to use tools, this time with slightly bigger brains that are less complicated than ours, programmed more ethically.

It's a long-range view indeed, but maybe there really is still hope for humankind.

Life: Half Full or Half Empty?

These quotes by Kurt Vonnegut are arranged chronologically. More precise attribution is in the Notes section at the back.

1945 Hey, Corporal Vonnegut, maybe you were wrong to be an optimist. Maybe pessimism is the thing.

1970 Everything is going to become unimaginably worse, and never get better again.

1973 I couldn't survive my own pessimism if I didn't have some kind of sunny little dream. That's mine, and don't tell me I'm wrong. Human beings *will* be happier...when they find ways to inhabit primitive communities again.

1974 For two thirds of my life I have been a pessimist. I am astonished to find myself an optimist now...Thank God we are beginning to dream of human communities which are designed to harmonize with what human beings really need and are.

1983 I'm really quite optimistic about human nature, but the constitution of our culture seems to be deadly.

1989 I think the human situation is hopeless, and so I've been working mainly on epitaphs for the human race.

1991 I'm pessimistic just 'cause the news is so awful, and you catch hell for noticing.

1995 It seems to me that it's no more trouble to be virtuous than to be vicious. I'm critical, but not a pessimist.

1997 I believe in original sin. I also believe in original virtue. Look around!

2005 I know now that there is not a chance in hell of America becoming humane and reasonable.

2005 I have to have been one of the luckiest persons alive...I can't begin to count the times I should have been dead or wished I were.

2006 There is nothing [young environmentalists] can do. It's over, my friend. The game is lost.

2007 My country is in ruins...I'm mostly just heartsick about this. There should have been hope. This should have been a great country. But we are despised all over the world now.

Chapter 5

A Great Time for Comedians

Jokes can be noble. Laughs are exactly as honorable as tears. Laughter and tears are both responses to frustration and exhaustion, to the futility of thinking and striving anymore. I myself prefer to laugh, since there is less cleaning up to do afterward—and since I can start thinking and striving again that much sooner.

Kurt Vonnegut, March 30, 1980

Kurt Vonnegut wavered between pessimism and optimism. As a humanist he had little choice. There are no guarantees we will preserve the planet or ensure our own survival or simply commit to kindness worldwide, so it's possible we never will. But we've solved some other big problems, so maybe we'll make it.

What's a reasonable response to those twin possibilities except to feel both dismayed by the first thought and buoyed by the second? Most of us feel different ways at different times.

No matter how you feel, humor can fit your mood. It is neither optimistic nor pessimistic by default. We associate it with laughter, but you can laugh out of cruelty as well as mirth. You can laugh at circumstances you find ridiculous rather than funny.

"I had to laugh like hell," a *Hocus Pocus* character says repeatedly without ever laughing.

Humor can be hurtful and offensive, and yet at its best it reminds us that we shouldn't take ourselves too seriously. When we're feeling good, it can complement our giddiness. When we're at low points, it can help us deal with them.

And when we're not sure how we feel, humor can inexplicably satisfy our uncertainty with its own ambiguity.

That's a pretty neat trick, to be useful in good times, bad times, and confusing times. That about covers everything.

Now, I've just inspected "Humanism and Its Aspirations" again, and I couldn't find anything in there about being funny. This is as close as it gets:

> We aim for our fullest possible development and animate our lives with a deep sense of purpose, finding wonder and awe in the joys and beauties of human existence, its challenges and tragedies, and even in the inevitability and finality of death.

Not exactly a barrel of laughs. Surely a little levity is a healthy part of "our fullest possible development," but nowhere in the whole aspirational statement does it say that humanists believe individual happiness is maximized by well-told jokes.

It isn't just the AHA document. Secular humanism progenitor Paul Kurtz (1925–2012) produced 21 bullet points in his "Affirmations of Humanism" without affirming the role of humor.

Acknowledging these absences is long overdue, it seems to me. Human beings' embrace of humor ought to be recognized as an essential, positive trait, even if it's unique to us only by degree. (Researchers report laughter-like reactions in everything from rats to dolphins—especially among apes—although their stand-up routines leave something to be desired.)

Laughter can occur involuntarily, like when you're tickled. It can also come on without a physical cause, suggesting a more complex response learned over years of living on Earth—a sense of humor.

It can even have practical applications.

"Laughter is…not simply a psychological relief valve, but a collective guard against despotism," British anthropologist Chris Knight wrote. "When moved to laugh by those around us, we reveal ourselves to be truly human."

I'm not thinking much about despotism when watching, say, Monty Python skits, but that British troupe's ridicule of pomposity does signify something important. The same is true of other comedians globally. If we're free to make the ruling class look silly, then the rulers are not completely in charge.

To its credit, "Humanism and Its Aspirations" doesn't say *not* to value humor. And although the document is also silent about sex, sports, and other recreational activity, surely it has no objection to *them*.

Maybe all of that will be included in the Humanist Manifesto Version IV.

The soul seeking some relief

I tried to show in the dueling quotes preceding this chapter that Vonnegut felt both hopeful and hopeless. He believed that, despite our many screw-ups, being human is not loathsome. It's just worth mocking.

This is a good place to follow where Vonnegut's humor leads us. His up-and-down inclinations will take us everywhere from slip-on-a-banana-peel comedy to knowing satire, through laughter and tears, optimism and pessimism, playfulness and cynicism.

Vonnegut was exclusively neither a winsome Winnie the Pooh nor a curmudgeonly Eeyore, but as he grew old, despair became more prominent in his writing and speaking. He was particularly disheartened regarding our species' failed stewardship of the planet. This attitude, he feared, made him less funny—that is, made him defenseless.

Pessimism gradually eroded his sense that humor was a useful reaction to some problems. Vonnegut pointed to his wartime experience as a factor.

In middle age, about a year after *Slaughterhouse-Five* had catapulted him to fame, Vonnegut reflected on how his youthful belief that "scientific truth was going to make us *so* happy and comfortable" had been challenged by the horrors of World War II—by the Holocaust, the aerial bombing of Dresden and other cities, the use of nuclear weapons on Japan, and so on.

"I have been a consistent pessimist ever since, with a few exceptions," he told an audience at Bennington College in 1970. After that, in his public comments he seldom called himself an optimist without attaching a qualifier.

Vonnegut and contemporaries like Noam Chomsky and Howard Zinn possessed what publisher Dan Simon called "earned optimism." As members of the "'Great Depression Generation' [who] saw it get really bad," Simon said, they had been "cleaned of false optimism even post-World War II."

A true pessimist could not have produced some two dozen books in a lifetime, son Mark Vonnegut said: "He had an odd kind of optimism that he doesn't get enough credit for."

This is hard to pin down, right? The perspective in Vonnegut's long fiction, too, is ever shifting. Look at the various moods in which he tries to leave readers.

Besides the *Galápagos* ending ("You'll learn, you'll learn.") that I mentioned in the last chapter, relatively upbeat conclusions can be found in Vonnegut's books both early and late in his career.

As *The Sirens of Titan*'s Malachi Constant dies, he heads to Paradise—at least in his mind. The title character of *God Bless You, Mr. Rosewater* redirects his imperiled fortune to anyone who claims to be his child, providing a solution to his predicament and a windfall for lots of people who need the money.

In *Bluebeard* the narrator, his body and soul having achieved harmony, exclaims without irony, "Oh, happy Meat. Oh, happy Soul. Oh, happy Rabo Karabekian."

Vonnegut's darker endings, however, perhaps have greater resonance. The presumed suicide of Howard W. Campbell Jr. in *Mother Night*, the icy apocalypse of *Cat's Cradle*, the teary self-doodle that places a period on *Breakfast of Champions* as Kilgore Trout cries out to be made young: Again and again, Vonnegut lays waste to cities, nations, and civilizations, along the way deflating their self-importance and many of the idealistic notions their inhabitants hold.

Deadeye Dick, the book right before hopeful *Galápagos*, leaves the reader with this downer: "We are still in the Dark Ages. The Dark Ages—they haven't ended yet." Vonnegut called his 1990 novel, *Hocus Pocus*, "a sardonic fable in a bed of gloom."

All of that darkness comes from a renowned humorist. Of course, that is not a contradiction. They say comedy is tragedy plus time. And Vonnegut was, after all, "a laughing prophet of doom." He knew that, if you do it correctly and your audience understands, you can make a good joke about anything.

Well, *almost* anything. "Some things aren't funny," Vonnegut wrote late in his life.

> I can't imagine a humorous book or skit about Auschwitz, for instance. And it's not possible for me to make a joke about the death of John F. Kennedy or Martin Luther King. Otherwise I can't think of any subject that I would steer away from, that I could do nothing with. Total catastrophes are terribly amusing, as Voltaire demonstrated. You know, the Lisbon earthquake is funny.
>
> I saw the destruction of Dresden. I saw the city before and then came out of an air-raid shelter and saw it afterward, and certainly one response was laughter. God knows, that's the soul seeking some relief.

And yet Vonnegut—that is, his characters—*did* joke about Auschwitz. It happens in *Mother Night*, where Vonnegut takes two approaches to notorious Nazi officials. One short passage, not about Auschwitz, is mild and gently amusing, harming no one. The other is told at the expense of the Nazis' victims and makes you want to punch somebody.

First, the gentler one. I've mentioned that *Mother Night* pretends to be Howard W. Campbell Jr.'s memoir, written in an Israeli cell while he awaits trial for war crimes. Also being held for trial in Israel—as he was in real life—is none other than Adolf Eichmann, who had been tasked with getting Jews to the death camps efficiently.

Eichmann lacks remorse. In fact, he seems content. He too is writing the story of his life. He slips Campbell a note: "Do you think a literary agent is absolutely necessary?"

Campbell's reply: "For book club and movie sales in the United States of America, absolutely."

Even though Eichmann is despicable, Vonnegut the author is winking at us, commenting not about human rights but intellectual property rights. Such mundane dialogue at that time and place, I think, is funny.

The other joke is not meant to be laughed at.

Campbell is conversing with Joseph Goebbels, the Reich Minister of Propaganda. Goebbels wants Campbell to write a pageant that he would produce, after the war, about the heroic Germans who died while defeating the Jewish uprising in Warsaw. This spectacle would be staged in the very ghetto where the triumph occurred.

The exchange, in which Auschwitz commandant Rudolf Hoess is mentioned for good measure, begins with Campbell seeking clarity.

> "There would be Jews in the pageant?" I asked him.
> "Certainly—" he said, "thousands of them."
> "May I ask, sir," I said, "where you expect to find any Jews after the war?"
> He saw the humor in this. "A very good question," he said, chuckling. "We'll have to take that up with Hoess," he said.
> "With whom?" I said. I hadn't yet been to Warsaw, hadn't yet met with brother Hoess.
> "He's running a little health resort for Jews in Poland," said Goebbels. "We must be sure to ask him to save us some."

Using an entirely different sort of humor than the lines about literary representation, Vonnegut makes it clear that Goebbels and by implication all Nazis who enabled the Holocaust were monsters. The intent is to chill rather than amuse, chide, ridicule, or insult.

And while Vonnegut places the Eichmann publishing quip at the end of a narrative passage—like a punchline—he inserts the Goebbels segment in the middle of one, as if to make it a bit less ghastly. Still, it packs a wallop.

Vonnegut has shown that he *can* "imagine a...skit about Auschwitz" by having one of his characters envision it. His humor's shock value is sparked by the friction between utterly abominable circumstances and the witty but contemptible reaction to them.

Writing about Eichmann, Hannah Arendt referred to "the banality of evil." How's this for banality: Eichmann used to be an oil salesman. He advanced from that to become a top Nazi official. And propaganda meister Goebbels, whose job was to sell genocide, really did write plays, newspaper articles, and a novel in his youth. He could have conceived of the pageant described in *Mother Night*, could have said the things that Vonnegut had him say.

Humanists tend to view evil as something committed by former salesmen, failed playwrights, and other ordinary people. Wrongdoers are pushed to action by inner demons, self-interest, charismatic leaders, and mob mentality rather than corrupted by a literal Satan opposing God.

Even the Nazis were ordinary for a while, Vonnegut is telling us. That's one of the lessons about Germany between the world wars: Don't think it can't happen here.

Only one way to get anybody's attention

When *Playboy* asked Vonnegut whether humor was his "way of dealing with sadness, of coming to terms with problems you can't solve," he replied,

> Well, I try. But laughter is a response to frustration, just as tears are, and it solves nothing, just as tears solve nothing. Laughing or crying is what a human being does when there's nothing else he can do.

Laughter and humor are by no means solely optimistic. "It is my serious belief," Vonnegut wrote, "that those of us who become humorists (suicidal or not) feel free (as most people do not) to speak of life itself as a dirty joke, even though life is all there is or ever can be."

That could be considered pessimistic or simply realistic.

Former *Washington Post* features writer Gene Weingarten called humor "an exaggeration of the truth, done to make fun of our fears so as to help cope with them." That's why, Weingarten explained, he can joke about dementia even though his father suffered from it terribly in the last two years of his life.

The author Erica Jong said "humor is one of the most serious tools we have for dealing with impossible situations."

Joking about serious moral matters is essential to Vonnegut's art. To novelist Jay McInerney he was "a satirist with a heart, a moralist with a whoopee cushion, a cynic who wants to believe."

Vonnegut surely placed great value in the humorous slant he gave his work, even declaring, "All I really wanted to do was give people the relief of laughing." This is the man who at age eighty-two revived his comment "We are here on Earth to fart around. Don't let anybody tell you any different."

Still, he fully realized that joking was about more than getting laughs. "The telling of jokes is an art of its own, and it always rises from some emotional threat," Vonnegut said in a 2002 interview. "The best jokes are dangerous, and dangerous because they are in some way truthful."

Vonnegut was heavily influenced by American comedians, calling them "often as brilliant and magical as our best jazz musicians" and asserting "they have probably done more to shape my thinking than any writer."

His comedic heroes were Stan Laurel and Oliver Hardy, who starred in dozens of short and feature-length movies between 1921 and 1951. He found them to be "screamingly adorable and funny" because they were constantly imperiled but "did their best with every test."

> I used to laugh and laugh at Laurel and Hardy. There is terrible tragedy there somehow. These men are too sweet to survive in this world and are in terrible danger all the time. They could be killed so easily.

Looming physical harm was common among the duo's contemporaries and immediate predecessors. Laurel and Hardy futilely pushed a piano up a ridiculously long set of stairs. Buster Keaton stood immobile while the front of a house collapsed around him. Harold Lloyd dangled from a clock high above a city street. A blindfolded Charles Chaplin roller-skated along the edge of a two-story drop.

All of them seemingly "could be killed so easily." With the help of cinematic trickery, they confronted peril in ways marvelously creative, athletic, graceful, and funny. They taught keen observers like Vonnegut that laughing is a way of triumphing, if only temporarily.

Physical humor might be silly, but we seem wired to respond to silliness. In *Galápagos* the narrator says that doesn't change in the far future.

> People still laugh about as much as they ever did, despite their shrunken brains. If a bunch of them are lying around on a beach, and one of them farts, everybody else laughs and laughs, just as people would have done a million years ago.

The comedians Vonnegut favored were popular during one of the country's most difficult periods. The Great Depression "was a great time for...the radio comedians. And a very bad time in the history of the country," he told an interviewer in 1966. "Fred Allen, Jack Benny, and so forth, you got your little dose of humor every day, and the people did cluster around radios to pick up an amount of encouragement, an amount of relief."

Relief. Vonnegut kept coming back to that serious effect of being funny. Early on, Vonnegut had been drawn to humor as a means to be heard in a household that included his parents and two older siblings.

"When I was the littlest kid at our supper table, there was only one way I could get anybody's attention, and that was to be funny," he recalled. "I had to specialize. I used to listen to radio comedians very intently, so I could learn how to make jokes."

Vonnegut came to think of humor as more than an attention-grabbing device. In the 1980 quote that tops this chapter, he said he preferred laughing to crying because "there is less cleaning up to do afterward." Then he could "start thinking and striving again that much sooner."

Thinking and striving are determined reactions to tragedy.

An air of defeat

The two significant tragedies of Vonnegut's life that I mentioned in previous chapters, he said, affected him more than did the cataclysm of Dresden. They help explain his pessimism while also going beyond it.

His sister Alice's death from cancer at age forty-one robbed him of the person for whom he said he wrote. They shared a similar outlook. When commenting about her demise, Vonnegut referred to the kind of humor he and his sister most appreciated.

> "Soap opera!" she said to my brother and me one time, when discussing her own impending death. She would be leaving four young boys behind, without any mother.
>
> "Slapstick," she said...
>
> Exhaustion, yes, and deep money worries, too, made her say toward the end that she guessed that she wasn't really very good at life.
>
> Then again: Neither were Laurel and Hardy.

The apparent suicide of Vonnegut's mother resonated with him in a different way. That incident and his father's "full retreat from life" meant that "an air of defeat has always been a companion of mine." Both of his parents had been defeated by the Depression, which dealt a severe blow to the family's quite healthy finances. Kurt Sr. lost architectural clients and the opportunity to do meaningful work. Edith lost much of her wealth and status.

They exemplified how not to face life's inevitable disappointments, Vonnegut said in his *Playboy* interview:

I'm damned if I'll pass their useless sadness on to my children if I can possibly help it.

Part of the trick for people my age, I'm certain, is to crawl out of the envying, life-hating mood of the Great Depression at last...I know this much: After I'm gone, I don't want my children to have to say about me what I have to say about my father: "He made wonderful jokes, but he was such an unhappy man."

There's the Great Depression, from which Kurt Sr. and Edith and much of the nation never recovered, and then there's depression, which Vonnegut said also affected them and him. "Unhappy"—a word Vonnegut hoped would not be applied to him—does not adequately describe depression. That clinical term entails more than a blue mood and manifests in ways other than pessimism.

During the 1973 interview, Vonnegut described depression that he attributed to both bad chemicals and the state of the world.

> Until recently, every twenty days, I blew my cork. I thought for a long time that I had perfectly good reasons for these periodic blowups; I thought people around me had it coming to them. But only recently have I realized that this has been happening regularly since I've been six years old. There wasn't much the people around me could do about it...
>
> I've been taking lessons in how to deal with it. I've been going to a doctor once a week. It isn't psychoanalysis; it's a more superficial sort of thing. I'm talking to her about depression, trying to understand its nature. And a lot of it is physiological....
>
> But for me, this year is a much better one than last year was. Depressions really had me, and they don't this year. I'm managing much better. I was really very down the last couple of years, and by working at it, I've gotten myself up again. I'm getting help from intelligent people who aren't Freudians....
>
> But any sadness I feel now grows out of frustration, because I think there is so much we can do—things that are cheap—that we're not doing. It has to do with ideas.

Incidentally, despite the line about followers of Freud, Vonnegut felt the father of psychoanalysis was correct about a particular kind of humor that applied to Vonnegut's own work. Rather than "black humor," as writer Bruce Jay Friedman and others called it, Vonnegut preferred the term Freud had written about: "gallows humor."

His fellow writer Vance Bourjaily agreed, calling Vonnegut a gallows humorist rather than a black humorist: "Gallows humor is nothing much like black humor because its intention is pure kindness," Bourjaily contended. "Black humor is ghoulish and sadistic; gallows humor is human and gallant."

Gallows humor is "people laughing in the middle of political helplessness," Vonnegut said. "It's humor about weak, intelligent people in hopeless situations. And I have customarily written about powerless people who felt there wasn't much they could do about their situations."

There is, of course, another way in which people react to situations they feel they can do nothing about. Vonnegut's mother ultimately may have reacted that way. And suicide is a plot point in much of Vonnegut's fiction.

> My fascination with it, the fascination of many people with it, may be a legacy from the Great Depression. That Depression has more to do with the American character than any war. People felt so useless for so long.

While Vonnegut refers to America's history and makeup, a more personal connection is indisputable.

"Sons of suicide seldom do well," the narrator of *God Bless You, Mr. Rosewater* declares. He is referring to the title character's cousin Fred, whose father "blew his brains out." Anyone who knows Vonnegut's circumstances can't help but take notice. It continues:

> Characteristically, they find life lacking a certain zing. They tend to feel more rootless than most, even in a notoriously rootless nation. They are squeamishly incurious about the past and numbly certain about the future to this grisly extent: they suspect that they, too, will kill themselves.

Vonnegut, the self-described "monopolar depressive descended from monopolar depressives," expresses at least that last fear in *Breakfast of Champions*. "Suicide is at the heart of the book," he told *Playboy*. At one point its narrator, an "I" who seems to be Vonnegut himself, is sitting in a cocktail lounge, looking through mirrored sunglasses ("leaks" into another universe) at some of the characters he has created. He is having an interior dialogue.

> "This is a very bad book you're writing," I said to myself behind my leaks.
> "I know," I said.
> "You're afraid you'll kill yourself the way your mother did," I said.
> "I know," I said.

> There in the cocktail lounge, peering out through my leaks at a world of my own invention, I mouthed this word: schizophrenia.

That passage is rich with allusions to the real Kurt Vonnegut Jr. and proved prescient about his self-destructive thoughts. In March 1984, eleven years after *Breakfast of Champions* was published, he ended up in a Greenwich Village hospital for eighteen days, having been found "unconscious from a combination of alcohol, sleeping pills, and antidepressants," according to biographer Shields. "Beside his bed was a note saying, in effect, his former and current wife could continue quarreling over his will without him."

Vonnegut was adamant about his intentions when he recounted the incident seven years later.

> I had tried to kill myself. It wasn't a cry for help. It wasn't a nervous breakdown. I wanted "The Big Sleep" (Raymond Chandler). I wanted to "Slam the Big Door" (John D. MacDonald). No more jokes and no more coffee and no more cigarettes.
>
> I wanted *out* of here.

An optimist posing as a pessimist

Mark Vonnegut is skeptical that his father "wanted *out* of here." As Kurt Vonnegut's oldest child, the coexecutor of his estate, a pediatrician, and the author of two books about his own struggles with mental illness and another about practicing medicine, Mark is the most-quoted family member when it comes to Kurt. He's dubious about the intent behind the overdose.

> There was a bizarre, surreal incident when he took too many pills and ended up in a psych hospital, but it never felt like he was in much danger. Within a day he was bouncing around the dayroom playing Ping-Pong and making friends. It seemed like he was doing a not very convincing imitation of someone with mental illness.

"Of all the medications he took," Mark Vonnegut wrote, "there wasn't a toxic level of anything. He had a barely therapeutic level of Tylenol."

Similarly, Mark finds diagnoses of depression in his father—including those by Kurt himself—to be unconvincing.

> He didn't want to be happy and he said a lot of depressing things, but I honestly don't think he was ever depressed.

He was like an extrovert who wanted to be an introvert, a very social guy who wanted to be a loner, a lucky person who would have preferred to be unlucky. An optimist posing as a pessimist, hoping people will take heed.

"He was more angry than depressed," Mark Vonnegut wrote to me.

His youngest sibling, Nanette Vonnegut, while believing their father was mildly depressed from time to time, agrees that mainly he was exasperated by human behavior. "As he aged, he had less resilience, as we all do," she told me.

The political climate at the end of his life enraged him, he put it on paper and gave amazing interviews. What one might see as bitterness in him, another might see as realistic cynicism. My father was not ever defeated or crippled by depression, but he was at times depressed.

As Vonnegut's time ran short, he seemed to grow more despondent. Mark Vonnegut recalled, "It wasn't until the Iraq War and the end of his life that he became sincerely gloomy."

Like many of us, Kurt Vonnegut found the days of his youth more enjoyable than current times. He believed that Americans' dreams, at least, were not what they used to be.

Many years ago I was so innocent I still considered it possible that we could become the humane and reasonable America so many members of my generation used to dream of. We dreamed of such an America during the Great Depression, when there were no jobs. And then we fought and often died for that dream during the Second World War, when there was no peace.

But I know now that there is not a chance in hell of America becoming humane and reasonable. Because power corrupts us, and absolute power corrupts us absolutely.

No tomorrow

To be sure, Vonnegut could be downbeat in his younger years too, but as an old man he sounded especially tired and, for the first time, certain he wasn't funny anymore.

He had predicted as much. This is what he said during a celebration at Mark Twain's refurbished house in Hartford, Connecticut, in April 1979, when he was fifty-six years old:

> Religious skeptics often become very bitter toward the end, as did Mark Twain. I do not propose to guess now as to why he became so bitter. I know why I will become bitter. I will finally realize that I have had it right all along: that I will not see God, that there is no heaven or Judgment Day.

Eleven years later to the month, now at age sixty-seven, Vonnegut made similar comments in a *New York Times* essay but focused on his identity as a humorist rather than a skeptic, his public role rather than his private thoughts.

> For whatever reason, American humorists or satirists or whatever you want to call them, those who choose to laugh rather than weep about demoralizing information, become intolerable pessimists if they live past a certain age...
>
> But jokesters are all through when they find themselves talking about challenges so real and immediate and appalling to their listeners that no amount of laughter can make the listeners feel safe and perfectly well again.

Among those "challenges so real and immediate and appalling" are the environmental threats that are common to industrial societies. Humanity's many failures to address those threats were perhaps the biggest contributors to Vonnegut's dejection.

He could laugh about world war, the menace of nuclear annihilation, the growing cynicism of American government, and general human folly.

Ruining Earth was too much.

A Man Without a Country, Vonnegut's wide-ranging series of essays published as a book two years prior to his death, contains prime examples of his humorless prognosis. "We have squandered our planet's resources, including air and water, as though there were no tomorrow," he laments. "So now there isn't going to be one."

Vonnegut had found something besides Auschwitz and the deaths of JKF and MLK that he could not joke about. He was eighty-two, and nothing was going to change before he died. Humor was not making the bad news any easier to take, and he felt unfunny anyway.

> The biggest truth to face now—what is probably making me unfunny now for the remainder of my life—is that I don't think people give a damn whether the planet goes on or not....
>
> It may be that I am no longer able to joke—that it is no longer a satisfactory defense mechanism. Some people are funny, and some are not. I used to be funny, and perhaps I'm not anymore.

There may have been so many shocks and disappointments that the defense of humor no longer works. It may be that I have become rather grumpy because I've seen so many things that have offended me that I cannot deal with it in terms of laughter.

Without laughter as a defense, the offensive becomes intolerable. More than mere pessimism, that creeps perilously close to fatalism, which is corrosive to the humanistic mindset.

Highest ideals

Is humanism optimistic or pessimistic? Humanists receive no instruction about whether to think one way or the other. If you believe we are on our own in figuring out how to solve our problems, you can call yourself a humanist—or at least dabble in humanism—no matter how likely you think we are to find and enact solutions.

Steven Pinker, the cognitive psychologist and linguist who was named Humanist of the Year in 2006, wants us to recognize that our many successes demonstrate our capabilities. His book *Enlightenment Now: The Case for Reason, Science, Humanism, and Progress* argues that human beings have the means to improve life on Earth, but even he does not find it inevitable that they *will* make those improvements.

"It would be a mistake to think the message of the book is that we should be optimistic," Pinker told the *Humanist* magazine. "The point of the book is that most measures of human wellbeing show that we have improved, that we should seek to understand what went right, and do more of that in the future."

Pinker makes the case that even our flawed institutions are valuable, if we use them properly.

> Certainly, if anyone were to propose that things will get better no matter what we do, there would undoubtedly be a moral hazard in that. I think the greater hazard is in excessive pessimism or cynicism. It can lead to fatalism—the sense that humanity is screwed no matter what we do, so we may as well just enjoy ourselves now, not have children, and so on. And [it can lead] to radicalism—the idea that society is so corrupt, degenerate, and duped that anything would be better, so we should destroy our institutions in the hope that whatever would replace it is bound to be better. That is a dangerous belief. It's what led to Nazism in Germany in the Weimar era.

The book has detractors who find, for example, that Pinker's championing of the Enlightenment is "unduly simplistic." A *New York Times* reviewer called *Enlightenment Now* "profoundly maddening," partly because Pinker "has little patience for individual tragedy; it's the aggregate that excites him."

Setting aside what may be valid criticism of Pinker's book, we can still consider his essential point that in reason, science, and compassion we have the tools we need to continue our progress. Our views on that help us determine whether to be optimistic or pessimistic—or, rather, what to be optimistic and pessimistic about.

Another factor in one's thinking about *this* life is belief in an afterlife. Most humanists lack such belief, so they focus on this world and our descendants. Those who trust in a plane of existence where souls live peacefully for eternity might decide that life on Earth is unimportant, even meaningless, because it's temporary.

While believers in an afterlife don't *have* to think that way—and many don't—there is logic, once you make the leap of faith, in favoring a limitless, perfect future over a limited, imperfect present. That's a moral hazard similar to what Pinker warns about when he rejects pessimism and cynicism.

So humanists pursue a different sort of faith: the position that human beings are capable of succeeding and must strive to solve problems.

I scolded "Humanism and Its Aspirations" for leaving out humor as a significant part of our lives. I was kidding, mostly. What it does include is plenty. Its six affirmations are both assertive and hopeful. They are choices based not on faith but on the conviction that they are the best ways to achieve happiness and peace. Here are three:

> Knowledge of the world is derived by observation, experimentation, and rational analysis.
>
> Humans are an integral part of nature, the result of unguided evolutionary change.
>
> Working to benefit society maximizes individual happiness.

Humanism, if not inherently optimistic, is ambitious. This is how the statement ends: "Thus engaged in the flow of life, we aspire to this vision with the informed conviction that humanity has the ability to progress toward its highest ideals. The responsibility for our lives and the kind of world in which we live is ours and ours alone."

After all, a manifesto that does not look forward isn't appealing, and that last line about responsibility is designed to embolden people into action.

On the other hand, someone could conclude that, if shaping our world really is up to only us—and if therefore we must depend on world leaders and the passion of enough motivated citizens to guide us in a direction that benefits people around the globe—we are doomed.

Even having "informed conviction" may be overly optimistic. Or maybe that conviction can coexist with the resignation that humanity likely will never truly "progress toward its highest ideals."

Some days, you think we will climb great heights. Other days, you think our shortcomings are insurmountable.

Fair enough. Just keep in mind the moral hazards of fatalism. It precedes cynicism. The next stage is apathy, which discourages action and leaves morality to the whims of those in power.

An aspirin tablet

For most of his life, Vonnegut avoided fatalism. Although he could sound resigned to human failure, he felt there was still a chance that something could be done to make the world better. He consistently used humor to help his readers—and himself—through the good times and the bad.

Did Vonnegut end up like Mark Twain, as he predicted? There's no telling what he found out about God, heaven, or Judgment Day once he entered the blue tunnel, but many of the friends he left behind, for what it's worth, did not find him personally bitter in his waning days.

"During the years of his friendship, though I was aware that he might be suffering private misery, Kurt scuttled his demons with élan," recalled writer/editor Sidney Offit. "I don't think it an exaggeration to suggest that I, as well as Kurt's other friends, felt that time with Kurt was a momentous gift no matter how light our conversation."

Among those friends were the likes of George Plimpton, Truman Capote, and Morley Safer—famous people who would not have felt fortunate to be in Vonnegut's company merely because of his celebrity. They noted that, much like his writing, his often droopy demeanor was punctuated by bursts of laughter.

"He looked really morose sometimes, but most of the time there was this kind of wonderfully mad twinkle in his eye," said Safer, the longtime CBS News correspondent.

"He was one of the most positive, enlightening men I'd ever been around," said conductor/composer Richard Auldon Clark, who collaborated with Vonnegut on a *Happy Birthday, Wanda June* opera and grew close to Vonnegut over the last 15 years of the author's life. "He had a very wicked sense of humor and he was very macabre, but bitter? No way. He just called it like he saw it. He found humor in it...Bitter is not a word I would use at all."

Vonnegut found humor in life even in his seventies and eighties, even though he figured nothing could be done to avert ecological ruin. Late-stage Vonnegut was not just a cranky old geezer after all.

Despite making baldly bitter statements in *A Man Without a Country* such as "Like my distinct betters Einstein and Twain, I now give up on people too," he looked forward to everyday pleasures. In the same book, he writes about taking enjoyable walks to buy envelopes and stamps, repeatedly praises the arts, and marvels, "How beautiful it is to get up and go out and do something."

Going out and doing something is like the thinking and striving that we saw Vonnegut talk about earlier. It's what happens once you clean up after laughing.

And for all of his moralizing, Vonnegut summarized his work as primarily that of a humorist who offered a respite from troubles. "Humor can be a relief, like an aspirin tablet," he wrote. "If a hundred years from now people are still laughing, I'd certainly be pleased."

Humor frequently is not optimistic, but using it the way Vonnegut did can be an optimistic act. Humanists need that kind of optimism. Vonnegut's humor, when it's not withering and mordant, shows that deep down he felt—or wanted to feel—at least somewhat upbeat about his fellow Earthlings.

"I think he always had the seeds of faith and hope in humanity. He was not as cynical as one might think," Nanette Vonnegut wrote to me. "He was consistent in his wish that people would be more humane and reasonable."

Chapter 6

A Man Within a Country

"The aborigines didn't know whether to shit or go blind until I showed up. And then I fixed everything."

Kurt Vonnegut, Fates Worse Than Death

Kurt Vonnegut tried to support humane and reasonable behavior in the real world. He lent his name and his time to nuclear disarmament, environmental protection, authors' rights, censorship-bucking libraries, and other causes he considered worthwhile. His occasional occupation—volunteer firefighter—placed him among America's most beloved helpers.

Once in a while he practiced something like journalism as a traveling correspondent. Travel allowed him to satisfy his fascination with unfamiliar cultures and to escape his comfort zone. Reporting satisfied something else.

Journalism, like firefighting, is not just another vocation. Thomas Jefferson and countless others have commented about the role of a "free press" in a free society.

Good journalism also is essential to humanism. It's a crucial way in which we find out about things. Most of us, for instance, are not scientists. We rely on reporting about science, as we depend on reporting about politics, societal trends, and especially the things that bureaucrats, corporation managers, and our elected leaders don't want us to know about.

Vonnegut often referred to "what's really going on." Uncovering that, of course, is the mission of good journalism. In his day, as in Jefferson's, that meant newspapers.

At Shortridge High School in Indianapolis, Vonnegut contributed columns and stories to a newspaper published every weekday. He worked for the paper at Cornell and after the war for the City News Bureau in Chicago. Deadline writing for a general audience honed his prose style.

Later, Vonnegut was ambivalent about being a reporter. He praised the work of the so-called New Journalists—fiction-inspired writers Tom Wolfe, Joan Didion, Hunter S. Thompson, and the like. He characterized them in humanistic terms, calling them "Populists screaming in pain [who] believe that it is easy and natural for Americans to be brotherly and just." But he did not aspire to be one of them.

> Am I a New Journalist? I guess....
>
> But I am not tempted to do much more of that sort of stuff. I have wavered some on this, but I am now persuaded again that acknowledged fiction is a much more truthful way of telling the truth than the New Journalism is. Or, to put it another way, the very finest New Journalism is fiction...The New Journalist isn't free to tell nearly as much as a fiction writer, to show as much.

Perhaps it's predictable for a master of metafiction to declare "the very finest New Journalism is fiction." But both fiction and nonfiction present the *appearance* of realism, as Vonnegut knew well. "In either case," he claimed, "the principal issue...is whether or not the person who is trying to tell the truth gives the impression of being an honest man."

When Vonnegut's fame drew invitations to write about what was really happening in farflung corners of the world, he relied on the skills he had developed while working for newspapers.

At times the result was humanistic journalism, an attempt to explain and report from a moral perspective rather than a political or purely informational one. Such reporting has been described as "stories and features that [are] focused on ordinary people and the conditions that loom large in their lives [and that] celebrate the deeds of people, institutions and organizations in nurturing community life."

On the infrequent occasions when Vonnegut practiced journalism, he pleaded for the community life of ordinary people to be protected from forces that were destroying it.

For our purposes, two trips to Africa are worth noting. Vonnegut's visits to Biafra and Mozambique produced journalistic essays that give the impression they were written by an honest man.

An admirable nation

Vonnegut and his friend Vance Bourjaily, the American novelist and writing instructor, were guided in Biafra by "a committee of one" named Miriam Reik for a week during the short-lived African republic's dying days in January 1970. Less than a week after they left, the secessionist state's leaders surrendered. Vonnegut wrote about the experience for *McCall's* magazine.

> I flew in from Gabon on the night of January 3, with bags of corns, beans, and powdered milk—aboard a blacked-out DC–6 chartered by Caritas, the Roman Catholic relief organization. I flew out six nights later on an empty DC–4 chartered by the French Red Cross. It was the last plane to leave Biafra that was not fired upon.

Largely prosperous and well-educated inhabitants of Nigeria's eastern region, principally Ibo villagers, had declared independence on May 30, 1967. Civil war had broken out a few weeks later. Since then, federal forces—supported by Russian and British planes, heavy artillery, and ammunition—had retaken about ninety percent of the land, and the Biafrans were being starved into submission. Somewhere between five hundred thousand and three million of them died during the war.

Confronted by hopeless conditions, Vonnegut took a cue from Reik, the guide, and determined that he would not "move readers to voluptuous tears with tales of innocent black children dying like flies, about rape and looting and murder and all that," but instead would describe "an admirable nation that lived for less than three years."

Vonnegut met the top Biafran leaders and other dignitaries. They were prosperous men with doctorates from Western universities and access to good food. They were Christian and spoke English. He noted that they smiled in spite of everything, and that their smiles dimmed—but did not entirely fade—as the prospects of securing independence dwindled to nothing.

The three Americans had private rooms and baths. They were guests at a dinner attended by some of the fledgling nation's countless professionals and artists. (Vonnegut wrote, perhaps with overstatement, that Biafra had "about one-third of all the black intellectuals in Africa.") Among the people they met was the famous Ibo writer Chinua Achebe, author of the novel *Things Fall Apart*.

They also encountered children who were desperate for anything to eat. The well-fed Americans told them "No chop," meaning they had no food to give.

"It was embarrassing," Vonnegut wrote. "Whenever we told a cadaverous beggar 'No chop,' it wasn't really true. We had plenty of chop, but it was all in our bellies."

And he cried a bit: "I did it three days after I got home—at two o'clock in the morning. I made grotesque little barking sounds for about a minute and a half, and that was that."

Vonnegut did write, after all, about things that could move readers to voluptuous tears—about brutal rape, devastating hunger, fatal malnutrition, senseless death. He was appalled: "It was like a free trip to Auschwitz when the ovens were still going full blast. I now feel lousy all the time."

The fate of these people was all the more anguishing to Vonnegut because they had been leading what he perceived as an idyllic existence. Much of what he saw in the Biafran people confirmed what Vonnegut the student of humankind had figured out, especially in the role played by extended families.

A community could be content and life could be pleasant if enough caring people were around, he believed.

> They all had the emotional and spiritual strength that an enormous family can give. We asked the general to tell us about his family, and he answered that it was three thousand members strong. He knew every member of it by face, by name, and by reputation.
>
> A more typical Biafran family might consist of a few hundred souls. And there were no orphanages, no old people's homes, no public charities—and, early in the war, there weren't even schemes for taking care of refugees. The families took care of their own—perfectly naturally.
>
> The families were rooted in land. There was no Biafran so poor that he did not own a garden.
>
> Lovely.

Vonnegut reported on the disintegration of this community in his accustomed way, seeking out poignant absurdities. By the time of his visit, the Biafran soldiers' lack of resources was material for comedy.

> We were taken to a training camp near Owerri. The soldiers had no live ammunition. In mock attacks, the riflemen shouted, "Bang!" The machine gunners shouted, "Bup-bup-bup!"

In facing the situation with joyless wisecracks, according to his *McCall's* account, Vonnegut resembled the Biafran generals whose gallows humor he admired. Vonnegut even said of Biafra's leader, General Odumegwu Ojukwu, "His humor was superb."

Bourjaily, the writer who accompanied Vonnegut to Biafra, gave an example of how his friend responded with humor even in the face of physical danger. The two of them and the aid worker Reik heard two shells land, first one and then the other, about a quarter mile to either side of them,

> and that goddam Vonnegut—he'd just lit a cigarette. He stood up. He ground out the cigarette under his foot.
> "Okay, Miriam," he said briskly. "You get over in the air-raid bunker, okay? Vance and I are going up on the roof, and we're going to go, 'Buppabuppabup. Buppabuppabup.'"

For this sort of thing, Reik admonished Vonnegut. It was like Mary O'Hare taking him to task over his approach to his World War II novel, although this time the rebuke was about making flippant remarks rather than seeking macho tales of adventure.

"You won't open your mouth unless you can make a joke," Reik told him.

"It was true," Vonnegut later commented. "Joking was my response to misery I couldn't do anything about."

In Biafra, Vonnegut saw his ideas about community being lived out—as the republic was disintegrating. There, according to Gary McMahon in *Kurt Vonnegut and the Centrifugal Force of Fate*, "he finally found a country that modeled his ideal of extended families beautifully, only to see it starved and destroyed. It haunted him. It was the last thing a suicidal pessimist needed to see."

A particularly maddening catastrophe

More than a million refugees were in Mozambique, on the longest coastline of Africa, in 1989 when Vonnegut and others accepted an invitation to visit from the relief organization CARE.

Only about fifteen million people lived in Mozambique, a nation twice the size of California. Communities could function well there, but again, as in Biafra, human beings often prevented that.

"This is a particularly maddening catastrophe because it's completely manmade," Vonnegut told TV talk-show host Dick Cavett shortly after returning home.

> It should be paradise, except it is an absolute nightmare, and the reason is political. It has nothing to do with lack of rainfall or overpopulation or anything...These people would all be happy farmers in an area where there's plenty of room for everybody,

there's decent rainfall, the soil is reasonably good, and the only reason they're starving to death is they've all been driven off their farms by this gang called RENAMO.

Mozambique had been a nation for fourteen years, since winning its independence from Portugal in 1975. RENAMO was the acronym for the National Resistance of Mozambique, a group of what Vonnegut said were perhaps forty-five thousand bandits that, he wrote for *Parade* magazine, "had been raping and murdering and pillaging and all that since 1976, when it was trained and equipped by white South Africans and Rhodesians."

Our own State Department estimates that RENAMO, virtually unopposed, has killed more than 100,000 Mozambicans since 1987 alone—including at least 8,000 children under the age of five, most of whom were driven into the bush, where they starved to death.

The CIA also helped finance RENAMO, Vonnegut claimed, and some US officials backed the so-called freedom fighters because aid from the Soviet Union had nudged Mozambique into becoming "that most awful of things, [which] is a Marxist state," at least at first. So Marxism found support among some Mozambicans for a while. After all, it's "very close to the Sermon on the Mount, except it hasn't worked very well in practice," Vonnegut told Cavett.

"They let their Government choose evil rather than good, so now they have only themselves to blame," he wrote in a *New York Times* op-ed piece with mock disapproval of the Mozambican people. "Never mind that most of them never heard of Karl Marx or Moscow."

Neither RENAMO nor Mozambique's military could care for the increasingly dispossessed citizenry. Cavett showed videotape of Vonnegut visiting a refugee center with, Vonnegut said, 180,000 people who had been driven off their farms. The country's poor army was unable to protect them, he explained, and every day an average of five arrivals to the center died. RENAMO bandits occasionally stole the refugees' food and burned their temporary housing.

And they did worse. On Cavett's show and several weeks later in the *Parade* article, Vonnegut described acts that stood out in their cruelty even counting the starvation he had witnessed during World War II and in Biafra. He told Cavett:

> "[W]hat is new—what I hadn't seen before—is people mutilated... They cut people's fingers off and ears off and noses off. It was a pretty standard thing to cut noses off."

Something else was different. Vonnegut himself had changed. By his own telling, he was becoming less affected witnessing human misfortune. Unlike his experiences in Biafra nearly two decades earlier, Vonnegut wrote, his trip to Mozambique prompted not even a brief, belated crying fit. He was unaffected even though he again was the father of a young child, six-year-old Lily, whom he and Jill Krementz had adopted as an infant.

Vonnegut expressed this dispassion to old high-school friend Herb Harrington.

> I confessed that something had happened to me since Biafra, that Mozambique had impressed me intellectually but not emotionally. I told Herb that I had seen little girls about the age of my own precious Lily drifting off to death, having been in the bush too long before reaching a refugee center, but that I felt hardly anything afterward.

Rather than seem heartless, this relates something about modern life and our increased awareness of suffering in the world.

Anyone with empathy—whether humanist, Christian, Muslim, Buddhist, or something else—is concerned about people everywhere, not just those living in our neighborhood or under the same flag or creed. We also realize that caring about everyone who deserves to be cared about is impossible.

What's more, we sometimes conclude that we cannot do anything to help. The corruption and ruthlessness of leadership combines with our species' damnable capacity for cruelty, and preventable catastrophes grow maddening and unsolveable.

So we don't cry about every atrocity. Feeling powerless, we often are not moved to act. And the atrocities continue. We become accustomed to our guilt and anguish.

In his Biafra and Mozambique essays, as usual, Vonnegut does not provide new facts or fresh lessons about the state of human beings in the world. He certainly does not offer solutions. How could he?

What he offers is all any writer can offer in response to injustice: testimony. Even when actual remedies are not possible, awareness is. Writers can provide that much. With enough awareness, relief might even be conceivable.

Vonnegut chronicled his personal Dresden experience best in a novel. He told the stories of Biafra and Mozambique, which he visited and then left, through journalism.

He found reporting less satisfying than novel writing, calling fiction "a much more truthful way of telling the truth." Whatever the merits of that phrasing, we know that, although Vonnegut's fiction primarily is what makes him worth reading today, his occasional reporting is informed by the same humanism found in his more celebrated work. His journalistic essays, among his best nonfiction, enhance awareness.

What did Vonnegut want us to be aware of? Increasingly throughout his life, it was about how government leaders let people down and how the promise of scientific progress goes unfulfilled. And he was not always referring to far-off African nations with flimsier foundations than that of the USA.

Chapter 7

Science Certainly Tried

In all of history only one country has actually been crazy enough to detonate atomic weapons in the midst of civilian populations.

Letter to *The New York Times* from Kurt Vonnegut, September 12, 2002

Kurt Vonnegut was disappointed by the direction America took in his lifetime. Surely many contemporaries were too. Anyone who lived through the "just war" that America fought in the 1940s and then through the Cold War, Korea, McCarthyism, Vietnam, Watergate, the Gulf War, and the terrorist attacks of September 11, 2001, must have felt that something had gone terribly wrong.

Even the gains made in civil rights were hard-fought victories that, if this were a truly moral nation, would not have been necessary. One of the signs that justice inches along in the land of the free is that federal law establishing that minorities nationwide have the same voting rights as whites was not enacted until a hundred years after the Civil War.

Think about that, Vonnegut might have written.

At the same time, science and technology advanced at a sometimes dizzying pace. Throughout the twentieth century there were faster, sleeker automobiles, airplanes, household appliances, and calculating machines. There were increasingly efficient, deadlier ships, jets, firearms, and missiles.

There was the atomic bomb.

Modern societies have a hard enough time maintaining an ethical course that respects human dignity. Then the people running them exalt technology even as it dehumanizes. Technology, the result of scientific processes, improves life in many ways, but it's also used to destroy life. Killing becomes easier and easier all the time.

We regard technological progress as inevitable, just as we accept that people will be left behind every step of the way—and that nothing can or even should be done about it.

Technology made Vonnegut uneasy, but assigning blame was complicated. In his fiction, at least, he tended to find fault with implacable forces, imperfect institutions, and innate human failings rather than with individuals.

He said his books lacked villains. Actually, that's what his father told him, according to the preface to Vonnegut's play *Happy Birthday, Wanda June*. Initially, he wrote, this resulted from observations he made as a child reading Edgar Lee Masters' *Spoon River Anthology*, a popular fictional collection of free verse narrated by dead people.

Young Vonnegut was struck by how none of the characters seemed to behave badly on purpose.

> I marveled at all the epitaphs in Masters' book when I was only twelve years old, and I was bound to say to myself, "My gosh—all those people had to be what they were."

This view was reinforced later in his collegiate studies, he told an audience of psychiatrists.

> I hold a master's degree in anthropology from the University of Chicago. Students of that branch of poetry are taught to seek explanations for human comfort or discomfort—wars, wounds, spectacular diseases, and natural disasters aside—in culture, society, and history. And I have just named the villains in my books, which are never individuals. The villains again: culture, society, and history.

(The master's was the one bestowed on Vonnegut for having published *Cat's Cradle* in 1963 and was awarded eight years later, after he had become famous. The conspicuous timing should not detract from his serious interest in "that branch of poetry.")

Outside his fiction, Vonnegut did aim criticism at presidents and others who in his opinion surrendered to technology. Political leaders and scientists failed Vonnegut—failed the country and the world, he felt—at the very end of World War II. Horrific but defendable, the war in its waning days unleashed a legacy from which we have not and perhaps cannot recover.

The most racist, nastiest act by this country, after human slavery, was the bombing of Nagasaki. Not of Hiroshima, which might have had some military significance. But Nagasaki was purely blowing away yellow men, women, and children. I'm glad I'm not a scientist because I'd feel so guilty now.

Good ways to kill more efficiently

Hiroshima, Japan, had become the Earth's first inhabited locale to be targeted with a nuclear bomb. On August 6, 1945—less than four months after President Harry S. Truman had taken on the duties of commander-in-chief upon the death of Franklin D. Roosevelt—a bomb containing one hundred forty-one pounds of uranium–235 was dropped on Hiroshima. The city was a key military supply, assembly, and communications center with a port and some 350,000 human occupants.

At least sixty-five thousand of them died as a result of the bombing, more than two-thirds of them civilians. Missing by eight hundred feet the bridge that had been targeted, the bomb detonated over a downtown surgical clinic. More than ninety percent of the city's doctors and nurses were killed or wounded.

Truman, in a speech given later that day, repeated warnings for Japanese leaders ("If they do not now accept our terms they may expect a rain of ruin from the air, the like of which has never been seen on this earth") and praised American scientific ingenuity.

"The battle of the laboratories held fateful risks for us," Truman said. "We have spent two billion dollars on the greatest scientific gamble in history—and won."

Three days later, there was more gambling and more winning. In Nagasaki, a strategically important seaport of more than 260,000 inhabitants, about one in seven people died after the second atomic bomb, containing fourteen pounds of plutonium, exploded over a tennis court.

Japan capitulated five days later, on August 14. Two of its representatives formally signed surrender papers on September 2. The war was effectively over. Science had played a major role in ending it, even as it made the future more uncertain.

Vonnegut deplored that second bombing but understood the first.

"Ask all those who would have been dead otherwise," he said in 1990 when addressing whether the atomic bomb should have been used initially.

Hiroshima was bombed, among other reasons that have been offered, to hasten the war's conclusion and to prevent tens of thousands or hundreds of thousands of additional Allied and Japanese casualties that would have occurred if, as an alternative, the home islands had been invaded.

The Soviet Union was planning to attack Japan in a major ground offensive, and it posed a significant threat to its fellow Allies if it were to grow apart from them (which of course soon happened). With the nuclear attacks, the USSR might have been the intended recipient of a pointed message about America's newfound warmaking prowess.

Saving lives is an enduring justification for the bombing of Hiroshima, though, and Vonnegut believed it. Hamburg, Germany, in 1943 was the only other defendable bombing in which the United States participated between World War II and Panama City (1989), in Vonnegut's estimation.

He went farther in 2003, which is when he called the Nagasaki bombing "the most racist, nastiest act by this country, after human slavery." That conclusion was reached after decades of reflection during which Vonnegut's attitudes about his country changed along with his feelings about technology.

Seeds of his mistrust were sown during that just war of the 1940s. Back then, he and buddies like Bernard V. O'Hare began to suspect that their conception of America was mistaken.

> During the '30s when we grew up, we did believe our Government and were such great enthusiasts for it because the economy was being reborn. We were such cooperative citizens that it turned out to be a relatively minor thing that made us decide that we couldn't believe our Government anymore—that we had caught it lying. It was quite something to catch your Government lying then. What it was all about was our bombing technique...There was no use of bombsights whatsoever, there was simply carpet bombing. And that was kept secret from the American people: the nature of the air raids and random bombings, the shooting and the blowing up of anything that moved.

Optimism about technology diminished as scientific advancements continued to result in mass destruction with the chiefly British attack on Dresden and then with America's actions, Vonnegut recalled in 1980.

> But for me it was terrible, after having believed so much in technology and having drawn so many pictures of dream automobiles and dream airplanes and dream human dwellings, to see the actual use of this technology in destroying a city and killing 135,000 [sic] people and then to see the even more sophisticated technology in the use of nuclear weapons on Japan. I was sickened by this use of the technology that I had had such great hopes for. And so I came to fear it. You know, it's like being a devout Christian and then seeing some horrible massacres conducted by

Christians after a victory. It was a spiritual horror of that sort which I still carry today.

Some scientistis wrestled with the same thoughts.

A much different sort of world order would have emerged if Nazis had been the first to deploy an atomic bomb. They had a head start, so the possibility was real: German scientists had helped Hitler compile the world's most lethal military technology, and a small team led by German chemist Otto Hahn had split the atom in late 1938.

A few physicists around the world—several of whom had fled or been forced out of Germany—understood the powerful and potentially terrible implications of Hahn's discovery, especially if a self-sustained chain reaction could be achieved. Select members of this community were tracked by Axis, Allied, and Communist operatives in the frenzied pursuit of nuclear weapons during and after World War II.

Hahn and other prominent scientists who remained in Germany later maintained that they opposed using nuclear energy as a weapon—at least, they were opposed to the Nazis using it. Some disputed accounts even suggest that German scientists thwarted their own country's research.

Another significant factor likely was that Germany devoted insufficient financial and technical resources to creating an atomic bomb, compared to massive American efforts, and that it lacked adequate facilities and internal communication for a well-coordinated mission.

After the war, Vonnegut in his time as a publicist at General Electric saw how military and scientific progress moved side by side. Those who were devoted to destroying the enemy seized upon technological breakthroughs as good ways to kill more efficiently. And researchers weren't given a pass. For Vonnegut, scientists bore some responsibility when they shared their discoveries with warmakers.

One man in particular influenced such thinking. The GE chemist/physicist Irving Langmuir was Vonnegut's model for the brilliant, disengaged Felix Hoenikker. In *Cat's Cradle* Hoenikker is the father of the atomic bomb and the inventor of ice-nine, the substance that causes a frosty apocalypse.

Unlike his fictional counterpart, Langmuir did not work on nuclear bombs. The Nobel Prize winner resembled Hoenikker, however, in his pursuit of knowledge without regard to consequences, according to Vonnegut.

> Langmuir was absolutely indifferent to the uses that might be made of the truths he dug out of the rock and handed out to whoever was around. But any truth he found was beautiful in its own right, and he didn't give a damn who got it next...That generation

[of scientists] was not cautious at all about what information it turned over to the Government, to the War Department, to the Secretary of the Army or whomever. But one member of that generation, Norbert Weiner, published an article in The Atlantic not long after the war was over, saying, "I'm not going to tell my Government anything anymore." And I think scientists have become more and more cautious since. I know my brother has.

Bernard Vonnegut, the eldest of Kurt's two siblings, achieved notoriety at GE with his groundbreaking research into seeding clouds with silver iodide to produce rain. Nine years older than Kurt, Bernard preceded his brother as a student of science in college and, along with their father, had all but forced Kurt to pursue a career in that field.

Kurt Vonnegut left Cornell to join the army. After the war, he did not resume his study of chemistry, eventually opting instead for anthropology. He continued to value his background in hard science long after he settled on writing as a profession.

> I'm no scientist at all. I'm glad, though, now that I was pressured into becoming a scientist by my father and my brother. I understand how scientific reasoning and playfulness work, even though I have no talent for joining in. I enjoy the company of scientists, am easily excited and entertained when they tell me what they're doing. I've spent a lot more time with scientists than with literary people.

Vonnegut especially admired those who, unlike Langmuir, chased knowledge with an eye on consequences—those like his brother. Bernard found that even his weather-related work at GE drew the interest of the US military. Author Ginger Strand described what Bernard must have been thinking.

> His research had intended to bring the benefits of water down from the sky, to create a kind of anti-Dresden, an anti-Hiroshima. An explosive showering of life, not death, from the clouds. Now the undersea warfare branch was negotiating with GE to have Bernie come work with it.
> Bernie didn't want to spend the rest of his life making someone's dreams of undersea warfare come true.

Bernard quit GE in 1952. Kurt had quit in late 1950 to write full time. People like Bernard, having achieved success in their field, may find vocational opportunities more easily than those who lack significant accomplishments. Vonnegut urged prospective scientists—and, really, anybody in any field—to be careful from the beginning. He told MIT graduates in 1985, "It can make quite a difference not just to you but to humanity: the sort of boss you choose, whose dreams you help come true."

That's a tall order, asking essentially powerless young people to help guide human destiny against its own relentless march toward violence on a large scale. It was a plea as much as an admonishment. Vonnegut was hoping that the choice he requested—to select, as one's career commences, only humane bosses—actually *could* be made.

Those bosses run corporations and governments that seek power in their own ways. They are the world leaders who determine when and how to use technology, and they are the heads of industries that supply the weapons.

Before those leaders can misuse technology, Vonnegut felt, scientists themselves could make sure there was nothing to misuse.

> A virtuous physicist is a humanistic physicist...What does a humanistic physicist do? Why, he watches people, listens to them, thinks about them, wishes them and their planet well. He wouldn't knowingly hurt people. He wouldn't knowingly help politicians or soldiers hurt people. If he comes across a technique that would obviously hurt people, he keeps it to himself. He knows that a scientist can be an accessory to murder most foul. That's simple enough, surely. That's surely clear.

Those words reveal a certain awe—even fear—in the power of science and a belief that sometimes it must be reined in.

Vonnegut saw signs that the message was getting through, although at the expense of scientific areas of study, he claimed with a dash of humor. Young people who considered becoming scientists, he said, "were afraid that careers in science could all too easily lead to the commission of war crimes...So they go into other fields. They become physicists who are so virtuous that they don't go into physics at all."

He said he took to heart a comment that a speech he gave at Valparaiso University flopped because he had told jokes instead of moralizing. Addressing students, whether they were budding scientists or not, was a chance to persuade them to behave for the benefit of the public good.

> I tell them not to take more than they need, not to be greedy. I tell them not to kill, even in self-defense. I tell them not to pollute water or the atmosphere. I tell them not to raid the public treasury. I tell them not to work for people who pollute water or the atmosphere, or who raid the public treasury. I tell them not to

commit war crimes or to help others to commit war crimes. These morals go over very well. They are, of course, echoes of what the young say to themselves.

Vonnegut understood "how scientific reasoning and playfulness work," but the self-described Luddite also realized that science is never the sole answer. Throughout *Cat's Cradle*, in particular, people are happiest when they cling to some of their most unscientific beliefs. In that novel, Schlichter von Koenigswald is an ex-Nazi doctor who tries to atone for his past by working at a hospital in the San Lorenzo jungles. Despite his medical training, he administers last Bokononist rites to "Papa" Monzano, saying:

> "I am a very bad scientist. I will do anything to make a human being feel better, even if it's unscientific. No scientist worthy of the name could say such a thing."

Rather than make people feel better, science applied dispassionately can make people feel worse.

Even apart from wartime applications, Vonnegut felt that science was being misused by the American government. He called one of the most celebrated government-run scientific pursuits, the NASA missions to the moon, a "space boondoggle" that merely reinforced "that there was only death and more death out there."

What's worse, Earth itself was suffering. The environmental degradation that Vonnegut deplored could be traced to the indiscriminate use of oil-guzzling automobiles, smoke-belching factories, water-polluting chemicals, and other hallmarks of industry that drove the national economy.

> Our children have inherited technologies whose byproducts, whether in war or peace, are rapidly destroying the whole planet as a breathable, drinkable system for supporting life of any kind. Anyone who has studied science and talks to scientists notices that we are in terrible danger now. Human beings, past and present, have trashed the joint.

Sandra Steingraber, the kind of ethical scientist Vonnegut admired, probably would agree—up to a point. The biologist, activist, and poet has sounded the alarm about the effects of environmental damage and chemical toxicity in her several books and many articles, papers, and interviews.

However, she would not permit herself to think, as Vonnegut had, that there's no hope.

Steingraber acknowledges that many people suffer from "well-informed futility syndrome." That term, credited to psychologist Gerhart Wiebe, describes the feeling of helplessness that set in while viewing daily TV news images of carnage during the Vietnam War.

"Awareness without corresponding political change leads to paralyzing despair," Steingraber wrote. "We feel helpless in the face of our knowledge, and we're not sure we want to know anything more."

This sounds like what afflicted Vonnegut in his statement to young environmentalists that I placed among his optimistic and pessimistic quotes. "It's over," he said. "The game is lost."

Steingraber's solution: "Action is the antidote to despair."

She was among the leaders of a movement that successfully opposed hydraulic fracturing, a.k.a. fracking. For years her Concerned Health Professionals of New York and other groups and individuals petitioned political leaders while the scientific literature linking health risks to fracking grew to more than 400 peer-reviewed studies. Those studies helped persuade the New York State Department of Health that extracting oil and natural gas from deep undergound at high pressure was a bad idea.

"Science alone did not stop fracking," Steingraber said during a victory speech about five weeks after Governor Andrew Cuomo banned fracking statewide. "The data received a big assist from a well-informed citizen movement that took the scientific evidence to the media, to the Department of Environmental Conservation, and to elected officials....

"Science alone is just a lot of black dots on white mathematical space. Like a musical score that sits on a shelf, it doesn't become a song until someone picks up the score and sings it."

Steingraber is a Quaker who has gotten herself arrested at least twice, demonstrating a commitment to her message. From jail, she's written about civil disobedience. Her devotion to pacifism and her relentless advocacy for a clean environment fit well with the aims of humanism.

The separate paths taken by Vonnegut, who was not lauded for public defiance outside the printed page, and liberty-sacrificing Steingraber intersect at written communication.

"I would not be interested in writing if I didn't feel that what I wrote was an act of good citizenship or an attempt, at any rate, to be a good citizen," Vonnegut said in 1973.

For Steingraber, crafting and publishing poems and both personal and educational essays are acts of good citizenship in which she has great interest.

"Writing and art are part of the intermediary between recognition of a social problem and the execution of a meaningful solution," she said in 2007. "Just as abolitionist writing played a role in ending slavery, I believe environmental writing can play a role in ending unsustainable economic practices."

Steingraber is occasionally vindicated in her belief that scientists can help lead economic and political change. Vonnegut felt that scientists could issue warnings and tell us what we ought to do, but he also realized that some of them invent or discover the tools that create the situations that others warn about.

He would have noticed that engineers, after all, used science when they devised fracking.

For all of its promise, science and the technology it helps create cannot always be trusted to benefit the populace, Vonnegut decided.

> I used to think that science would save us, and science certainly tried. But we can't stand any more tremendous explosions, either for or against democracy.

Something we started to do to ourselves

"It isn't knowledge that's making trouble, but the uses it's put to," says the Rev. James J. Lasher, the revolutionary leader in *Player Piano*. There's machinery, and there's the political machine. The latter can resemble the former, with human input leading to occurrences that seem inevitable even when they're not.

Technology and science do not act on their own. Nor do scientists. When and how technology is employed are up to government, military, and corporate leaders, and Vonnegut believed they have let us down.

Heads of state, who wield the power of life and death, especially in wartime, are culpable:

> I think the trouble with Dresden was restraint surely, or lack of restraint, and I don't regard technocrats as having gone mad. I think the politicians went mad, as they often do. The man responsible for the bombing of Dresden against a lot of advice was Winston Churchill. It's the brain of one man, the rage of one man, the pride of one man, and I really can't hold scientists particularly responsible for that.

If restraint was lacking in the case of Dresden, the same must be true of Hiroshima and even truer of Nagasaki. Ever since, it's been easy to assume that superpowerful weapons will be used even when the result is tens of thousands of civilian deaths. That is, to say the least, a troubling legacy from the supposedly justified war.

As the Vonnegut short story "Thanasphere" from 1950 put it, "Science had given humanity forces enough to destroy the earth, and politics had given humanity a fair assurance that the forces would be used."

When those forces are used, the secret-keeping and lying that Vonnegut first noted in his government during World War II is at its most contemptible, because countless innocent lives are at stake. He would complain about foolish, destructive actions taken by American political leaders the rest of his life.

He did this sometimes with a joke, sometimes with blunt seriousness.

In May 1972, he observed comically that people "rising to the top of society who are not only indifferent to the arts, but to jokes and cheerful sex, and to all sorts of human playfulness" must be "flying saucer creatures from Pluto."

> My guess is that Plutonians began to arrive and reproduce and hold jobs in our government just as the Second World War was ending. Our last three presidents may have been Plutonians. Most of them, however, are in the Pentagon.
>
> We would perhaps welcome them, if it weren't for their humorlessness and pitilessness, and their blather about national honor—and for their love of war...To them, our hatred for one another, our unwillingness to touch one another, have been votes in the ballot box and money in the bank.

The Korean War and the Cold War had carried on a trend. And the Vietnam War had "broken our hearts.

> It prolonged something we started to do to ourselves at Hiroshima; it's simply a continuation of that: an awareness of how ruthless we are. And it's taken away the illusion that we have some control over our Government...Quite possibly, the Government has never been interested, but it has never made it so clear before that our opinions don't matter.

By the time Vonnegut turned fifty, he wrote the year after reaching that age, he "had become more and more enraged and mystified by the idiot decisions made by my countrymen."

Vietnam had "made our leadership and our motives seem so scruffy and essentially stupid."

President Nixon had "taught us to resent the poor for not solving their own problems [and] to like prosperous people more than unprosperous people."

The last book that Vonnegut published while he was alive, *A Man Without a Country*, in places is a screed against the last presidential administration of his lifetime, that of two-term George W. Bush, who after the terrorist attacks of September 11, 2001, led the United States into two wars.

Technology played its usual role in Bush's march toward deadly conflicts. A significant factor surely was this: The enemy could be bombed from farther away than ever.

"C-Students from Yale" and "psychopathic personalities," Vonnegut called Bush and his Cabinet, "haters of information" and "unelected leaders" who gained power "as the result of a shamelessly rigged election in Florida."

Vonnegut accused the Bush administration of a serious offense: disregard for facts, which are fundamental to the knowledge-gathering processes of science and academic study and journalism.

"Our leaders are sick of all the solid information that has been dumped on humanity by honest research and excellent scholarship and investigative reporting," Vonnegut complained to *Rolling Stone* in 2006. "They want to put us back on the snake oil standard."

"This borders on the outrageous"

He went farther after *A Man Without a Country* was published. Having just turned eighty-three, Vonnegut still was capable of provoking. He gained some infamy for what detractors said was his defense of terrorism in a November 2005 interview with Australian journalist David Nason.

Asked whether he harbored "any ill will towards" the Germans who had captured him during World War II, Vonnegut told Nason, "Not at all…And I regard anybody who is a soldier in any army that is at war as a brother of mine."

Even terrorists are soldiers, Vonnegut said: "I regard them as very brave people."

But surely the suicide bombers are "mad," Nason countered. Vonnegut reminded him that President Truman ordered an atomic bomb to be dropped on an entire city, adding,

> "What George Bush and his gang did not realise was that people fight back…It is sweet and noble—sweet and honourable I guess it is—to die for what you believe in."

Vonnegut in his old age apparently found nothing bad to say about the Nazis who had taken him prisoner sixty years earlier or about the al-Qaeda fanatics whose actions had resulted in the deaths of more than 2,900 Americans only four years earlier. He was identifying with soldiers and speaking approvingly, as he sometimes did, about death.

Nason was taken aback ("This borders on the outrageous"). He offered that terrorists, with their "twisted religious" beliefs, must be wrong.

> Vonnegut fires back[:] "It's a terrible thing to deprive someone of their self-respect. It's [like] your culture is nothing, your race is nothing, you're nothing." . . .
> [Vonnegut] says: "It must be an amazing high."
> "What?" I ask. "Strapping a bomb to yourself," he says. "You would know death is going to be painless, so the anticipation... must be an amazing high."

It was too much for Nason ("At this point, I give up"). Others were troubled too. "Kurt Vonnegut Lauds Suicide Bombers," at the website Middle East Forum, was a typical reaction. Vonnegut's anti-Gulf War, anti-Bush stance was recast as pro-terrorist.

A month later, Mark Vonnegut shot back at such conclusions about his father.

> Kurt, every so often, will play with people a little.
> What Kurt can do better than most people is reframe things and turn them around in a way that creates a new perspective. Even if you disagree with that perspective, the plausibility and novelty of his vision are enough to make you think. We need to think a little more, not less.

Perhaps the elder Vonnegut's comments to Nason were a failed attempt to spur thought. On the other hand, they were similar to what he had written back in 1966: "If I'd been born in Germany, I suppose I would have *been* a Nazi."

In calling terrorists "brave," Vonnegut's point was not to condone murderous behavior. His humanistic impulse was to try to understand it. Rather than explain terrorism as simply the "mad" actions of a "twisted religion," he put himself in the place of people who might go to such lengths.

They are people, he pointed out, who lack self-respect, just the kind of individuals who are exploited by fanatical leaders. The kind who will die for what they believe.

Pointedly, Vonnegut regarded terrorists as soldiers and therefore part of his community. Throughout his career he had portrayed soldiers not as heroes but as pawns—and yet as "very brave people" in the way they face mortality as they defend their beliefs.

What Vonnegut left out—and here is where criticsm could be best directed—is that terrorists also are willing to *kill* for what they believe. Killing noncombatants calls the bravery into question. Still, Vonnegut the humanist, not Vonnegut the soldier, wanted to know why.

The conviction to kill for one's beliefs, combined with the technology that allows even one person with modest resources to end lives on a mass scale, makes us all vulnerable to extremism. As author Adam Gopnik put it, "The opposite of humanism is not theism but fanaticism."

While Vonnegut could be clever in provoking humanistic discussions, he sometimes got his facts wrong. It's well established that the Dresden death count of 135,000 that he kept citing is probably much too high. And in his early eighties (again) he misstepped at least twice while invoking a subject that frequently betrays oversimplification: The head Nazi himself.

Vonnegut said this in 2006: "The only difference between Bush and Hitler is that Hitler was elected."

He published this in 2005: "Our president is a Christian? So was Hitler." Well, maybe not.

While Nazis did collect the most seats in the Reichstag through a democratic process in 1932, there was no parliamentary majority and Hitler was actually *appointed* chancellor in 1933.

And, although Bush apparently *is* a Christian, "Hitler clearly thought that anyone should be able to figure out that he was not a Christian," wrote scholar Richard Weikart. (Hitler was confirmed in his mother's Roman Catholic faith. Still, he can't be considered an exemplar of Christian devotion, even setting aside his being a mass murderer.)

So Vonnegut occasionally stood on shaky ground when he played historian.

Far more often, though, his insights into human behavior were built on a strong moral foundation.

So dependable and efficient and tireless

Getting back to the issue of self-respect (or lack of it) so important to Vonnegut's perspective, technology can be a source of great anxiety to people. Machines can be viewed as both dangerous—because they're in the hands of leaders whose self-interests put a habitable world on the precipice of annihilation—and dehumanizing.

David Simon, the writer and TV producer, makes the case that institutions increasingly devalued human beings after the Industrial Revolution, despite the promise that technology once held for Vonnegut and other Americans.

"We may feel, in this sort of postmodern age, that some of us are worth more and that there are extraordinary opportunities in life, but the truth is that labor is worth less, automation is taking over," Simon says while commenting about director Stanley Kubrick's World War I film *Paths of Glory*.

Kubrick's film is not even about the direct effects of machines. It's about hapless soldiers being blamed for the failure of their power-seeking leaders' poorly planned suicide mission. Simon's point is that the cruel military bureaucracy depicted in *Paths of Glory* and the opportunistic corporate embrace of mechanization that ascended in America share a disregard for human dignity.

That the lack of dignity eats away at self-respect is a constant.

Judging from his first novel, Vonnegut would agree. *Player Piano*, while lacking the distinctive authorial style that bloomed in his next book seven years later, establishes the effects of technology as one of Vonnegut's most enduring themes. Marketed as science fiction along the lines of Aldous Huxley's *Brave New World* or George Orwell's *1984*, it was intended not as dystopic futurism but as a satire of what already was happening in Schenectady, New York.

It chronicles a time when ever-dependable, ever-cheaper machines "are taking the halfway decent jobs from human beings....

"You can't fight progress. The best you can do is ignore it, until it finally takes your livelihood and self-respect away."

Vonnegut did not condemn all manufacturers for thinking that automation was good, for wishing to save money and improve efficiency. That idea of progress, however, left behind a growing number of displaced workers.

> To have a little clicking box make all the decisions wasn't a vicious thing to do. But it was too bad for the human beings who got their dignity from their jobs.

Paul Proteus, the novel's thirty-five-year-old protagonist, rebels against the loss of dignity. He sees self-respect being stripped from employees as the huge operation he manages advances mechanization over human output.

People are willing to let it happen. After all, technology "was the miracle that won the war—production with almost no manpower." The war in this case is ill-defined and fictitious, but its reliance on an engineered solution resembles that of the real conflict in which Vonnegut had fought.

The Ilium Works of *Player Piano* stands in for General Electric, the kind of place that holds a companywide morale-boosting retreat every year while its employees search for methods and devices that will make themselves obsolete. Proteus is enlisted as the reluctant leader of a revolutionary movement called the Ghost Shirt Society. Its name refers to the actual cotton garments that some Lakota warriors of the late nineteenth century believed would offer protection from white occupiers' gunfire.

The fictional Ghost Shirt Society's manifesto is written and distributed by the rebels' intellectual agitator, Professor Ludwig von Neumann, and signed with Proteus's name. It makes the case for considering the needs of human beings: "Replacement is not necessarily bad, but to do it without regard for the wishes of men is lawlessness." The letter lays out admittedly "radical proposals, extremely difficult to put into effect."

> "I propose that men and women be returned to work as controllers of machines, and that the control of people by machines be curtailed. I propose, further, that the effects of changes in technology and organization on life patterns be taken into careful consideration, and that the changes be withheld or introduced on the basis of this consideration....
>
> "I hold, and the members of the Ghost Shirt Society hold[, that] there must be virtue in imperfection, for Man is imperfect, and Man is a creation of God....
>
> "You perhaps disagree with the antique and vain notion of Man's being a creation of God.
>
> "But I find it a far more defensible belief than the one implicit in intemperate faith in lawless technological progress—namely, that man is on earth to create more durable and efficient images of himself, and, hence, to eliminate any justification at all for his own continued existence."

As shown by the "little clicking box" quote above, those words are an extension of Vonnegut's own perspective. It seemed to him that replacement—what GE and other business giants considered progress—was a significant part of corporate culture. Regarding the wishes of the people who were replaced was not as important.

In Vonnegut's next-to-last novel, *Hocus Pocus* (1990), narrator Eugene Debs Hartke realizes that inmates of the prison across the lake from Tarkington College, where he is a professor, once were providers of cheap labor but later were not even that. Hartke writes that "poor and powerless people, no matter how docile, were no longer of use to canny investors. What they used to do was now being done by heroic and uncomplaining machinery."

Those people had been sent off to fight in Vietnam, had been tasked with drudgery that sustains the comfortable lives of their supposed betters. With machines increasingly providing the drudgery, unpleasant work disappeared and left no work at all. The prison in *Hocus Pocus* is just another corporation, another form of industry.

Like science and politics, industry takes on a soul-crushing life of its own. Like science, it's driven forward by the search for knowledge and improvement. Like politics, it's affected by other forces—the lust for power or money, the desire to maintain influence—that can push aside human beings' need for a sense of purpose.

People themselves give in to the thinking. They can't help it. As *Player Piano* ends, the rebels have destroyed all the automated machinery, but the revolution has failed. Still, a few workers tinker with a damaged soda dispenser, eventually getting it to operate again. That makes them happy. Proteus observes with a shrug that they "are already eager to recreate the same old nightmare."

The thing is, curiosity and the desire to improve are perfectly fine human attributes. Leaders and willing followers who simply take advantage of those attributes are taking us in the wrong direction.

Misguided leadership had America's own citizens wondering whether the nation stood for anything anymore. But, in one of his more optimistic observations about the state of the country, Vonnegut used a machine metaphor and talked like one of the workers making repairs at the end of *Player Piano*:

> I was raised to be bughouse about the Constitution, and to be very excited about the United States of America as a Utopia. It still seems utterly workable to me and I keep thinking of ways to fix it, to see what the hell went wrong, to see if we can get the thing to really run right.

Chapter 8

Good for the Common Man

"My politics in a nutshell: let's stop giving corporations and newfangled contraptions what they need, and get back to giving human beings what we need."

Kurt Vonnegut, February 17, 1994

The tinkerers at the end of *Player Piano* hope they can recreate society by rebuilding broken machines. You get the sense that everything that just happened, guided by technology and curiosity, will happen again.

Other Vonnegut characters have more grandiose ideas for improving people's lives. They usually fail, sometimes spectacularly.

Bokonon's attempt to "ma[k]e this sad world a par-a-dise" in *Cat's Cradle* results in a functioning civilization for a while, but ultimately human ingenuity combines with the lust for power to wipe out nearly all life on Earth, thanks to ice-nine.

In *The Sirens of Titan* Rumfoord's manipulations that are designed to "change the World in a significant way" don't result in an apocalypse, but they create a social order that, like the one in Vonnegut's later story "Harrison Bergeron," is egalitarian to a fault.

Wilbur and Eliza Swain, the genius twins of *Slapstick*, seek a major overhaul too, but their master plan, implemented by Wilbur after Eliza dies and he becomes president of the United States, relies on compassion rather than curiosity or authoritarianism. "Lonesome no more!" is Wilbur's rallying cry. He simply wants a kinder society. He wants community, so he imposes it upon the nation.

Eliot Rosewater's attempts seem rooted in a society more resembling our own, not that of a remote island nation or a postapocalyptic world. His intention to manage everybody's problems one at a time might be the most ambitious even though it's focused on the less-favored inhabitants of a single town.

Mary Kathleen O'Looney, the extraordinarily rich widow in *Jailbird* (1979), aims higher, but her efforts, like Rosewater's, ultimately help only a small group of people. The peaceful economic revolution that O'Looney seeks is thwarted after her death. Neither the United States government nor its corporate institutions prove capable of dividing her late husband's enormous conglomerate "on behalf of the people."

Before looking at some of those characters' plans more closely, let's see where Vonnegut's notions came from.

Concern about community, particularly in the form of extended families, shows up in Vonnegut's fiction repeatedly. He must have been thinking about long summer days in his youth spent with his parents, siblings, and other relatives in cottages along Lake Maxinkuckee, up in the Indiana countryside.

He was also thinking about an anthropology course taught by Robert Redfield at the University of Chicago, where Vonnegut studied after the war. Redfield's lectures identifying a developmental stage that many cultures have in common amounted to the "one plausible, romantic theory about humanity" that Vonnegut said he took from his time at the university.

> Dr. Redfield's theory of the Folk Society...has been the starting point for my politics, such as they are.
>
> My politics in a nutshell: let's stop giving corporations and newfangled contraptions what they need, and get back to giving human beings what we need....
>
> A Folk Society, he said, was a relatively small number of persons bonded by kinship and a common history of some duration, with a territory uncontested or easily defended, and sufficiently isolated so as to be little influenced by the cultures of other societies.

Such societies, Vonnegut reasoned, "might be regarded as petri dishes in which human beings might demonstrate certain apparently basic human needs other than food, shelter, clothing, and sex."

> For want of a better word, I will call such needs spiritual, by which I mean only that they are invisible, un-smellable, inaudible, intangible, and inedible.

Was it possible, I wondered, that certain features common to all of them not only revealed spiritual needs of all human beings [but also showed] us methods for satisfying those needs, theatrical performances, if you will, which human beings, by their nature, can ill-afford to do without?

When Vonnegut put some of those "theatrical" components together, his conclusions could sound like a call to action, as in a 1972 commencement address.

We must become a family in order to take care of one another the way families do. Now, nearly two hundred years after the signing of the Declaration of Independence, written by a man who owned human slaves, I think we understand that our politicians and millionaires can do very little for us, except to take our money. There are sound reasons for this, I'm sure. I mean to study economics some day.

Meanwhile, we must love one another and care for one another as best we can, and we must organize....

And if our government persists in being as wrong-headed as it is today, you must threaten it with...a general strike.

(It looks selfish for Vonnegut to have said *we* must love but *you* must strike. He meant that young people should be the lead organizers who make the threat, since they have the most to gain.)

Within a community, intangible needs can be filled by "theatrical performances" like religion, politics, and art. To Vonnegut, Redfield's concept of the folk society, found among "a relatively small number of persons" within a collective, expanded to become a theory of everything.

Simple enough and reasonable enough

From the first time he voted, Vonnegut cast ballots for Socialist Party nominees. In 1944, that meant selecting perennial candidate Norman Thomas for president. The following summer, back from the war but still in uniform and thinking about getting involved in union causes once the conflict ended, Vonnegut met Indianapolis labor leader and former gubernatorial candidate Powers Hapgood (1899–1949). He called Hapgood "a typical Hoosier idealist."

"Socialism," he continued, "is idealistic."

Vonnegut's expressed views about socialism are idealistic. They're not much concerned about theory and party politics, which among socialists of his younger days already were falling out of fashion anyway, as the movement itself languished.

Socialism in the United States hung in there as the economy struggled to recover from the Great Depression, which began shortly before Vonnegut's seventh birthday. Throughout the 1930s unemployment ranged from about fifteen to twenty-five percent. Capitalism was exposed, some believed, as a severely flawed concept that ought to be reconsidered or even replaced. Hundreds of thousands of voters like Vonnegut were receptive to alternative candidates who routinely appeared on ballots along with Democrats and Republicans.

> I imagined that I was a socialist. I believed that socialism would be good for the common man. As a private first class in the infantry, I was surely a common man.

Socialism's relative popularity in the early part of the twentieth century is sometimes forgotten today. Although socialism nearly disappeared in America during Vonnegut's lifetime, he fondly recalled when, much like religion, it offered hope to the beleaguered masses.

> Most Americans don't know what the socialists did during the first half of the past century with art, with eloquence, with organizing skills, to elevate the self-respect, the dignity and political acumen of American wage earners, of our working class..."Socialism" is no more an evil word than "Christianity." Socialism no more prescribed Joseph Stalin and his secret police and shuttered churches than Christianity prescribed the Spanish Inquisition. Christianity and socialism alike, in fact, prescribe a society dedicated to the proposition that all men, women, and children are created equal and shall not starve.

Vonnegut and his family had reason to regard the promise of capitalism as fragile. They'd been wealthy until their financial fortunes suffered during the Depression, souring Vonnegut's father and demoralizing his mother prior to her overdose.

As an organized political movement, however, socialism was waning in popularity. Responding to real and perceived threats posed by Bolshevism and anarchists—the first Red Scare—a series of federal, state, and municipal crackdowns had reduced the ranks even before Vonnegut was born.

The Socialist Party of America itself had been splintered by Communist factions. Socialist presidential candidates of the 1940s still were drawing tens of thousands of votes, but the totals were declining badly from the heights of 1912. That year, SPA membership peaked at about 118,000 and Vonnegut's hero Eugene V. Debs collected six percent of the nation's popular vote.

By the time Vonnegut began to ponder socialist notions, the "tales of labor's sufferings and derring-do" inherent in those notions were fading from mainstream acceptance. He recalled in the prologue to *Jailbird* that "labor history was pornography of a sort in those days, and even more so in these days."

American supporters of socialism, then as today, typically don't call for a system matching its theory's radical dictionary definition, with the state owning property and the means of production. Instead, worker rights are emphasized within a capitalistic framework—a subject "pretty much taboo" primarily when it seems to promote a revolutionary subversion of ownership, a stepping stone to communism.

When it's about bosses and workers, the subject can be more palatable. One example is when Vonnegut's *Jailbird* character Kenneth Whistler, modeled on Hapgood, criticizes a power structure that gives an employer an unfair measure of authority.

> "The laws that say he can fire anybody who stands up for the basic rights of workers—those are loaded dice. The policemen who will protect his property rights but not your human rights—those are loaded dice."

In such a rigged system, even that employer is not entirely blameworthy, Whistler contends, because that man "never attended a lecture, never wrote a paper, never read a book" before being kicked out of Harvard, and therefore, "How else could he ever amount to anything if he did not use loaded dice?"

A socialist who casts the rich not as villains but as (conveniently) clueless role players within a larger injustice is being ethically relativistic—or compassionate, or simply realistic. Vonnegut, through Whistler, again is accusing culture, society, and history...or being sarcastic.

Years after Vonnegut's death, Vermont senator Bernie Sanders brought new enthusiasm for a tempered kind of American socialism by addressing an unfair system. The democratic socialist (or socialist Democrat) won twenty-three primaries and caucuses in his ultimately unsuccessful challenge to Hillary Clinton for the Democratic Party's presidential nomination in 2016.

Sanders didn't get as far as he did by preaching Marxist displacement of capitalism.

"I don't believe government should take over the grocery store down the street or own the means of production, but I do believe that the middle class and the working families of this country who produce the wealth of this country deserve a decent standard of living and that their incomes should go up, not down."

Similarly, Vonnegut "believed in free enterprise," biographer Shields concluded. "It had made his forebearers rich. And he recognized that many ideas of Western freedom are intrinsically tied to capitalism."

What's more, citing correspondence to which he had access, Shields wrote that Vonnegut "personally invested heavily" in enterprises that included "a strip mining company, a shopping center development, and the manufacturer of napalm."

As I noted in the introduction, Mark Vonnegut particularly objected to that last claim about his father's investments. We are left to draw our own conclusions. Might Kurt Vonnegut's financial transactions be an area of hypocrisy on his part, to some degree?

Shields does not go that far. Vonnegut was not even being inconsistent, he felt.

> What he objected to was capitalist ideology, combined with Christian pieties, to justify the power of the rich over the poor...
>
> The system, Vonnegut would say, is not the problem; it's the tendency to blame the poor as a way of shifting responsibility away from the rich.

Well, Vonnegut did not cast economic systems as villains, just culture, society, and history. However, it seems as though capitalism easily could be mixed in with the others. Even so, it's still up to people to repair the system's broken parts.

For what it's worth, Vonnegut himself publicly described a different approach to his money managing than is suggested by investments in soulless building projects and an anti-union mining concern and Dow Chemical. Once Vonnegut became wealthy, he claimed in 1983, he felt obligated not to support a system that thrived when people of modest means were pushed aside.

> I made a lot of money, a lot for me, about 12 years ago—and my publisher took me over to the Chase Manhattan Bank to meet a money manager. I decided not to sign up with him, but he promised to do his best to make my money grow, even as the planet became poorer. It would keep pace with inflation and then some. As though to reassure me, he declared that he would not,

in effect, allow his judgment to be addled by patriotism. If the United States turned out to be a relatively inhospitable place for my money, with workers getting high wages and expensive social benefits and so on, he would send it overseas. How fast could he do this? In two shakes of a lamb's tail.

So long, Youngstown, Ohio. Hello, Seoul.

When writing and speaking to the public, Vonnegut did not map out a precise political and economic system or concern himself much with ideological niceties. He appealed to fairness as he saw it.

And like a campaigning politician full of big ideas and short on details about how to achieve them, he was quite capable of passionate exhortation. At times he urged taking action to make the country better. He sounded like a rabble rouser, telling college graduates that, when they are old enough to make an impact, they should "work for a socialist form of government."

> Free Enterprise is much too hard on the old and the sick and the shy and the poor and the stupid, and on people nobody likes. They just can't cut the mustard under Free Enterprise....
>
> So let's divide up the wealth more fairly than we have divided it up so far...It isn't moonbeams to talk of modest plenty for all. They have it in Sweden. We can have it here.

How exactly to divide up the wealth and how specifically to work for which kind of government were left to the young people in Vonnegut's audience to figure out. In the same vein, his character Eugene Debs Hartke does not craft the reform proposals of his socialist grandfather, but he does know that he opposes wealthy authoritarians.

> I think any form of government, not just Capitalism, is whatever the people who have all our money, drunk or sober, sane or insane, decide to do today.

Hapgood, that Hoosier idealist, "was a middle-class person who thought there could be more economic justice in this country," Vonnegut wrote. "He wanted a better country, that's all."

Vonnegut sought and communicated the kind of simplicity summed up by "a better country, that's all," or perhaps a better world or a better life, guided by plain decency—that's all—expressed in a secular "heartfelt moral code."

We sure need such a thing, and it should be simple enough and reasonable enough for anyone to understand.

In the actions and words of Eliot Rosewater, Vonnegut created a character through which to express that code.

"How can we help you?"

The protagonist of *God Bless You, Mr. Rosewater* (1965) is a wildly rich, deeply troubled but compassionate man conducting a social experiment: What if someone with great means tries to help fellow human beings who have very few means, one by one?

Vonnegut said he once shared an office atop a liquor store with an accountant, "a man who is that *kind*" although he was poor.

> I could hear him comforting people who had very little income, calling everybody "dear" and giving love and understanding instead of money...I took this very sweet man and in a book gave him millions and millions to play with.

That multimillionaire character, Eliot Rosewater, sits in his office in downtown Rosewater atop a lunchroom and a liquor store across from a fire station, answering the phone ("This is the Rosewater Foundation. How can we help you?"), ready to give callers what they need. That might mean a few kind words, some money, or just an ear with which to hear their troubles.

He shows concern about Diana Moon Glampers' ailing feet. He helps someone pay off a motor scooter. He awards $300 to a suicidal man whose child has cerebral palsy. His most common prescription is an aspirin tablet and a glass of wine.

"There, there," he tells his callers and visitors gently. "Now, now."

Rosewater County's downtrodden citizens revere him.

His father, a United States senator who would not be caught dead in the hick Indiana town of his heritage, thinks Eliot is wasting his time and misusing the limitless Rosewater Foundation funds. Relatives and family lawyers think Eliot is crazy. Much of the time, he is drunk.

You would *have* to be off your rocker, wouldn't you, to give away small pieces of your vast wealth to people who will always need more of it? What sane person would abandon a life of leisure and a chance at dignified accomplishment to consort with, as his father calls them, "the maggots in the slime on the bottom of the human garbage pail"?

Eliot used to attend the opera, buy paintings for museums, oversee large contributions to respectable institutions. He still gives Harvard, where he earned a law degree, $300,000 a year. His portfolio swells by $10,000 a day whether he does anything or not.

So Eliot does something. He does not renounce his fortune or disinherit himself. Instead, he uses the foundation to help people less fortunate than he is, which in his namesake county is everybody.

Why does he do this? Guilt, to some extent. During the war, minutes after killing three Germans in a smoke-filled clarinet factory—the two oldest with a grenade and the third, a 14-year-old boy, with a bayonet to the throat—he realized he'd slain innocent firefighters, not enemy soldiers. Then "he calmly lay down in front of a moving truck," which stopped just in time.

Eliot is not only scarred by witnessing carnage in the war. He has perpetrated it.

Also, he was steering the boat when his mother was accidentally killed while sailing with him.

"She was a wise and amusing person, with very sincere anxieties about the condition of the poor," Eliot recalls. He has inherited those anxieties. He knows his great-grandfather built the family's fortune on opportunism and greed and that the massive assets have been sustained by decades of ignorance and presumed privilege.

Back from the war, Eliot had taken control of the Rosewater Foundation, a New York City-based tax shelter and benefactor of countless charitable organizations. After a few years, he drifted, traveling the country, drunkenly carousing with firefighters, bonding with them as he once did with fellow soldiers—two kinships Vonnegut shared. Eliot transformed the foundation into the source of small gifts that he distributes to down-on-their-luck nobodies in Rosewater.

This behavior perplexes his close relatives, particularly his father.

In a sealed letter to the eventual inheritor of his wealth, whoever that might be, Eliot calls America "this Utopia gone bust" and complains that "every grotesquely rich American represents property, privileges, and pleasures that have been denied the many." He expresses such contempt for "rapacious citizens [who have] come to control all that was worth controlling in America" that we can see why he has different ideas about what to do with Rosewater riches.

He goes beyond socialism, as he explains in a difficult phone call with his father, who asks point-blank whether Eliot is a communist.

> "Oh, I have what a lot of people would probably call communistic thoughts," said Eliot artlessly, "but for heaven's sakes, Father, nobody can work with the poor and not fall over Karl Marx from time to time—or just fall over the Bible, as far as that goes. I think it's terrible the way people don't share things in this coun-

try. I think it's a heartless government that will let one baby be born owning a big piece of the country, the way I was born, and let another baby be born without owning anything. The least a government could do, it seems to me, is to divide things up fairly among the babies. Life is hard enough, without people having to worry themselves sick about money, too. There's plenty for everybody in this country, if we'll only share more."

"And just what do you think that would do to incentive?"

"You mean fright about not getting enough to eat, about not being able to pay the doctor, about not being able to give your family nice clothes, a safe, cheerful, comfortable place to live, a decent education, and a few good times? You mean shame about not knowing where the Money River is?"

"The *what?*"

"The Money River, where the wealth of the nation flows. We were born on the banks of it—and so were most of the mediocre people we grew up with, went to private schools with, sailed and played tennis with. We can slurp from that mighty river to our hearts' content. And we even take slurping lessons, so we can slurp more efficiently."

"Slurping lessons?"

"From lawyers! From tax consultants! From customers' men! We're born close enough to the river to drown ourselves and the next ten generations in wealth, simply using dippers and buckets. But we still hire the experts to teach us the use of the aqueducts, dams, reservoirs, siphons, bucket brigades, and the Archimedes' screw. And our teachers in turn become rich, and their children become buyers of lessons in slurping...When one of us claims that there is no such thing as the Money River I think to myself, 'My gosh, but that's a dishonest and tasteless thing to say.' "

Most Americans, Eliot is saying, are declared winners and losers at birth. And the winners get to decide who wins and who loses.

Swimmers and sinkers

Senator Lister Ames Rosewater is exasperated by his son's conception of how the world should work. He correctly asserts that, in trying to love everyone, Eliot is cutting off the people closest to him. Vonnegut knew better than to claim there were flawless solutions to humanity's failings, and Eliot's enterprise is shown to be, if not quite insane, then at least the product of a damaged soul desperate to find purpose.

Although he's right that his son's search for meaning has repercussions for those who love him, the blustering Senator Rosewater serves as the foil to Eliot's (and Vonnegut's) longing for mercy from society's self-determined victors. During a speech on the Senate floor, he points out that brutal oppression preceded the so-called Golden Age of Rome. Something similar can be achieved, he says, with the carrot-and-stick system that he contends the Founding Fathers believed would ensure a properly functioning nation.

But Senator Rosewater laments that "do-gooders, who thought people shouldn't ever have to struggle for anything, had buggered the logic of the system beyond all recognition."

The senator's determinism is how Eliot and Vonnegut assume the winners want the economy to run.

> "I see two alternatives before us. We can write morals into law, and enforce those morals harshly, or we can return to a true Free Enterprise System, which has the sink-or-swim justice of Caesar Augustus built into it. I emphatically favor the latter alternative. We must be hard, for we must become again a nation of swimmers, with the sinkers quietly disposing of themselves."

Those are human beings the senator is talking about "disposing of themselves" so that he need not think about them anymore. Winners and losers. Swimmers and sinkers. Vonnegut was certain the world is divided that way.

> I just know that there are plenty of people who are in terrible trouble and can't get out. And so I'm impatient with those who think that it's easy for people to get out of trouble. I think there are some people who really need a lot of help. I worry about stupid people, dumb people. Somebody has to take care of them, because they can't hack it.

That was rather blunt talk for Vonnegut's *Playboy* interview, patronizing toward certain losers even while defending them. His point was that especially needy people should be treated with compassion, not be allowed to dispose of themselves.

In *Rosewater* Eliot is not the only person who's ashamed about his fortune. Vonnegut revisits the matter with another discussion between two characters on opposite sides. The winners' side dominates.

Stewart Buntline, another well-heeled client of the Rosewaters' lawyers, turns out much different from Eliot, even though at one time he too was appalled by the bounty into which he was born. We learn that, having completed a year at Harvard, Buntline had marched into the firm's office, declared that "the free enterprise system was wrong" and announced that he wanted "to buy decent food and clothing and housing for the poor, and right away."

The senior partner in charge of Buntline's $14 million inheritance—"a miracle," the lawyer calls it—was ready with a counter argument to the young man's naïve notions:

> "Giving away a fortune is a futile and destructive thing. It makes whiners of the poor, without making them rich or even comfortable. And the donor and his descendents become undistinguished members of the whining poor...Money is dehydrated Utopia. This is a dog's life for almost everybody, as your professors have taken such pains to point out. But, because of your miracle, life for you and yours can be a paradise! Let me see you smile!"

That reasoning worked on Buntline. Twenty years later, he is still "on the path of conservatism." More than that, he makes his servants swear a loyalty oath every Sunday before dinner. The oath demonstrates their gratitude for being rescued from an orphanage owned by the Buntlines:

> "I will be grateful to those who employ me, and will never complain about wages and hours, but will ask myself instead, 'What more can I do for my employer, my republic, and my God?' "

Vonnegut has drawn us into the debate about winners' responsibility toward losers. We assume he's on the side of the servants, but like Whistler in *Jailbird* he does not flatly condemn their bosses, as ridiculous and cruel as they sometimes appear.

The poor and their advocates believe in the Money River. The economy's top achievers, whether they've climbed to the summit through hard work or arrived there by limousine, may instead view success as a goal to strive for, no matter where you're starting from.

Vonnegut lets the winners have their say. It might be the only perspective they've ever been taught about a properly run society: When exposed to the good life, the less fortunate will work hard to achieve it for themselves and will benefit many others.

That version of the American Dream remains popular today. Both swimmers and sinkers believe it.

Howard W. Campbell Jr., who narrates *Mother Night*, has a cameo role in *Slaughterhouse-Five* in which he comments about the sink-or-swim lessons taught by capitalism. He writes in a monograph:

America is the wealthiest nation on Earth, but its people are mainly poor, and poor Americans are urged to hate themselves... They mock themselves and glorify their betters...This inward blame has been a treasure for the rich and powerful, who have had to do less for their poor, publicly and privately, than any other ruling class since, say, Napoleonic times.

Jesús Ortiz, a young bartender in *Galápagos*, is a sinker who wants to be a swimmer. He is delivering two filet mignon suppers to wealthy guests of the hotel where he works, justifying the extravagance even though the island they're occupying is suffering through famine.

Ortiz's brain was so big that it could show him movies in his head which starred him and his dependents as millionaires. And this man, little more than a boy, was so innocent that he believed the dream could come true, since he had no bad habits and was willing to work so hard, if only he could get some hints on succeeding in life from people who were already millionaires....

He thought this about the steaks, too, as he knocked on [the] door: The people inside there deserved them, and that he would deserve them, too, once he had become a millionaire.

But the man in the room tells him, "Uncover the steaks and put them both on the floor for the dog, and then get out of here." Startled, Ortiz is forced to reconsider his "opinion of himself, humanity, the past and future, and the nature of the universe."

"We must find a cure"

Humanists, if they are concerned about all people, cannot avoid having at least an internal discussion about income disparity in the United States. They may find themselves longing for a system that discourages economic inequality, whether that's more compassionate capitalism, socialism within a free-enterprise framework, radical communism, or some other way that helps lessen poverty and otherwise benefits the public.

Dutch philosophy professor Ingrid Robeyns, for example, promotes limitarianism, a newer theory advocating "that there should be upper limits to the amount of income and wealth a person can hold." A group of rich people called the Patriotic Millionaires seeks to mitigate the harms of extreme wealth by fixing a tax code that unfairly favors them.

The Patriotic Millionaires—now *there's* a group I'd like to join someday.

Ahem. It might be useful here to turn to the Humanist Manifesto of 2003, not as an infallible text but as a reference point for what someone calling herself a humanist may want to consider.

That document offers no specific direction about social welfare, no evaluation of the deterministic mentality of Senator Rosewater or an older Stewart Buntline. But it does contain this passage:

> **Working to benefit society maximizes individual happiness...** We seek to minimize the inequities of circumstance and ability, and we support a just distribution of nature's resources and the fruits of human effort so that as many as possible can enjoy a good life.

Humanists must decide for themselves what it means to justly distribute "nature's resources and the fruits of human effort," let alone how to do that.

Vonnegut's heart is with Eliot Rosewater more than with Senator Rosewater. His comment to *Playboy* about taking care of people who "can't hack it" echoes words he put into Eliot's mouth. "I'm going to love these discarded Americans, even though they're useless and unattractive," Eliot tells his befuddled wife. "*That* is going to be my work of art."

Vonnegut's work of art known as *God Bless You, Mr. Rosewater* prompts the reader to think about a society in which human beings are valued no matter who they are, and to consider the chances that such a society has to be realized.

There's only one way it can ever happen, Vonnegut advises us through Eliot in perhaps the most oft-quoted passage from his novels. It's more of Eliot's words to his soon-to-be-ex-wife, this time explaining what he will say upon baptizing the newborn twins of a client who has begged him to conduct the ritual. It's sober and frustrated and urgent and insistent:

> "Hello, babies. Welcome to Earth. It's hot in the summer and cold in the winter. It's round and wet and crowded. At the outset, babies, you've got about a hundred years here. There's only one rule that I know of, babies—:
>
> "God damn it, you've got to be kind."

Ultimately, Vonnegut is kind to his character. Eliot first goes through some more trauma, though. So do the people who rely on him, when they learn he is leaving town to baptize the babies and then going to Indianapolis to meet his wife for perhaps the last time.

Diana Moon Glampers is distraught, fearing Eliot will never return to Rosewater. She tells him, "You're my *only* friend."

"You can make more, surely," Eliot suggested hopefully.
"Oh God!" she cried.
"You could join some church group, perhaps."
"You're my church group! You're my everything! You're my government. You're my husband. You're my friends."

But it's time for Eliot to find his destiny elsewhere. His departure can be viewed as a kind of failure. It's an acknowledgment that one person can do only so much, and it's even a comment about where not to put one's faith.

Eliot's social experiment, however, does not conclude with his exodus, although there is a lengthy detour. On the bus out of Rosewater, he reads a Kilgore Trout novel, has the fiery vision of Indianapolis we saw earlier, and blacks out. He is still trying to shake away his mental fog a year later, one day before a hearing at which he must prove his sanity despite being institutionalized, or else lose much of his fortune to a Rosewater cousin in Pisquontuit, Rhode Island.

Trout himself shows up and helps embolden Eliot, telling him that "if we can't find reasons and methods for treasuring human beings because they are *human beings*, then we might as well, as has so often been suggested, rub them out."

Clean-shaven and outwardly respectable for the benefit of the upcoming court proceeding, Trout reminds the amnesiac Eliot why his abandoned charitable work in Rosewater County was so important.

> "Poverty is a relatively mild disease for even a very flimsy American soul, but uselessness will kill strong and weak souls alike, and kill every time.
>
> "We must find a cure....
>
> "It seems to me...that the main lesson Eliot learned is that people can use all the uncritical love they can get...It's news that a man was able to give that kind of love over a long period of time. If one man can do it, perhaps others can do it, too. It means that our hatred of useless human beings and the cruelties we inflict upon them for their own good need not be parts of human nature. Thanks to the example of Eliot Rosewater, millions upon millions of people may learn to love and help whomever they see."

Eliot's experiment is revived—and ultimately succeeds—due to an inspired twist. Embracing false paternity charges from dozens of women who have been bribed by a calculating lawyer, Eliot becomes a de facto father who now has progeny onto which he can pass his inheritance.

This decision empowers Eliot to distribute the fruits of his ancestors' greedy efforts. It's one of the most hopeful endings Vonnegut ever wrote.

> "Let their names be Rosewater from this moment on. And tell them that their father loves them, no matter what they may turn out to be."

This, Eliot Rosewater might well have determined, not only benefits the family name but is exactly what *he* needs. Instantaneously, he has created a community, an extended family.

Lonesome no more!

Vonnegut knew Sargent Shriver a little. Shriver was the Democratic vice presidential candidate during George McGovern's 1972 bid for the presidency. When Shriver asked for advice on the campaign trail, Vonnegut told him to say this:

> "You're not happy, are you? Nobody in this country is happy but the rich people. Something is wrong. I'll tell you what's wrong: We're lonesome! We're being kept apart from our neighbors. Why? Because the rich people can go on taking our money away if we don't hang together. They can go on taking our power away. They want us lonesome; they want us huddled in our houses with just our wives and kids, watching television, because they can manipulate us then. They can make us buy anything, they can make us vote any way they want. How did Americans beat the Great Depression? We banded together. In those days, members of unions called each other 'brother' and 'sister,' and they meant it. We're going to bring that spirit back. Brother and sister! We're going to vote in George McGovern, and then we're going to get this country on the road again. We are going to band together with our neighbors to clean up our neighborhoods, to get the crooks out of the unions, to get the prices down in the meat markets. Here's a war cry for the American people: 'Lonesome no more!' "

So there's more socialism, this time wrapped in the rhetoric of a stump speech. (Shriver did not use it, by the way, and McGovern lost handily to incumbent Richard Nixon.) "Nobody in this country is happy but the rich people" might inspire the troops, but it does not sound like the more nuanced views of the rich that appear elsewhere in Vonnegut's novels.

After all, Eliot Rosewater is traumatized by combat shock and his mother's death. Wilbur Daffodil-11 Swain is disconnected from the sibling to whom he is fundamentally attached. Mary Kathleen O'Looney grows so isolated and so suspicious of the people around her that she stuffs her immense riches into her basketball shoes and moves literally underground.

All of these swimmers are, it turns out, as vulnerable and lonely as the sinkers to whom Shriver's would-be speech is addressed.

Pep-rally polemics aside, in the Shriver speech Vonnegut again praises community as a way to ease our misery. *Lonesome no more!* became the subtitle for Vonnegut's 1976 novel, *Slapstick*, and a campaign slogan, after all, for that book's own presidential candidate, Wilbur Swain.

> I spoke of American loneliness. It was the only subject I needed for victory, which was lucky. It was the only subject I had...I said that all the damaging excesses of Americans in the past were motivated by loneliness rather than a fondness for sin.

Wilbur pledges to make "Lonesome no more!" a reality. When he wins the presidency, another social experiment gets underway, a "Utopian scheme for reorganizing America."

Prior to their forced separation years earlier, Wilbur and his sister, Eliza—monstrous "neanderthaloids" who were preternaturally intelligent when together, telepathic when their heads touched—had privately developed a critique of the nation's founders.

> We said it was possible that the framers of the Constitution were blind to the beauty of persons who were without great wealth or powerful friends or public office, but who were nonetheless genuinely strong.

Wilbur and Eliza diagnosed the problem: "The framers had not noticed that it was natural, and therefore almost inevitable, that human beings in extraordinary and enduring situations should think of themselves as composing new families."

Thus, they "proposed that the Constitution be amended so as to guarantee that every citizen, no matter how humble or crazy or incompetent or deformed, somehow be given membership in some family."

As president, Wilbur works out the details. Every American is randomly assigned a new middle name and a number, such as Hollyhock-13 or Uranium-3. In Wilbur's case, it's Daffodil-11. All Americans who share the same word would be cousins. All who share the same word-and-number combination would be siblings.

Thousands of brothers and sisters for everyone! Tens of thousands of relatives! Connections like that would improve people's lives a lot more than "bad sorts of extended families," such as a professional association, which appears "nearly insane to outsiders." Such "a seeming team that was meaningless in terms of the ways God gets things done"—as *Cat's Cradle* identified a *granfalloon*—is deemed insufficient.

Wilbur unearths a written statement in which he and Eliza further explain their reasoning.

> "An ideal extended family...should give proportional representation to all sorts of Americans, according to their numbers. The creation of ten thousand such families, say, would provide America with ten thousand parliaments, so to speak, which would discuss sincerely and expertly what only a few hypocrites now discuss with passion, which is the welfare of all mankind."

Vonnegut is practically quoting himself there. A couple years earlier, he had written this in the preface to his nonfiction collection *Wampeters, Foma & Granfalloons*:

> My longer-range schemes have to do with providing all Americans with artificial extended families of a thousand members or more. Only when we have overcome loneliness can we begin to share wealth and work more fairly. I honestly believe that we will have those families by-and-by, and I hope they will become international.

We still await in America the kind of nurturing folk society that Vonnegut heard about in Robert Redfield's lectures, witnessed in Biafra, and imagined in *Slapstick*.

It would be a flowering of ideas planted by another humanist author, E. M. Forster. The main character in his 1910 novel *Howards End* urges "Only connect!," and Forster in his 1938 essay "What I Believe" identifies which qualities would flourish if personal relationships were valued above faith and causes: "Tolerance, good temper and sympathy—they are what matter really."

What becomes of Wilbur Swain's attempt to promote tolerance, good temper, and sympathy, his program of allotted familial ties?

It seems to help matters even as epidemics decimate the country.

Instant kinships are made among people who don't have bloodlines or anything else in common. Here and there in the ravaged nation, democratic enclaves manage to care for, support, and censure their own. Swain himself joins a gathering of Daffodils in Indianapolis led by an 11-year-old African American girl. States ruled by self-appointed dictators are fighting one another, but the Daffodils, like other "families," carry on with their business.

A young man who cries at a meeting of Daffodils, "There's nothing I'd rather do than kill me some 'Sooners' " is "scolded by several speakers for his military ardor." To the north, a battle has been waged at Lake Maxinkuckee, the site of many of Vonnegut's fondest childhood memories. Swain brings mixed but hopeful news from that front:

> I saw several people killed. I also saw many people embracing, and there seemed to be a great deal of deserting and surrendering going on....
> It is no massacre.

In Vonnegut's fictional decaying United States, even war cannot overcome the combatants' innate goodwill. Families are not fighting families, so "there's no such thing as a battle between strangers any more."

"Because we're just families, and not a nation any more," Swain says, "it's much easier for us to give and receive mercy in war."

As in *Rosewater*, Vonnegut gives us an imperfectly satisfying ending, the only kind of resolution he can muster for his scheme of overcoming loneliness through community.

People wishing to imitate Christ

The folk society that Vonnegut favored may be "just families, and not a nation," but we'll be stuck with nations and their flawed leaders for a while. So politics remain important. Although less than fully fleshed out in Vonnegut's work, his politics spring from thinking those leaders and their citizenry should behave like caring communities more than like indifferent organizations.

Religion is not going away either. Vonnegut's thoughts about religion harbor the same wish as his political leanings, and they go straight to the source. He told an interviewer in February 2003, "Socialism is, in fact, a form of Christianity, people wishing to imitate Christ."

The Hoosier socialist labor hero Powers Hapgood, to whom Vonnegut was introduced as a young man by his conservative and favorite uncle, Alex Vonnegut, provided an anecdote that further made the point. I will end this chapter with it.

Hapgood arrived late to a lunchtime meeting with Vonnegut, Vonnegut's father, and Uncle Alex. He'd been testifying in court about some picket-line trouble in which he had not been personally involved.

Hapgood had been educated at Harvard, where he'd met Alex, but after that "had chosen to endure death threats, beatings, and stints as a Debsian jailbird." The judge that morning had asked a question that prompted a response Vonnegut found perfectly lovely.

"Mr. Hapgood," he said, "why would a man from such a distinguished family and with such a fine education choose to live as you do?"

"Why?" said Hapgood, according to Hapgood. "Because of the Sermon on the Mount, sir."

The Gospel of Matthew, Chapter 5
The Sermon on the Mount

"The Sermon on the Mount suggests a mercifulness that can never waver or fade."

    Kurt Vonnegut, St. Clement's Episcopal Church, March 30, 1980

The Beatitudes

And seeing the multitudes, He went up on a mountain, and when He was seated His disciples came to Him. ² Then He opened His mouth and taught them, saying:

³ "Blessed are the poor in spirit,
For theirs is the kingdom of heaven.

⁴ Blessed are those who mourn,
For they shall be comforted.

⁵ Blessed are the meek,
For they shall inherit the earth.

⁶ Blessed are those who hunger and thirst for righteousness,
For they shall be filled.

⁷ Blessed are the merciful,
For they shall obtain mercy.

⁸ Blessed are the pure in heart,
For they shall see God.

⁹ Blessed are the peacemakers,
For they shall be called sons of God.

¹⁰ Blessed are those who are persecuted for righteousness' sake,
For theirs is the kingdom of heaven.

¹¹ Blessed are you when they revile and persecute you, and say all kinds of evil against you falsely for My sake. ¹²Rejoice and be exceedingly glad, for great is your reward in heaven, for so they persecuted the prophets who were before you."

New King James Version

Chapter 9

Christ Worshiper

"I say with all my American ancestors, 'If what Jesus said was good, and so much of it was absolutely beautiful, what does it matter if he was God or not?'"

Kurt Vonnegut, May 15, 1999

To understand Kurt Vonnegut's humanism, you have to make sense of one seemingly incongruous phrase he uttered while delivering the annual Palm Sunday guest sermon at St. Clement's Episcopal Church, New York, in 1980. He called himself "a Christ-worshiping agnostic."

First, let's be clear again about Vonnegut's ancestral background:

> My family has been religiously skeptical as far back as I can trace it. My people have always been agnostics, and wilder of the elements have been atheists...And so if I declare that God is dead, it's no turning point in my personal history or in the history of my family. We've always found this meant an agreeable situation, to be on our own and to behave virtuously within the biological limits of being human beings. They say there are no atheists in foxholes. I was certainly one, and it was a comfort to me.

Atheism gave Vonnegut comfort. So why did he "worship" the man whom Christians believe to be the Son of God?

One explanation: More comfort, this time for others.

Consider *which* Christ he "worshiped"—that is, *admired*. It's not the figure who in the New Testament is born of a virgin and is crucified and rises from his tomb to save humankind from its sins and reopen the gates of heaven. Vonnegut showed no interest in a supernatural Jesus who views the world through the eyes of God Almighty (except for juvenile readers—see the last section of this chapter).

No, Vonnegut was fascinated by the Jesus who embodied the best *human* traits he could imagine, personal qualities worthy of worship: mercy, compassion, and goodwill. It's the Jesus who preached from the mountaintop in the Gospel according to Matthew.

This came up during the St. Clement's sermon. "I am enchanted by the Sermon on the Mount," Vonnegut said. "Being merciful, it seems to me, is the only good idea we have received so far."

In the Gospels according to Matthew and Luke—in the latter it's called the Sermon on the Plain—Christ tells a crowd of his disciples and other followers about the type of people who are favored by God. Their attributes are included in a list commonly called the Beatitudes, beginning with "Blessed are the poor in spirit...."

The notion that the world's least materially successful inhabitants are worthwhile motivates many a charitable cause, whether religious or secular, and it inspired Vonnegut.

> What, exactly, was the Sermon on the Mount? It was the prediction by Jesus Christ that the poor in spirit would receive the Kingdom of Heaven; that all who mourned would be comforted; that the meek would inherit the Earth; that those who hungered for righteousness would find it; that the merciful would be treated mercifully; that the pure in heart would see God; that the peacemakers would be called the sons of God; that those who were persecuted for righteousness' sake would also receive the Kingdom of Heaven; and on and on.

That hopeful message sounded just fine to Vonnegut. It's the ultimate comforting lie: Jesus is in the corner of every hapless soldier, every Biafran refugee, every Diana Moon Glampers whom Vonnegut ever encountered or created. And the ultrarich, compassionate Eliot Rosewaters of the world—if there are any—are not enough. Since Jesus' lie is about heaven, then a sweet afterlife is an opiate for the masses.

Atheists and skeptics typically regard such conceptions of the universe and the promise of eternal peace after death as fairy tales.

Among the unbelievers are the so-called New Atheists, a group of European American male intellectuals—Richard Dawkins, Daniel Dennett, Sam Harris, and the late Christopher Hitchens—whose books extolling life without religious faith began to grace best-seller lists in the early twenty-first century. (Perhaps they're not so new anymore.)

They arrived at the same conclusion as the British philosopher and mathematician Bertrand Russell. In the 1920s Russell wrote:

> I do not believe that, on the balance, religious belief has been a force for good. Although I am prepared to admit that in certain times and places it has had some good effects, I regard it as belonging to the infancy of human reason, and to a stage of development which we are now outgrowing.

Hitchens was even less forgiving. "*Religion poisons everything*," he wrote. "As well as a menace to civilization, it has become a threat to human survival."

Vonnegut in his writings and public comments was not concerned with blazing a path for nonbelief. Reason and logic are fine, Vonnegut felt, but he was troubled by their limitations, by *science's* capacity for harm more than religion's. He urged kindness, and he knew it's common for human beings alive on Earth to be inspired to act kindly through God or Jesus or whichever supernatural means works for them.

The amateur anthropologist in Vonnegut said that, if we're going to be stuck with irrational belief for a while, let's make the best of it. And he knew Christ is the religious figure with whom his American readership, believers and nonbelievers alike, was most familiar.

> In America, it's easy to form a large clump of people who know something about Christianity, since there has always been so much talk about Christianity around. It wouldn't be easy to get a large clump of Zoroastrians, for instance. But there are very big clumps of Christianity. There are very big clumps of race hatred. It's easy to make either one of them grow, especially in a society as lonesome as this one is.

When you look at it that way, Jesus' message of mercy is worth promoting. That won't get you credit for helping to push reason to the forefront of human morality like the New Atheists and a lot of humanists want, but you'll be advocating for the humane behavior they want more than anything.

What you believe is your business. What you *do* actually makes a difference. The way Scottish-American comedian Craig Ferguson expressed the point would more likely get a nod from Vonnegut than from some of the New Atheists.

> I believe that religion is actually a neutral force. Like any other neutral force, from time to nuclear physics, the user is the one who determines whether the outcome is good or bad....
> It doesn't matter what you believe; it only matters how you behave. Or as it so succinctly says in Christian scripture, "Faith without works is dead."

And faith *with* works can benefit everyone. Imagine what would happen, Vonnegut asked, if Christians demanded that their government representatives obey the Sermon on the Mount. Acting upon those comforting lies might very well improve the nation, and perhaps the world.

> For some reason, the most vocal Christians among us never mention the Beatitudes. But, often with tears in their eyes, they demand the Ten Commandments be posted in public buildings. And of course that's Moses, not Jesus. I haven't heard one of them demand the Sermon on the Mount, the Beatitudes, be posted anywhere.
> "Blessed are the merciful" posted in a courtroom? "Blessed are the peacemakers" in the Pentagon? Give me a break!

Vonnegut was not impressed with George W. Bush-era Republicans' public regard for Christ. "I don't think they've ever paid any attention to him," he told TV talk-show host Bill Maher. In another interview, he called Bush "a phony Christian."

Elected officials were not the only phonies, in Vonnegut's estimation. So were religious leaders throughout history. Christianity, he told a group of Unitarian Universalists in Rochester, New York, in June 1986, "was nothing but a poor people's religion, a servant's religion, a slave's religion, a woman's religion, a child's religion, and would have remained such if it hadn't stopped taking the Sermon on the Mount seriously and joined forces with the vain and rich and violent."

The same speech tracked the effects of those joined forces, calling human beings to task collectively for saying they believe in Jesus' message of love and then dropping bombs on Dresden and Nagasaki.

Vonnegut opened his exploration by echoing a passage from *Slaughterhouse-Five*. He asked the same question posed by Tralfamadorians in Kilgore Trout's *Gospel from Outer Space*.

> Now what is it, do you think, that makes Christians so bloodthirsty?...I think the problem is linguistic, and might be repaired, if the evangelists would only allow it, with startling simplicity. The Christian preachers exhort their listeners to love one another and to love their neighbors and so on. Love is simply too strong a

word to be of much use in ordinary, day-to-day relationships. Love is for Romeo and Juliet.

I'm to love my neighbor? How can I do that when I'm not even speaking to my wife and kids today?... I like to think that Jesus said in Aramaic, "Ye shall respect one another." That would be a sign to me that He really wanted to help us here on Earth, and not just in the Afterlife...

And look at the spectrum of emotions we think of automatically when we hear the word "love." If you can't love your neighbor, then you can at least like him. If you can't like him, you can at least not give a damn about him. If you can't ignore him, then you have to hate him, right? You've exhausted all the other possibilities. That's a quick trip to hate, isn't it? And it starts with love...That is my explanation of why hatred is so common in that part of the world dominated by Christianity. There are all these people who have been told to do their best at loving. They fail, most of them. And why wouldn't they fail, since loving is extremely difficult? And when they fail to love, day after day, year in and year out, come one, come all, the logic of the language leads them to the seemingly inevitable conclusion that they must hate instead....

So there you have my scheme for making Christianity, which has killed so many people so horribly, a little less homicidal: substituting the word "respect" for the word "love."...The Christian quick trip from love to hate to murder is our principal entertainment. We might call it "Christianity Fails Again," and how satisfying so many of us have been trained to find it when it fails and fails.

Vonnegut left out tolerating your neighbor, which ought to be slotted between liking and ignoring, still a bit short of respecting. And if there's a "spectrum of emotions" with love at one end, the continuum beyond ignoring one's neighbor would include disrespect, disdain, and contempt along the way to hatred.

In any event, "Ye shall respect" does sound more workable than "Ye shall love."

Vonnegut recognized other flaws in organized religion. It requires faith, and the wrong kind of faith leads to hatred and even murder and war rather than to love—I mean, *respect*.

Howard W. Campbell Jr., the American spy and Nazi propagandist from *Mother Night*, is certain about faith. Often the last sentence of the following excerpt from the book is quoted (and we saw a few pieces of this passage several chapters ago), but it's useful to include a bit more:

> I had hoped, as a broadcaster, to be merely ludicrous, but this is a hard world to be ludicrous in, with so many human beings so reluctant to laugh, so incapable of thought, so eager to believe and snarl and hate. So many people wanted to believe me!
> Say what you will about the sweet miracle of unquestioning faith, I consider a capacity for it terrifying and absolutely vile.

If you believe something merely because you *want* to believe it, Campbell infers, then you might be open to any suggestion, no matter how unreasonable, that seems to support your belief. You're controllable, and the controllers have an easy time of it.

It can be risky even to believe in something nice and seemingly positive, such as a loving Creator of the Universe who appeared on Earth to wash our souls clean and remove our fear of death. How far are you willing to take your faith in such an entity?

More to the point: Do you think those who don't share your faith are inferior? That they should be punished? Their views declared illegal? Do you want others to punish them on your behalf?

Believers and unbelievers alike have to challenge themselves from time to time. We all have to decide how far to take our convictions.

Tolerance must be a part of contemporary religious discourse, if we're going to coexist in spite of our differences. The public correspondence in 2007 between Andrew Sullivan, a Christian conservative blogger, and Harris, one of the New Atheists, demonstrated such civil tolerance. In defense of "a Truth that may yet be beyond our understanding," Sullivan wrote:

> You ask legitimately: how can I, convinced of this truth, resist imposing it on others? The answer is: humility and doubt. I may believe these things, but I am aware that others may not; and I respect their own existential decision to believe something else. I respect their decision because I respect my own, and realize it is indescribable to those who have not directly experienced it. That's why I am such a dogged defender of pluralism and secularism—because I believe secularism alone does justice to the profundity of the claims of religion.

Sullivan's last point—that a secular society actually protects, not threatens, individual religious belief—is anathema to many believers. One notable such view came in 2019 from then-United States Attorney General William P. Barr, who like Sullivan is Catholic. "We must be vigilant," Barr said, "to resist efforts by the forces of secularization to drive religious viewpoints from the public square and to impinge upon the free exercise of our faith."

Sullivan defends pluralism in the public square while maintaining a deep-seated sense of personal Truth emanating from faith in Christ. Vonnegut never claimed to know the truth or the Truth, or even to be seeking it.

In fact, to him untruths were allowable if their intent was kindness. While Bokonon's lies seek to preserve society and Winston Niles Rumfoord's lies aim to direct history, another Vonnegut character has mercy in mind, more like Jesus did.

Eugene Debs Hartke, the atheist narrator of *Hocus Pocus*, asks: "Why argue somebody else out of the expectation of some sort of an Afterlife?" In the prison where he teaches remedial English, Hartke breaks institutional policy by informing lifers about the facility's surroundings.

> And of course, this enriched their dreams of escaping, but what were those but what we could call in any other context the virtue hope? I never thought they would ever really get out of here and make use of the knowledge I had given them of the countryside, and neither did they.
>
> I used to do the same sort of thing in Vietnam, too, helping mortally wounded soldiers believe that they would soon be well and home again.
>
> Why not?

Full of white magic

It would be easy enough to say that "faith" as commonly understood is another word for "the virtue hope," a longing for something desirable to occur or to be true. Hebrews Chapter 11 begins by calling faith "the substance of things hoped for, the evidence of things not seen." Scholars probe a critical question about this passage: Does it *define* faith, or does it describe its *effects*? Does "things hoped for" simply mean wishes, or does the phrase more fundamentally concern the Word of God?

The answer depends on the level of your faith, or lack of it.

Throughout the Bible, how the original Hebrew, Aramaic, and Greek are translated can vary, and therefore so does modern interpretation. Fine points can be altered depending upon whether a word means *this* or *that*.

A humanistic reading of Hebrews 11:1 would accept the sentence as plainly stating the tight, often indistinguishable connection between faith and hope.

Humanists do not believe that faith—uncritical belief—is essential. Believers contend that their faith is profound and therefore *is* essential, to them and possibly to all people. Both, however, would agree that life without *hope* can be miserable.

But here's Vonnegut the contrarian in a 1976 interview with Robert L. Short, a minister who wrote books of Christian apologetics for popular consumption. Vonnegut tells Short he lives "without...hope of paradise."

> I love sleep; so sleep is fine with me...But I've done fine living without hope. One clear hope I had was that I'd be able to—it's a middle-class hope—to give good education to my children. And that I've been able to do...But once I fulfilled that hope—'cause they're all out of college now—and I've got a lot of money, and there's nothing much I want to do with—there's no hope to fulfill.

Note the distinction between the earthbound hope that Vonnegut had and the otherworldly "hope of paradise" that sounds more like faith. While his wealth helped Vonnegut fulfill the one clear hope he mentioned having, he believed most people lack hope in this world and thus rely on the comforting lies of religion.

Czech writer and president Václev Havel talked about the importance of hope, which he called "the certainty that something makes sense, regardless of how it turns out...

> I think that the deepest and most important form of hope, the only one that can keep us above water and urge us to good works, and the only true source of the breathtaking dimension of the human spirit and its efforts, is something we get, as it were, from "elsewhere."

Faith's positive effects on many people impressed Vonnegut, and as we've seen he was not a strident atheist looking for a fight. Most humanists are not, he contended.

> Are we enemies of organized religion? No. My great war buddy Bernard V. O'Hare, now dead, lost his faith as a Roman Catholic during World War Two. I didn't like that. I thought that was too much to lose.
>
> I had never had faith like that, because I had been raised by interesting and moral people who, like Thomas Jefferson and Benjamin Franklin, were nonetheless skeptics about what preachers said was going on. But I knew Bernie had lost something important and honorable.
>
> Again, I did not like that, did not like it because I liked *him* so much.

Instead of rejoicing that O'Hare had cast aside notions about resurrection and the eternal soul and the Holy Eucharist to join Vonnegut's "team," Vonnegut was sorry because his friend "had lost something important and honorable."

Could his comments reveal a bit of envy about being *able* to believe in something that would make this life more bearable?

This admiration for achieving contentment through personal belief extended to concepts that most atheists find ridiculous. Vonnegut told a college audience in 1970 that astrology and palm-reading "are good because they make people feel vivid and full of possibilities."

He was not going to bash something outright if it seemed harmless and made people feel better.

Vonnegut the social observer understood people's desire for spiritual fulfillment as a way to seek community within a folk society. He struck those familiar notes while talking to a Unitarian assemblage in 1980.

> What is so comical about religious people in modern times? They believe so many things which science has proved to be unknowable or absolutely wrong.
>
> How on earth can religious people believe in so much arbitrary, clearly invented balderdash? For one thing, I guess, the balderdash is usually more beautiful—and therefore echoes excitingly in the more primitive lobes of our brains, where knowledge counts for nothing.
>
> More important, though: the acceptance of a creed, any creed, entitles the acceptor to membership in the sort of artificial extended family we call a congregation. It is a way to fight loneliness. Any time I see a person fleeing from reason and into religion, I think to myself, There goes a person who simply cannot stand being so goddamned lonely anymore.

If Vonnegut found comfort in atheism even while in a foxhole, he realized that many people, including a few to whom he was closest, found no refuge in nonbelief. In print, at least, Vonnegut expressed understanding about those who, unlike O'Hare, kept their religious faith or converted to it.

Both of his daughters spurned their ancestral skepticism in favor of religion. Vonnegut claimed he did not object. He told the Unitarians about the first such conversion.

> Living alone and far from home, she has memorized an arbitrary Christian creed, Trinitarianism, by chance. She now has her human dignity regularly confirmed by the friendly nods of a

congregation. I am glad that she is not so lonely anymore. This is more than all right with me.

Vonnegut's most touching remarks about faith involve his first wife, Jane. Her religious explorations were "painful" to him even though her "alliances with the supernatural [fulfilled] her need to increase her strength and understanding—and happiness and health."

Eventually Jane, like their daughters, arrived at born-again Christianity. They were, Vonnegut wrote,

> working white magic through rituals and prayers. That's all right. I would be a fool to say that the Free Thinker ideas of Clemens Vonnegut remain as enchanting and encouraging as ever—not after the mortal poisoning of the planet, not after two world wars, with more to come.

As his marriage wobbled in the 1960s, Vonnegut wrote in *Palm Sunday,* "it was mainly religion in a broad sense that Jane and I fought about." Friends since childhood, they married in 1945, separated in 1970, divorced in 1979. Jane remarried in 1984 while suffering from terminal ovarian cancer.

Vonnegut spoke to her on the phone two weeks before she died in December 1986. He recounted the conversation lovingly. This is one of the most affectionate things he wrote about anyone:

> Jane could believe with all her heart anything that made being alive seem full of white magic. That was her strength. She was raised a Quaker, but stopped going to meetings of Friends after her four happy years at Swarthmore. She became an Episcopalian after marrying Adam, who remained a Jew. She died believing in the Trinity and Heaven and Hell and all the rest of it. I'm so glad. Why? Because I loved her.

"His sort of divinity is attainable by us"

Vonnegut knew that Jesus was important to a large clump of Americans and to a small clump of people close to Vonnegut himself. Whether Jesus was deemed a savior or a teacher, Vonnegut defended him.

A good example occurs in Vonnegut's magazine article about the Hindu spiritual leader Maharishi Mahesh Yogi.

The Maharishi developed and trademarked the Transcendental Meditation technique. He took his instructions on global tours beginning in 1958, and ten years later his popularity was boosted when the Beatles and other celebrities visited him in Rishikesh, India. He was alternately revered, accused of inappropriate (and unverified) sexual advances, welcomed as a TV show guest, and dismissed as an opportunistic salesman.

Among his claims was that TM and levitation and so forth would bring self-fulfillment and, if done by enough people, help achieve world peace. Vonnegut expressed skepticism as he, his wife, and their oldest daughter caught the Maharishi's act in Cambridge, Massachusetts.

One result of that January 1968 encounter was a satirical essay Vonnegut published in *Esquire*. He did not consider the Maharishi a fake, but he felt the alleged holy man sounded "like a General Electric engineer" in responding to a reporter's question about the plight of Americans seeking civil rights. They ought to try harder and meditate so they'll perform better in the job market, His Holiness seemed to be saying.

What bothered Vonnegut more during a crowded hotel-room press conference were the Maharishi's comments about Jesus. They were unenlightened, Vonnegut wrote.

> Maharishi was asked his opinions of Jesus Christ. He had some. He prefaced them with this dependent clause: "From what people have told me about Him—"
>
> Here was a man who had unselfishly spent years of his life in American and northern European hotel rooms, teaching Christians how to save the world. There had to be Gideon Bibles in most of those rooms. Yet, Maharishi had never opened one to find out what Jesus said, exactly.
>
> Some searching mind....
>
> A few moments later he said that Jesus and the early Christian saints had mistakenly allowed their minds to wander. "You must have control," he said. The wandering minds of Jesus and the saints had led to what Maharishi called "an absurdity," an emphasis on faith...
>
> I went outside the hotel after that, liking Jesus better than I had ever liked Him before. I wanted to see a crucifix, so I could say to it, "You know why You're up there? It's Your own fault. You should have practiced Transcendental Meditation, which is easy as pie. You would also have been a better carpenter."

So Vonnegut the non-Christian imagines chatting with an approachable Christ, whom he feels he understands better than does the robed guru who's drawing huge, worshipful crowds. The Maharishi would know Jesus better by reading the same Christian scripture that Vonnegut had read, text that contains "what Jesus said, exactly."

Those words persuaded Vonnegut that even an unsupernatural Jesus, far from allowing his mind to wander too much, was an excellent and relevant ethical guide. Vonnegut explained this to a clergyman from Transylvania University in Kentucky. The Rev. Paul H. Jones had read *Hocus Pocus* and wanted to know about its author's "religious persuasion." In 1990 Vonnegut replied in a letter.

> Jesus is particularly stimulating to me, since he noticed what I can't help noticing, that life is so hard most people are losers or feel like losers, so that a skill essential to most of us, if we are to retain some shred of dignity, is to show grace in defeat. That to me is the lesson he taught while up on the cross, whether he was God or not. And he was neither the first nor the last human being, if that is what he was, to teach that while in unbelievable agony.
>
> As for the teaching of formal Christianity, I am all for it... What I can't stand are sermons which say that to believe in the divinity of Jesus is a way to *win*.

The grace Jesus showed on the cross, as far as Vonnegut was concerned, derived from what he *didn't* do as much as what he did. Vonnegut spoke that way even about the message of forgiveness in the Lord's Prayer.

> When Jesus Christ was nailed to a cross, he said, "Forgive them, Father, they know not what they do." What kind of a man was that? Any real man...would have said, "Kill them, Dad, and all their friends and relatives, and make their deaths slow and painful."
>
> His greatest legacy to us, in my humble opinion, consists of only twelve words...Jesus of Nazareth told us to say these twelve words when we prayed: "Forgive us our trespasses as we forgive those who trespass against us."...
>
> And for those words alone, he deserves to be called "the Prince of Peace."

A church pastor could hardly put it better during a Sunday sermon to emphasize Christ's otherworldly nature. Vonnegut found greatness in a mortal Jesus. "He was another human being, and his sort of divinity is attainable by us," Vonnegut said in the interview with Short. "He had no superior connections or equipment."

Jesus was so human, Vonnegut contended, he was capable of humor. That was Vonnegut's conclusion upon reading chapter 12 of the Gospel according to John. It describes a dinner made for Jesus by the sisters of Lazarus, who recently had been raised from the dead by Jesus and who also was seated at the supper table. It says,

> Then Mary took a pound of very costly oil of spikenard, anointed the feet of Jesus, and wiped His feet with her hair. And the house was filled with the fragrance of the oil.
> But one of His disciples, Judas Iscariot, Simon's son, who would betray Him, said, "Why was this fragrant oil not sold for three hundred denarii and given to the poor?"

That's about a year's wages for a worker of the time, by the way. The passage concludes:

> But Jesus said, "Let her alone; she has kept this for the day of My burial. For the poor you have with you always, but Me you do not have always."

This made Vonnegut think back to his childhood. Growing up in Indianapolis, he had heard even his presumably non-Christian relatives twist Jesus' teachings when convenient. Looking back as an adult, he disliked the way they interpreted what Jesus said to Judas.

> Whenever anybody out that way began to worry a lot about the poor people when I was young, some eminently respectable Hoosier, possibly an uncle or an aunt, would say that Jesus himself had given up on doing much about the poor. He or she would paraphrase John twelve, Verse eight: "The poor people are hopeless. We'll always be stuck with them."...
> If those Hoosiers were still alive, which they are not, I would tell them now that Jesus was only joking, and that he was not even thinking much about the poor.

Vonnegut explained in a 1981 interview why he thought Jesus was joking. Partly it was the English-language version failing to capture the nuance of Jesus' reply, turning it into a resigned acceptance of poverty that sounded correct to many people, including Vonnegut's relatives in Indianapolis.

"This line has self-pity in it, which seems out of character for Jesus," Vonnegut said in examining the Christ quote.

> I feel it's a very bad translation...and so I thought that there was a possibility that Jesus was making the sort of kind joke that Abraham Lincoln might have made under the same circumstances, or Mark Twain, and so what I think Jesus really said, which was mistranslated, was, "Judas, don't worry about it, there'll be plenty

of poor people left long after I'm gone," which is a very nice American frontier joke.

A verse in John, chapter 12, not mentioned by Vonnegut supports his claim that Jesus' response "For the poor you have with you always, but Me you do not have always" was meant ironically. No mistranslation is to blame. This is how John explains Judas' complaint that the expensive oil was not sold to benefit the poor:

> This he said, not that he cared for the poor, but because he was a thief, and had the money box; and he used to take what was put in it.

The remark by Jesus immediately follows. It could have been a particular kind of humor: a knowing barb directed straight at Judas, the frontier joke Vonnegut suspected.

Selective editing

Several quotes ago, Vonnegut referred to two of the Founding Fathers, Jefferson and Franklin, as "skeptics about what preachers said was going on." Those two are among the Founders who are considered deists; that is, they believed in God as a clockmaker who created the world and then left it to progress on its own. Heavily influenced by the Enlightenment, they commonly rejected the divine nature of Jesus.

Jefferson left physical evidence of his skepticism. During and after his presidency, he cut and pasted his own version of the Gospels in four languages, removing mention of Jesus' miracles and other supernatural occurrences while retaining his moral teachings.

In an 1803 letter to his friend Benjamin Rush, a more conventional Christian who at the time was Treasurer of the United States Mint, Jefferson was clear about his perception of Christianity as flawed and of Jesus as a human being who was not the Son of God.

> To the corruptions of Christianity, I am indeed opposed; but not to the genuine precepts of Jesus himself. I am a Christian, in the only sense in which he wished any one to be; sincerely attached to his doctrines, in preference to all others; ascribing to himself every human excellence, and believing he never claimed any other.

You might be tempted to call Jefferson a Christ-worshiping agnostic. An accurate characterization would be more nuanced, but I think we can say his views of Jesus and Vonnegut's are similar.

What was extracted from the New Testament in the so-called Jefferson Bible? "In general,...passages that reflect violence, magic or the allegedly divine empowerment of ordinary humans" were excised, according to the American Humanist Association's modern reprinting of the text. Jesus' mother was not a virgin. He performed no miracles. When he died, he stayed dead.

Significantly, the Sermon on the Mount avoided Jefferson's razor.

Close to two centuries later, unlike America's third president, Vonnegut did not remove troubling and conflicting Bible passages about Jesus. He ignored them.

These would include Jesus promising harsh judgment on people who did not repent despite his miracles (Matthew 11:20–24), saying he has "not come to bring peace but a sword" (Matthew 10:34), and warning that with him around "father will be divided against son and son against father, mother against daughter and daughter against mother" (Luke 12:53). In much of John 8 and elsewhere, Jesus haughtily uses circular reasoning to equate himself with God Almighty and demands that others follow, know, and believe him and live according to his teaching rather than urge them to exhibit kindness for its own sake.

It's no wonder Vonnegut did not cite such accounts of a figure who believes he is at least God's representative on Earth, if not God himself. And beyond the four Gospels, the epistles of Paul, John, and others occasionally depict an even more unworldly, more demanding Jesus that is not the one Vonnegut celebrated.

Actually, Vonnegut addressed at least one fiery warning from Jesus, but it's a character rather than the author who dismisses the statement as a sign of temporary insanity.

The verse is in Matthew 25, which previews what Jesus will say on Judgment Day. His favored sheep, those who fed the hungry, clothed the naked, and otherwise helped "the least of these [his] brethren," are told they will inherit the Kingdom of God. But, according to Matthew, Jesus will tell those who ignored such unfortunates, "Depart from Me, you cursed, into the everlasting fire prepared for the devil and his angels."

In *Jailbird*, Emil Larkin, the fictional born-again hatchet man and Watergate criminal (obviously based on the real-life Chuck Colson), quotes that passage while attempting to save narrator Walter Starbuck from hell. Starbuck comes up with an explanation.

> These words appalled me then, and they appall me now. They are surely the inspiration for the notorious cruelty of Christians.
>
> "Jesus may have said that," I told Larkin, "but it is so unlike most of what else He said that I have to conclude that He was slightly crazy that day."

When Jesus' message strayed from that of his Sermon on the Mount, Vonnegut or a fictional surrogate chalked up the difference to a joke or a misstatement.

It might seem hypocritical for Vonnegut to accept that Jesus was gentle and merciful yet not that he was truly holy. But even among the faithful, only the most devoted literalists believe *everything* in the Bible. Instead, like Vonnegut, most Christians take from the New Testament only as much or as little as they need.

I mean that in a positive sense, assuming that religion fills a spiritual requirement.

Is behaving decently enough?

While Jefferson radically altered Christian scripture, Vonnegut performed a different sort of revision of text that, although not considered as sacred as the Bible, was not the sort of thing that Christians tampered with: The pope-approved sixteenth century Latin Mass.

At the world premiere of British composer Andrew Lloyd Webber's *Requiem*, a soaring musical piece for the Mass, Vonnegut was in the audience. The four-century-old lyrics were sung in Latin, but the program booklet included an English translation. Vonnegut found the words "sadistic and masochistic," as they were "promising a Paradise indistinguishable from the Spanish Inquisition."

After the show, he went home and wrote new lyrics, addressing not the Lord but the Cosmos. Where the groveling old text says

> A day of wrath, that day,
> it will dissolve the world into glowing ashes,
> as attested by David together with the Sibyl....
> My prayers are not worthy;
> but Thou, of Thy goodness, deal generously with me,
> that I burn not in the everlasting fire.

Vonnegut's Mass instead says

> A day of wrath, that day:
> We shall dissolve the world into glowing ashes,
> as attested by our weapons for wars
> in the names of gods unknowable....
> My prayers are unheard,
> but Thy sublime indifference will ensure
> that I burn not in some everlasting fire.

In a hundred and eighteen meditative lines, Vonnegut produced a poetic statement to complement the 1900 pamphlet *A Proposed Guide for Instruction of Morals* written by his great-grandfather Clemens, a co-founder of the Freethinkers Society in Indianapolis.

Vonnegut later found people to translate his requiem into Latin, write new music, and stage it three years after he'd seen Lloyd Webber's.

Both requiems refer to the "everlasting fire," although Vonnegut's Mass rejects the existence of hell. The alternative to heaven, and what Jesus said about it, is debated even among Christians. If Jesus warned about everlasting damnation as a consequence of rejecting his divinity—as many Christians believe—what kind of savior is he, and what kind of supreme being is God?

American popular culture typically refers to hell as never-ending punishment for transgressions. That conception does not aways match the opinions of New Testament experts.

John 3:18 says, "He who believes in Him is not condemned; but he who does not believe is condemned already, because he has not believed in the name of the only begotten Son of God." An easy and widespread interpretation is that *condemned* means doomed to suffer forever—that is, in hell.

But some scholars interpret the passage differently, replacing eternal torment with garden-variety mortality and the absence of God. If you don't accept Jesus as savior, then, damnation occurs not after death but *here* and *now*.

Without defining hell, Vonnegut's references to it generally agree with mainstream opinion, that it's a place in the afterlife for bad people. He implies as much in his "tried to behave decently without any expectation of rewards or punishments" quote.

A good example from his fiction: His character Kilgore Trout (we'll see a lot more of him in the next chapter) tells a gullible woman that if she did "more bad things instead of good things, that's too bad for you, because you'll burn forever and ever."

In any case, whether rewriting *Requiem* or having one of his characters dismiss the passage in Matthew, Vonnegut himself rejects the existence of hell. He finds Trout's version ridiculous too.

However, most Christians *do* believe in something like the perpetual punishment that Trout describes.

More than six in ten American adults—and about eight in ten Christian American adults—believe in hell, according to a Pew Research poll with more than six thousand respondents in September 2021. Believers don't necessarily envision souls on fire, but what they do believe is bad enough.

About half of all U.S. adults—the vast majority of the 62 percent who believe in hell—say that people in hell definitely or probably experience psychological suffering, become aware of the suffering they created in the world, experience physical suffering, and are prevented from having a relationship with God.

That "Depart from me, you cursed" verse in Matthew apparently has made quite an impression.

So even most Christians see hell as a place to which the souls of misbehavers are consigned on Judgment Day and not as what the author Short calls "a reality that exists in *this* lifetime" because death has been conquered.

That's how a Campus Crusade for Christ recruiter presented it to me on one of my first days in college. I was *already* going to heaven because Jesus died for my sins, this nice young man explained while buying me a bagel.

I had doubts. What I'd been told about Jesus in 13 years of Catholic schooling and church attendance seemed less and less likely to be true. So I didn't join CCC or come around to the nice young man's way of thinking. Later, though, I did give that organization occasional space on the op-ed page that I edited for the student newspaper. I let non-Christians have their say too.

Why not?

To be taken seriously

Vonnegut had some idea about the theological parsing of hell. But he realized what most Americans believed, and he wrote and spoke to that.

But the Christ he worshiped—that is, admired—is not the one whose story Americans knew so well, the one in whom faith leads to redemption of one's immortal soul. For all of Vonnegut's promotion of Jesus' words, his trying "to behave decently without any expectation of rewards or punishments" is not enough for those who believe in salvation.

It *can* be enough for people who see Jesus as less than the Holy Redeemer.

Christians and committed humanists both strive to behave decently. Christian doctrine posits that good deeds inevitably result from and supplement faith but on their own are not sufficient for salvation. Humanists believe good deeds will lead to a better world, regardless of what the deeds are attributed to.

If they were attributed to Jesus, Vonnegut would have no quarrel.

He identified at least two people who carried Christ's message into modern times. One was Indianapolis native Powers Hapgood, the Sermon on the Mount proponent we met in the previous chapter. The other was another Hoosier labor leader, Eugene V. Debs, namesake of the *Hocus Pocus* narrator. Debs, the Socialist presidential candidate, served two terms in federal prison for leading a railyard strike and speaking publicly against US involvement in World War I.

Vonnegut felt Debs and Jesus shared a commitment to those whom society vilifies and overlooks.

> I still quote Eugene Debs (1855-1926), late of Terre Haute, Indiana, five times the Socialist Party's candidate for President, in every speech:
> "While there is a lower class I am in it, while there is a criminal element I am of it; while there is a soul in prison, I am not free."
> In recent years, I've found it prudent to say before quoting Debs that he is to be taken seriously. Otherwise many in the audience will start to laugh. They are being nice, not mean, knowing I like to be funny. But it is also a sign of these times that such a moving echo of the Sermon on the Mount can be perceived as outdated, wholly discredited horsecrap.
> Which it is not.

For Vonnegut, Jesus and his Sermon on the Mount epitomized kindness. Even when writing about Christmas in one of his few published poems (not counting verse such as his Bokononist calypsos and his requiem), Vonnegut makes a wholly secular point.

> I will dream of a baby,
> A boy and a man,
> Who taught simple kindness;
> I'll learn it if I can.
> I'm sorry they killed you,
> I'm glad you were born.
> I'll be a mild Christian
> On mild Christmas morn.

Vonnegut wrote a Christmas carol too, for the composer Lukas Foss. Unproduced for the stage, it focused on the Nativity.

> Those who would kill Him
> Are near, are near.
> So keep Him a secret,
> So dear, so dear.
> And the Mother's name is May-ree.

Even if it wasn't true, the Biblical account of Jesus, Vonnegut felt, was "one hell of a story."

Christ for kids

Throughout his career, Vonnegut wrote of Christ favorably but mostly as no more holy than a caring, merciful, quite mortal teacher. Twice, however, he wrote unabashed Christ-centered pieces that resemble Sunday School lessons. These oddities within Vonnegut's half-century of published output are even more puzzling when compared to the free-thinking content for which he is known.

They work best with an impressionable juvenile audience in mind. Both rely on the image of Baby Jesus.

First was a disarmingly innocent "original playlet for children to perform." It was published by *Better Homes and Gardens* in 1962, when Vonnegut still was trying to establish himself as a writer while supporting a wife and six kids.

"The Very First Christmas Morning" concerns five hungry children who, after some internal discussion, give their last morsels of bread to Mary, Joseph, and the couple's newborn baby. An approving archangel declares, "From now on, good children like you shall receive gifts on the anniversary of this holy day."

Removing any doubt about the baby's identity, the archangel tells the children, "For unto you is born this day in the city of David a Saviour, which is Christ the Lord." A choir of angels sings hosannas.

The piece is so unaffectedly pious that, were it to be staged by schoolchildren, it could become a perennial favorite among faithful Christians.

More improbably, in 1980, long after Vonnegut had become a fixture on the best-seller lists and better able to choose among publishing opportunities, he wrote the text for a 64-page children's book called *Sun Moon Star* from the perspective of the infant savior as he is born.

Illustrator Ivan Chermayeff, whose famous designs include the NBC peacock and the Smithsonian Institution's circled sun, first supplied two dozen or so drawings. They resembled crude cutouts shaped like the celestial objects of the book's title. It was up to Vonnegut to write whatever accompanying words he wished.

Sun Moon Star begins with the epigraph "*Behold, / a virgin shall be with child, / and shall bring forth a son, / and they shall call his name Emanuel, / which being interpreted is, / God with us.*" It ends with "And life went on. Amen."

Various conclusions can be drawn from these diversions. To me the most likely one is that, both before he was well established and even a decade afterward, Vonnegut would step outside his belief system to make a buck if he had a suitable idea. He was trying to attract and keep a mainstream audience that, if not exclusively Christian, was at least familiar with Christianity.

That explains it, I suppose. But what if it doesn't?

You could play amateur psychologist and conclude that "The Very First Christmas Morning" and *Sun Moon Star* are signs that Vonnegut wanted to believe Jesus was God on Earth. Perhaps Vonnegut's unwillingness to criticize Christianity (which he admired "more than anything...as symbolized by gentle people sharing a common bowl") and his embrace of it in these two examples come from envy. Remember how he felt about his friend O'Hare losing his faith.

Christianity supplies a ready-made community, the kind of extended family Vonnegut valued so much. That could be reason enough for him to long for religious faith, if the juvenile stories are glimpses into his psyche rather than playful outliers.

A tantalizing comment appears in the Shields biography. Leaving Vonnegut's company for what turned out to be the last time, Shields asked Vonnegut whether he believed in God. The eighty-four-year-old Vonnegut's reply, according to the biographer: "I don't know, but who couldn't?"

That's enigmatic enough to leave you wondering. And there was no follow-up discussion, for only a few hours later Vonnegut fell while descending the steps outside his brownstone, striking his head and lapsing into unconsciousness from which he did not recover. Just under a month later, he was dead.

Chapter 10

The Eyes and Ears and Conscience of the Creator of the Universe

His prose was frightful. Only his ideas were good.

Narrator describing the books of Kilgore Trout, Slaughterhouse-Five

Kilgore Trout wrote 209 novels, the last one unfinished. He graduated from Thomas Jefferson High School in Dayton, Ohio. Both his father and his son were named Leo. He was born in Bermuda in 1907 and died in 1981. Two years before his death, he was awarded the Nobel Prize for Medicine. By the time of his passing, he was recognized for his scientific and artistic talent, and for popularizing the word *leak* to refer to a mirror. He wore a full black beard.

Or rather, Kilgore Trout shaved daily. He never graduated from high school, although he often quoted Shakespeare. He was born in 1916 and died in 2001. When he was twelve years old, his father, Raymond, killed Kilgore's mother. He had a son named Leon. He wrote perhaps 2,500 short stories, most of which he threw away before hitting the road, homeless for years. He served in Europe during World War II and was discharged from the US Army in 1945.

No, not the army. Kilgore Trout was a marine. And his publication totals were more like a hundred books and a thousand short stories.

Wait a minute. Wasn't "Kilgore Trout" merely a pen name for a prison lifer who had been convicted of treason?

And didn't he look just like the actor Albert Finney in his sixties? Actually, all of the above is true, if we believe Kurt Vonnegut's novels. (Well, except the last bit. Finney played Trout in the 1999 *Breakfast of Champions* movie. Vonnegut was not involved.)

At his best, Trout is a consistently moral voice who has a profound though not always positive effect on a few protagonists. Through him, Vonnegut probes responsibility, humankind's place in the universe, the worth and worthlessness of literature, free will, and other big topics that interest humanists.

At one point, Trout even provides an answer to the question "What is the purpose of life?"

Vonnegut's most famous character debuts in *God Bless You, Mr. Rosewater*. He returns in *Slaughterhouse-Five*, has a leading role in *Breakfast of Champions*, and appears, more or less, in three more Vonnegut novels after that. He stars in Vonnegut's ramshackle final novel, barely holding it together.

These appearances are accompanied by roughly forty Vonnegutian parables in the form of synopses of tales written by Trout. Impoverished and obscure, disheveled and cranky, Trout sometimes comes off as a grouchy lunatic, but the story summaries reveal his insights into the perilous yet salvageable existence of humans on Earth.

At times, his spoken words are refrains of conscience.

Trout changes at least slightly from one appearance to the next. This throws the careful reader, who customarily assigns importance to details like what a person looks like and the dates and circumstances of his birth and death. Those sorts of facts are mutable in the arc of the recurring character Kilgore Trout.

"Vonnegut's chief avatar of human transformation," critic Kathryn Hume called him. "Trout is a means for Vonnegut to deal with problems that affect him as artist, and those problems shift throughout his life...Trout is a metaphor, so his changes are not realistic and novelistic, but symbolic."

Trout isn't the only one. Other Vonnegut characters who seem quite similar—even those that share a name—are not the same.

Diana Moon Glampers is the Handicapper General of the United States who brings "Harrison Bergeron," perhaps Vonnegut's best-known short story, to a violent climax. She is not the illiterate, perpetually frightened Diana Moon Glampers who is Eliot's most frequent caller in *God Bless You, Mr. Rosewater*.

Bernie O'Hare is a middleweight boxer in Vonnegut's 1954 short story "A Present for Big Saint Nick." Bernard B. O'Hare is Howard W. Campbell Jr.'s wartime captor and would-be assassin in *Mother Night*.

Capt. Bernard O'Hare is a helicopter pilot in *Slapstick*. And, of course, Bernard V. O'Hare was Vonnegut's longtime real-life friend.

Vonnegut did not map out a stable universe in which all of his creations co-existed. He sounded unconcerned about such inconsistencies when an interviewer in 1974 asked whether there was "any conscious intent behind these changes."

> Well, no, only a perversity to not look in a former book. I don't look in a former book. And it's just a perversity that comes from having written so long, I guess. Just fuck it, it doesn't really matter what their names are.

Nor did it matter, apparently, whether Kilgore Trout was born in 1907 or 1916. So to study Trout is, possibly, to be frustrated by such untidiness. Once you get over that, you realize the contradictions don't matter.

From the beginning, though, Trout has definable characteristics with each appearance. He's similar to Vonnegut's comic heroes, Laurel and Hardy, who essentially played a version of their personas every time.

Vonnegut repeatedly runs his ideas through Trout. They are alike in many ways, down to the humanistic focus of their writing, Vonnegut acknowledged.

> "If I'd wasted my time creating characters," Trout said, "I would never have gotten around to calling attention to things that really matter: irresistible forces in nature, and cruel inventions, and cockamamie ideals and governments and economies that make heroes and heroines alike feel like something the cat drug in."
>
> Trout might have said, and it can be said of me as well, that he created caricatures rather than characters.

Beyond writing stories concerned with life's major questions, there are other similarities between the character and his creator: being an army scout in World War II, being hard to get to know, being born on November 11.

Oh, and living to age eighty-four.

Even so, over the years Trout is at least a little different each time—as was Vonnegut, as is anyone.

How to love people who have no use

The first two times Trout appears in Vonnegut's fiction, he is associated with bleeding-heart millionaire Eliot Rosewater, who at first is his only fan. Right away, Trout the ignored writer embodies a fate that Vonnegut feared for himself: Being regarded as a sci-fi hack who, despite writing stories and books he considers worthwhile, is unread, out of print, and destined to be forgotten.

That's not far from Vonnegut's fitful financial position for nearly two decades, until he took a teaching position at the University of Iowa in 1965 and signed a new three-book contract.

"Kilgore Trout is the lonesome and unappreciated writer I thought I might become," Vonnegut admitted.

First, there was the genre problem. Vonnegut wrote *Player Piano* to comment about General Electric in the present day, but in 1952 the book was marketed and reviewed, scantly, as futuristic. Reissued in paperback, it was consigned to drugstore spinner racks, its title changed to *Utopia 14*, its cover exclaiming MAN'S REVOLT AGAINST A GLITTERING, MECHANIZED TOMORROW.

In an essay published the same year as *God Bless You, Mr. Rosewater*, Vonnegut complains, "I have been a soreheaded occupant of a file drawer labeled 'science fiction' ever since, and I would like out, particularly since so many serious critics regularly mistake the drawer for a urinal."

Then there's the related matter of sales. Both *Player Piano* and its follow-up seven years later, *The Sirens of Titan*, released as a paperback original with another lurid cover, moved only a few thousand copies. Vonnegut's satirical science fiction with literary aspirations, it seemed, lacked the commercial appeal of cheap SF even when packaged that way.

Novel number three, *Mother Night*, decidedly *not* science fiction, was another paperback debut in 1961, and another poor seller. *Cat's Cradle*, an astonishingly original work now regarded as one of Vonnegut's best, did little better in 1963.

Two years after that, yet another of his books failed to even approach the best-seller list. *God Bless You, Mr. Rosewater* was the only Vonnegut novel in print at the time, and aside from a few favorable reviews—a positive development, at least—his reputation as a serious writer languished.

Even that modest level of accomplishment outdoes Trout's extreme anonymity in the publishing world. But for all he lacks in career success, Trout is a rousingly effective, passionate spokesperson for moral awareness.

His main choice of genre for promoting such awareness, in a perversely Vonnegutian twist, is the very realm his creator longed to escape. Eliot Rosewater, apparently the only devoted reader Trout has, knows why speculative fiction is a good venue for sweeping analysis of human activity. "I love you sons of bitches," he tells a convention of science fiction authors.

"You're all I read anymore. You're the only ones who'll talk about the really terrific changes going on...You're the only ones with guts enough to really care about the future, who really notice what machines do to us, what war does to us, what cities do to us, what big, simple ideas do to us, what tremendous misunderstandings, mistakes, accidents and catastrophes do to us. You're the only ones zany enough to agonize over time and distance without limit, over mysteries that will never die, over the fact that we are right now determining whether the space voyage for the next billion years or so is going to be Heaven or Hell."

Eliot's idol is not at the gathering. Trout is a destitute clerk in a stamp redemption center and can't afford the trip from Hyannis. In ten thousand years, Eliot tells the writers, "the only hero of our time still remembered will be the author of *2BR02B*." He is referring, of course, to Kilgore Trout.

The two do not meet until the novel's final scene. Emerging groggily from a yearlong blackout, Eliot is with his father and others who are plotting his defense against an insanity charge leveled by an opportunistic lawyer who works for a Rosewater cousin. The accusers see a chance to grab a large chunk of the family fortune. Eliot's giveaway of so many other chunks is going to be offered as proof of his mental instability.

Senator Rosewater has joined forces with a man whom he consulted in desperation. "You said Trout could explain the meaning of everything you'd done in Rosewater, even if you couldn't," he tells his son, "and calling him in is the smartest thing I ever did."

The senator does not truly grasp the ethical foundation beneath the writer's pronouncements, but he believes they will sound good at Eliot's hearing. He admires Trout as a clever public relations man, "a rascal who could rationalize anything, not understanding that Trout had never tried to tell anything but the truth."

That's the omniscient narrator characterizing Trout. That's Vonnegut telling us to pay attention to what Trout says.

And what Trout says would make a fine humanistic statement.

He first assures Eliot,

"What you did in Rosewater County was far from insane. It was quite possibly the most important social experiment of our time, for it dealt on a very small scale with a problem whose queasy horrors will eventually be made world-wide by the sophistication of machines. The problem is this: How to love people who have no use?"

Vonnegut asked that question throughout his career. He raises it in *Player Piano* through that novel's innocent abroad, the Shah of Bratpuhr. Referring to a supercomputer that supposedly can reply to any query, the Shah says to his American hosts, "Please, would you ask EPICAC what people are for?"

The question comes up again in one of the Trout story summaries in *God Bless You, Mr. Rosewater*. His novel *2BR02B,* it turns out, concerns Ethical Suicide Parlors where patriotic Americans go to die, since the eradication of disease has caused serious overpopulation. As a death stewardess straps in one of the characters, he asks her, "What in hell are people *for*?"

We don't know if that character receives an answer, but as we saw earlier Trout tells the senator that poverty must be wiped out because it leads to uselessness, which "will kill strong and weak souls alike."

His model for compassionate institutions that can provide such a cure is volunteer fire departments. Vonnegut himself belonged to one in Alplaus, New York. Trout says, "There we have people treasuring people as people. It's extremely rare. So from this we must learn."

Why Christians find it so easy to be cruel

In the next novel, *Slaughterhouse-Five,* Trout gains another fan, protagonist Billy Pilgrim, who is influenced by his roommate in a veterans' hospital: none other than Eliot Rosewater.

This Kilgore Trout is rougher than the one in *God Bless You, Mr. Rosewater*. His "unpopularity was deserved," we're told. "His prose was frightful. Only his ideas were good." He does not deliver speeches about how people ought to behave and how society ought to work. He's more likely to mock than to edify.

He is, after all, "a bitter man."

At a party for Billy's eighteenth wedding anniversary, Trout is a boisterous object of attention. He chats with Maggie White, a former dental assistant who doesn't read much. Trout declares that everything he publishes *has* to be true. If it isn't true, he says, "I could go to jail. That's *fraud*."

Maggie believes him. He then warns her that, if she isn't careful about what she says, God's judgment might cause her to burn for eternity.

> Poor Maggie turned gray. She believed that, too, and was petrified.
> Kilgore Trout laughed uproariously. A salmon egg flew out of his mouth and landed in Maggie's cleavage.

Trout provides more than comic jabs at gullibility, though, in *Slaughterhouse-Five*. Synopses of his plots continue Vonnegut's own tendencies, including affinity for an ordinary albeit uncommonly merciful Jesus.

One of Trout's books features a time traveler who watches twelve-year-old Jesus learning carpentry from his father and building "a cross to be used in the execution of a rabble-rouser." Nikos Kazantzakis had used that same occupational irony—minus the time traveler—in his 1953 novel, *The Last Temptation of Christ*. Director Martin Scorsese and screenwriter Paul Schrader later did the same in their 1988 film adaptation.

Speaking of which, another Trout summary from *Slaughterhouse-Five*, fleshed out into more than 350 words, might be the best alternate version of the crucifixion outside of Kazantzakis's book.

In Trout's *The Gospel from Outer Space*, an alien visitor to Earth rewrites the "slipshod storytelling in the New Testament" so that its moral is clearer. The problem with the existing text, the alien explains, is that readers know all along that Jesus is the Son of the Most Powerful Being in the Universe.

The implication is that lynching Jesus is wrong because he's so "well connected," and therefore lynching a troublemaker who is not well connected might be OK. In part, the alien concludes, that's "why Christians found it so easy to be cruel."

In the alien's revised Gospel, Jesus is a nobody who is adopted by God at the last moment and saved from crucifixion. "*From this moment on*," the parable concludes, God "*will punish horribly anybody who torments a bum who has no connections!*"

Now, there's a supreme being whose wrath is well placed for a change.

It's also a blasphemy that—along with passages containing coarse language uttered by soldiers in wartime and the revelations that pornography exists and people enjoy sex—often gets *Slaughterhouse-Five* in trouble with alarmed parents and education officials.

Even so, Vonnegut liked the idea of a very human, crucified Jesus enough to return to it years later. He told a gathering of Unitarians in 1980 that he was writing "a passion play...which leaves God out entirely, but which manages to be spiritual anyway."

That's right, we're still not finished with the Christ-worshiping agnostic.

In the last scene of his never-published passion play, Vonnegut said, Jesus is hanging on the cross and is approached by "a group of ordinary people" who wish to lend comfort but by law cannot touch him. They gather at the foot of the cross and "talk to him, sing to him, in the hopes that some of it will help a little. They say how sorry they are. They try to feel some of his pain—as though whatever they could feel of it he would not have to feel."

They talk, sing, and express sorrow for a while, then fall to their knees, exhausted. A wealthy Roman tourist happens upon the unusual scene. "My goodness!" he says. "The way you are worshiping him, you would think he was the Son of your God."

> A spokesperson for the kneelers, perhaps Mary Magdalene, says to him, "Oh no, sir. If he were the Son of our God, he would not need us. It is because he is a common human being exactly like us that we are here—doing, as common people must, what little we can."

Doesn't that illustrate our need to connect with one another as well as the New Testament illustrates its claims about our duty to worship the Creator of the Universe?

"The message, please"

The Creator and Trout are at it again in Vonnegut's next novel, *Breakfast of Champions*. Rather than contribute from a supporting role, Trout is one of two main characters destined to meet in a Holiday Inn cocktail lounge. The other is Dwayne Hoover, a Midland City, Ohio, auto dealer who becomes Trout's latest—and most dangerous—fan.

Though still "a nobody at the time [who] supposed his life was over," Trout is destined for big things. Due to events subsequent to his meeting with Hoover, Trout becomes "one of the most beloved and respected human beings in history."

As for the Creator, Trout has an idea about that. He sees this penciled on the men's room wall in an X-rated movie theater: "What is the purpose of life?"

His reply is not similarly inscribed on the restroom tile. Trout has nothing to write with. But the omniscient narrator—the "I" we are to assume is Kurt Vonnegut—tells us "what [Trout] would have written":

> To be
> the eyes
> and ears
> and conscience
> of the Creator of the Universe,
> you fool.

The novel includes more than a dozen synopses of Trout stories and books, everything from "a dialogue between two pieces of yeast" to the tragically misunderstood communication efforts of a creature from "a planet where the natives conversed by means of farts and tap dancing."

And, yes, there are Vonnegut's crude drawings of an asshole, a bucket of fried chicken, a beaver (both kinds), a pair of underpants, and so on.

Despite all the silliness in *Breakfast of Champions*, it presents plenty to think about. How much more are we than the sum of our physical bodies, with chemicals in control of so much? How much are bad ideas to blame for our misery, and where do those ideas come from?

As in many Vonnegut novels, we're left to wonder to what extent people are responsible for their actions.

Dwayne surely is affected by bad chemicals and by a very bad idea to which Kilgore Trout inadvertently exposes him. Dwayne's mind is already bedeviled by hallucinations and paranoia when he meets Trout in the cocktail lounge. "Give me the message," he demands. "The message, please."

Dwayne is losing his grip on reality, but his search for meaning, Vonnegut is telling us, is much like that of all Americans, who are fed faulty information, are victims of natural human failings, and are "doing their best to live like people invented in story books."

Perhaps because he has been thrown off guard, Trout fails to instruct Dwayne to be the eyes and ears and conscience of the Creator of the Universe. Dwayne grabs a copy of Trout's *And Now It Can Be Told* and instead receives a destructive variant of that message. "You are an experiment by the Creator of the Universe," begins Trout's novel.

> You are the only creature in the entire Universe who has free will. You are the only one who has to figure out what to do next—and why. Everybody else is a robot, a machine.

Dwayne administers several beatings. He pummels his son, punches two women, assaults eight other people. He bites off the tip of Trout's ring finger. He acts without conscience because of a singularly bad idea: That he and no one else can feel anything.

We don't experience the entire arc of Trout's public redemption after that but are told that it results from Dwayne's meltdown.

Eventually, Trout is acclaimed for his wisdom. The narrator, in the future of the 1980s or later, reveals that Trout "became a pioneer in the field of mental health [who] advanced his theories disguised as science-fiction." Trout won the Nobel Prize for Medicine in 1979 and by the time of his death two years later was "recognized as a great artist and scientist."

A sentence from Trout's unfinished 209th novel is inscribed on a monument placed atop his ashes: "We are healthy only to the extent that our ideas are humane."

That other message of Trout's—the one no one ever saw because he had nothing to write with, the one that implores human beings to be "the eyes and ears and conscience of the Creator of the Universe"—echoes what we heard Vonnegut entreat of the Bennington College graduates three years before *Breakfast of Champions* was published.

Remember? He urged them to believe and make others believe "that humanity is at the center of the universe, the fulfiller or the frustrator of the grandest dreams of God Almighty."

This, like Christ-worshiping agnosticism, is at the heart of Vonnegut's humanism.

For him, as for his most famous character, a loving supreme being was an aspiration rather than a given. Trout's "eyes and ears and conscience" and Vonnegut's fulfiller/frustrator have much in common. Those lines do not so much assert the existence of a Creator of the Universe as define what that Creator ought to be and declare what human beings have to do with it.

In the philosophy of both Kilgore Trout and Kurt Vonnegut, you fulfill the dreams of the Creator by acting with moral awareness. You frustrate those dreams by failing to do so.

He's back, more or less

Vonnegut bids farewell to Trout in *Breakfast of Champions*. "I am going to set at liberty all the literary characters who have served me so loyally during my writing career," the "I" who has been telling us the story says at the end. He informs Trout that he created him and is releasing him. (Trout, it turns out, suspected all along that he was a character in a book.)

"Arise, Mr. Trout, you are free, you are *free*," the narrator—Kurt Vonnegut, we presume—tells him.

Trout has the face and the skinny, varicose-veined legs of the narrator's father as an old man. He also has the father's voice. He cries out, "*Make me young, make me young, make me young!*"

Vonnegut apparently never does make Trout young, and Trout in fact is missing from Vonnegut's next novel, *Slapstick*, but he returns—sort of—in *Jailbird*, published six years after his emancipation.

The *Jailbird* version of Trout is vexing for readers who expect fictional personages to be portrayed with at least *some* consistency across multiple appearances. There might be a way around that problem.

But first: In *Jailbird*'s prologue, where Vonnegut seems to comment as himself, he immediately informs us that "Kilgore Trout is back again. He could not make it on the outside." Trout again is a character in a book, controlled by Vonnegut but this time never meeting his creator and possibly never really appearing in the book at hand.

The thing is, the Kilgore Trout in *Jailbird* is a pen name employed by another science fiction writer, one Dr. Robert Fender. This man, "the only American to have been convicted of treason during the Korean War," is serving a life term for his crime. He is in the federal prison where the novel's narrator, Watergate flunky Walter F. Starbuck, is incarcerated for a while.

This prisoner Fender—this Trout—plays Edith Piaf records all day in the supply room where he works. He has a doctorate in veterinary science. He is "tall and big-boned," a farmer who looks like Charles Lindbergh. Bob Fender does not at all resemble any previous or subsequent physical description of Kilgore Trout.

Fender is imprisoned because, when he was an army first lieutenant, he fell for a Piaf impersonator who turned out to be a North Korean spy. He is nice enough and keeps busy in prison.

But he is not the man who comments wisely about science fiction writers and Eliot Rosewater, who writes compassionate parables about a mortal Jesus, who has a worthwhile response to questions about the meaning of life.

So Fender lacks the qualities that, more than being an unknown genre storyteller, define the relevant, humanistic Kilgore Trout.

Fender does write Troutlike stories such as "Asleep at the Switch," in which auditors outside the Pearly Gates assert life's inherent fairness by reminding even heaven's most wretched entrants about business opportunities that they, through no fault of the Almighty, failed to recognize.

Vonnegut believed that luck plays a bigger role in a person's fortunes than many are willing to admit. (Eugene Debs Hartke in *Hocus Pocus*: "The 2 prime movers in the Universe are Time and Luck.") "Asleep at the Switch" shines a light on that idea by negating it.

Another, untitled Fender tale—under the pen name Francis X. Barlow but certainly in the style of Trout—is about a ghostly visitor from the planet Vicuna who, without realizing it would be permanent, inhabits the body of a man he believes to be a happy philosopher. Actually, the man is a white-collar criminal trying to clear his mind by reciting in his head a song that begins,

> Sally in the garden,
> Sifting cinders,
> Lifted up her leg
> And farted like a man...

The Eyes and Ears and Conscience

The ending is silly, but there's a lesson. Inhabitants of Vicuna are wondrous beings who can leave their bodies and become "silent awarenesses and sensibilities," pure music, something like the creatures called harmoniums in *The Sirens of Titan*. But their scientists find a way to capture time as a resource, which Vicunans waste. They have to flee the planet, leading the alien to Earth and the song and his unfortunate fate.

It's a message worthy of Trout, or Vonnegut. But there the similarities end.

A telling difference not mentioned so far: Fender presents modest gifts to fellow prisoners upon their release, such as getting the large hole in Starbuck's suit pants mended, using "all the money he made from his science-fiction tales." The Trout we know earned doodley squat, as Vonnegut would put it, from his writing.

You could deplore this and the other significant departures from the Trout canon, such as it is, as unforgiveable breaks with continuity. Or you could accept them the way you accept yet another actor playing James Bond, or Laurel and Hardy playing another pair of characters. Or you could view *Jailbird* as an alternate universe.

Someone who is unwilling to do any of that could ignore the fine literary analysis about Trout as metaphor that was quoted earlier and reach a different conclusion—that Fender was using the name of an existing author. The fly-by-night publishers and smut mag owners who peddle Trout's stories would not notice or care. Trout himself might not ever find out.

Fender's appropriation then could be an unauthorized act spoofing what the real science fiction writer Philip José Farmer had done. With Vonnegut's reluctant and later regretted permission, Farmer in 1974 published *Venus on the Half-Shell* under the name Kilgore Trout.

The Magazine of Fantasy and Science Fiction presented the novel in two parts. Dell Publishing went along with the ruse in 1975 and had a paperback hit.

If Vonnegut character Fender has lifted Vonnegut character Trout's name and writing style, then Trout's disjointed personal history from earlier novels is preserved by *Jailbird*, not thrown into irredeemable chaos as it otherwise seems to be. Whichever way you look at it, the Kilgore Trout in *Jailbird* is more like a concept than a figure who'd been developed by his creator over a few iterations.

That figure has a message steeped in humanism. He has ideas and advice that might prove useful to people living on Earth. Fender does not. He's a minor diversion.

A Trout-related tease even less essential than Fender's pseudonym turns up in Vonnegut's *Hocus Pocus*, published in 1990. It's worth mentioning for the sake of completeness.

Trout's name is nowhere to be found in *Hocus Pocus*, but another summary of what might well be a Trout story is in there. Across two chapters, Eugene Debs Hartke (yet another jailed memoirist) describes a tale he has read, "The Protocols of the Elders of Tralfamadore." It's about the titular "intelligent threads of energy trillions of light-years long" who direct activities on Earth by taking advantage of human vanity and foolishness.

To promote the spread of microscopic life throughout the universe, these beings caused the woman (yes, woman) who first wrote down the story of Adam and Eve to finish it by having God command humans to exert dominion over everything on the planet.

That way, germs would have a harder time conquering Earth, but through their struggles they eventually would grow strong enough to claim the planet for their own. Then they'd catch a ride on the next meteor that collides with Earth, and off they would go, spreading themselves far beyond the Milky Way.

It's convoluted, but the point is that the Elders' plan depends upon Earthlings believing in manifest destiny for all of humankind—that is, for their *own* kind of human.

"It appeared to the Elders," the synopsis goes, "that the people here would believe anything about themselves, no matter how preposterous, as long as it was flattering."

"I wish I knew his name," Hartke says of the story's author. Such coyness from Vonnegut. But he provides a clue: The short fiction is printed in a skin mag.

> The story was very likely pirated from some other publication, so the omission of the author's name may have been intentional. What sort of writer, after all, would submit a work of fiction for possible publication in Black Garterbelt?

Nature's experiment with cynicism

The Kilgore Trout to whom we had become accustomed, the essentially unknown science fiction writer who was in three consecutive novels that culminated with *Breakfast of Champions,* appeared twice after that book.

First is a small role in *Galápagos.* Six years after his cameo in *Jailbird* as the familiar name but not the familiar persona, he shows up as more or less a version of himself, trying to persuade his son, named Leon rather than Leo this time, to join him in the afterlife.

Yes, Kilgore Trout is dead. He would have to be, since the novel covers a million years of human evolution.

The Eyes and Ears and Conscience

In *Galápagos* Vonnegut anticipates by five years the supposition within the anonymous *Hocus Pocus* story that microorganisms have the inside track on world domination. The novel's narrator—none other than the ghost of Leon Trotsky Trout, you'll recall—comments upon the opportunity for other forms of life to establish primacy as humanity slides toward extinction: "Truth be told, the planet's most victorious organisms have always been microscopic."

Kilgore Trout's writing thrives on that kind of concept as well as its flip side, that larger animals with bigger brains thwart their own assumed superiority.

Galápagos presents this position not in a story written by Trout but in a Troutlike tale told by the ineffectual Captain von Kleist. The captain invents a fable to amuse a furry young progenitor of human beings' next stage of development: In a million years, Maine lobsters have evolved and taken charge of Earth, but they become entangled in the complications of civilization and long for a simpler time when all they had to worry about was being boiled alive.

"The moral of the story," Leon Trout explains, "was that the lobsters were doing exactly what human beings had done, which was to make a mess of everything."

That could have been written by Kilgore Trout.

We do get two actual, albeit brief, Trout plot summaries in *Galápagos*. One concerns a novel that chronicles the fate of humanoids who have ruined their planet's ecosystem and imperiled their chances of survival. Their deformed offspring are "Nature's experiments with creatures which might, as a matter of luck, be better planetary citizens than the humanoids."

Leon does not reveal how that turns out, but the novel's title, Leon feels, sums up the late twentieth century: *The Era of Hopeful Monsters*.

An unnamed Trout story is about an inventor who makes sports-playing robots that execute their tasks perfectly. Nobody thinks the robots serve any useful purpose until the inventor announces they're available for ad endorsements.

"He made a fortune, according to my father, because so many sports enthusiasts wanted to be exactly like those robots," Leon says about Kilgore's story. "Don't ask me why."

Besides being a dig at idol-worshiping Americans who are content to be a nation of consumers, the robot tale provides Leon/Vonnegut a chance to lament how readily people of our time enable "the craze…for having machines do everything that human beings did—and I mean *everything*."

In our era—that is, in 1986, when a series of unplanned events initiate human evolution of the next million years—Leon meets his father in the blue tunnel. Kilgore wants his son to enter the tunnel, but Leon, already a ghost, asks for five more years to complete his research and satisfy his curiosity "about what life is really like, how it really works, what it's really all about."

"The more you learn about people," the misanthropic Kilgore tells him, "the more disgusted you'll become."

He mocks his son for believing, like his late mother, "that human beings are good animals, who will eventually solve all their problems and make earth into a Garden of Eden again."

He reviews humanity's sins for Leon: warring endlessly, creating weapons that can wipe out everything, wrecking the planet. He warns his son that, unless he abandons his futile study of people and heads to the afterlife immediately, the blue tunnel will be closed to Leon for a million years. Which is what happens.

The Kilgore Trout in *Galápagos* is not the character who comes up with moralizing aphorisms, who punctuates a soliloquy about unconditional love by uttering "Joy," who has important things to say about awareness, who links health with humane behavior.

He is instead what Leon calls "Nature's experiment with cynicism," lacking the humorous antics, crusty wisdom, and even occasional optimism of a few of his other appearances. He is the bitter, mocking professional failure in *Slaughterhouse-Five* whose good ideas are in his books, not in his spoken words.

Kilgore's encounter with Leon makes us think about pessimism versus optimism again. You can't deny that both father and son have a point. Which way the scale tips in your estimation, and how far, helps determine how much value you place in humanism.

If the Kilgore Trout of *Galápagos* is a detour where *Jailbird*'s is a dead end, his final appearance in a Vonnegut novel is a valedictory performance in which, once more, he might be the only person on the planet who knows what's really going on.

Kilgore's Creed

The last time Vonnegut depicts Kilgore Trout with any depth, he presents a more well-formed character. Trout in *Timequake* spins written parables like the Trout of old. This time, however, he is the toast of the literary set, drawing laughter in a gathering of people who are in Vonnegut's real-life circle.

What's more, Trout acts decisively (eventually) once he figures out that humans have regained some semblance of autonomy after enduring ten years on repeat because of a cosmic anomaly.

"Wake up! Wake up!" he tells Dudley Prince. "You've got free will again, and there's work to do!"

Prince, a security guard, had been sentenced to two life terms for murders he did not commit and later was freed by DNA evidence. But then he was zapped back into years of incarceration because of a space-time hiccup that caused everyone on the planet to relive the past decade, aware but unable to change a moment. Now the timequake has abruptly ended, and people need to be roused from their stupor.

Trout does his best, turning an enclave for the homeless into a shelter for people injured in the restart, firing a bazooka at unoccupied vehicles to silence their cacophonous alarms, rousing Prince and others to the new reality.

To be sure, at first Trout was not being selfless.

> The old science fiction writer wanted to galvanize the armed and uniformed Dudley Prince into action, he later confessed, so that he himself wouldn't have to do anything. "Free will! Free will! Fire! Fire!" he shouted at Prince.

Free will? Trout remembers that he doesn't believe in it, so he amends his message:

"You were sick, but now you're well, and there's work to do."

Vonnegut has addressed free will before. The visitors from Tralfamadore find the concept comical, and therefore so does Billy Pilgrim. Their perception of time, with everything happening simultaneously, leads to extreme determinism: No one can do anything about anything.

Harrison Bergeron and the ballerina practice free will and pay with their lives.

Dwayne Hoover's rampage is so destructive because, compelled by chemicals and his misguided reading of a Trout novel, he is convinced he's the only living human who possesses free will.

It's a fraught topic. Often the term is used vaguely, and discussions about whether free will exists can be unsatisfying. Philosophical conclusions abound, but they can be unhelpful if you're trying to figure out what we're supposed to *do*.

Humanists disagree about whether there is such a thing as free will. To me, the more productive discourse is not about *whether* but about *how much*. Choices, to the extent that we can act on them, define my idea of free will. Some people have more choices available to them than others have. The more choices, the more control. The more control, the better the chance of achieving a desired outcome.

There are no guarantees no matter how many choices are available, but I have to believe that people—some more than others, to be sure—can act wilfully, if not free will-fully.

If everything we do, every choice we make, is inevitable due to upbringing, genetics, fundamental human behavioral traits, and every other unchangeable prior condition and occurrence that make us unique—a position that denies free will—then wilful action is impossible, the very idea of choice a mirage.

That's where I think the conversation becomes unproductive.

Even so, I agree with Malachi Contant, who in *The Sirens of Titan* says he "was a victim of a series of accidents...as are we all.," and with *Hocus Pocus* narrator Eugene Debs Hartke, who as mentioned a few pages ago says that "the 2 prime movers in the Universe are Time and Luck."

Those are reasonable conclusions about the big picture, but they're not codes to live by here on our little planet. Whatever they believe, humanists contend that moral action is necessary.

Kilgore Trout, who does not believe in free will, concurs. There's his flurry of activity as soon as the timequake is over. Later, his reaction to a play at which he is a stagehand points away from philosophical musings and toward the sentiment that Vonnegut hopes will compel us toward good behavior.

The play is a real one: Robert E. Sherwood's *Abe Lincoln in Illinois*. Trout's lone role behind the scenes is to blow an old steam whistle as the play ends, to simulate the noise a departing train makes. Lincoln is on that train, bound for his inauguration in Washington, DC, in February 1861.

Lincoln has just given a moving speech about his future, and the nation's, when civil war seems imminent. He calls the United States "the fulfillment of an ancient dream, which men have held through all time, that they might one day shake off their chains and find freedom in the brotherhood of life. We gained democracy, and now there is the question of whether it is fit to survive."

Acknowledging that the phrase "And this too shall pass away" may well provide comfort in such troubled times, Lincoln declares that it isn't enough.

> "And yet—let us believe that it is not true! Let us live to prove that we can cultivate the natural world that is about us, and the intellectual and moral world that is within us, so that we may secure an individual, social and political prosperity, whose course shall be forward, and which, while the earth endures, shall not pass away."

Sherwood used multiple sources to craft a longer speech than Lincoln's original. His Lincoln lays out a path of action by which the vision of a "moral world" can be made real, a path that humanists would find appealing.

Vonnegut regarded Lincoln as "the greatest President this country will ever have." He reveals in *Timequake* that Lincoln's assassination "was a major event" in an earlier, discarded version of the novel, which he struggled mightily to complete. He laments that Americans' grasp of history is being loosened by television and its fixation on the very recent past:

"Who is there left under the age of sixty, and not in a History Department, to give a damn?"

Lincoln's speech in the Sherwood play certainly affects Vonnegut's old science fiction writer, who blows the mournful whistle on cue to close the production.

> As the curtain descended, there was a sob backstage. It wasn't in the playbook. It was ad lib. It was about beauty. It came from Kilgore Trout.

Dudley Prince spreads Trout's message, shorn of reference to free will, and it becomes a mantra. It becomes Kilgore's Creed. Again: "You were sick, but now you're well, and there's work to do."

In *Galápagos*, Trout's urgency is expressed as a plea for his son to join him in the afterlife. In *Timequake* it's a plea to rejoin everyone else here and now, a rallying cry imbued with positivity.

They are the first hopeful words we've heard from Trout in nearly a quarter century. They're uttered by a man who still declares, even this late, that "being alive is a crock of shit." When readers think of Trout as a crusty but compassionate prophet, it's this depiction they're considering, along with those in *God Bless You, Mr. Rosewater* and *Breakfast of Champions*.

Vonnegut makes use of Trout a couple more times after *Timequake*, more as a mouthpiece for Vonnegut's dismay about the course of world events than an expansion of the character.

A supposed interview in one of Vonnegut's WNYC radio spots gives Trout the chance to say, "All that good people can do about the disease of ethnic cleansing, now always a fait accompli, is to rescue the survivors. And watch out for Christians!"

Finally, in *A Man Without a Country*, Vonnegut writes of a phone call he got from Trout. Vonnegut does almost all the talking, telling Trout that "the planet is trying to get rid of us, but I think it's too late."

So *Timequake* is the last word on Trout as the eyes and ears and conscience of the Creator of the Universe. In spite of his disdain for life as "a crock of shit," his philosophy in that final novel amounts to what critic Wilson Taylor calls "transcendent humanism."

Kilgore's Creed, Vonnegut suggests, could inaugurate a new human history of justice and prosperity (which Vonnegut mourns as forgotten political ideals). Vonnegut's invitation to heal the self, the community, and the planet underscores the moral obligation to do so. Reformulating the nightmare of history as a disease, from which humanity can recover, presents a messianic arc of history through the awakening of a sublime humanism. Humanity must realize itself as a healer and redeemer in order to inaugurate a sacred counter-history, a new history that has yet to be realized or written. And a writer of fiction shall lead them.

In *Timequake,* one writer of fiction meets another. That is, Kurt Vonnegut meets Kilgore Trout on a beach where Vonnegut and several of his friends and associates have gathered for an *Abe Lincoln in Illinois* cast party.

Creator meets creation again, as in *Breakfast of Champions*. This time, Trout is ready. In a sweet gesture, Vonnegut makes him the hit of the clambake: "There on the beach, whatever Trout said produced laughter and applause...People told him he was as witty as Oscar Wilde!" Trout takes control. He asks Vonnegut to pick out two twinkling stars in the night sky, and to "look precisely at one, and then precisely at the other."

The expanding universe has rendered the speed of light and the distance it travels meaningless, Trout contends. Another, much faster force passed between the stars as Vonnegut looked at them.

> "Your awareness," [Trout] said. "That is a new quality in the Universe, which exists only because there are human beings. Physicists must from now on, when pondering the secrets of the Cosmos, factor in not only energy and matter and time, but something very new and beautiful, which is human awareness...I have thought of a better word than awareness," he said. "Let us call it soul."

Chapter 11

Becoming

"I now believe that the only way in which Americans can rise above their ordinariness, can mature sufficiently to rescue themselves and to help rescue their planet, is through enthusiastic intimacy with works of their own imaginations."

Kurt Vonnegut, Wampeters, Foma & Granfalloons

Art is singled out in the *Humanist* magazine's description of humanism, which it calls "a rational philosophy informed by science, inspired by art, and motivated by compassion."

A distinction is implied: Inspiration need not come from a sacred text, a prophet, a revelation, a televangelist's daydream, a visit by extraterrestrials, or whatever. In the worldview called humanism, works of the imagination fill an essential role.

Kurt Vonnegut considered art an essential part of life, with an important function. He said that "a plausible mission of artists [is to] make people appreciate being alive at least a little bit."

Not that he felt professionals like him were the only ones capable of eliciting such appreciation. People could do it themselves. "The arts are not a way to make a living," he wrote decades after establishing a career in the arts. "They are a very human way of making life more bearable."

Creativity ran through Vonnegut's family, even though, at the turn of the twentieth century, the Vonneguts' hometown of Indianapolis was, he believed, a place "where the practice of the arts was regarded as an evasion of real life by means of parlor tricks."

Family legend claimed that Vonnegut's paternal grandfather, Bernard, while a boy working in the Vonnegut hardware store, broke down in tears one day. Vonnegut wrote, "He was asked what the trouble was, and he said that he didn't want to work in a store. He said he wanted to be an artist instead."

While Bernard Vonnegut never realized his wish to be a theatrical designer, he did become an architect in New York City before moving back to Indianapolis. And he painted.

Vonnegut's father was an excellent architect who took up painting as a hobby. Vonnegut's mother wrote well and submitted fiction to the same markets in which her youngest son later found success—however, none of her stories sold, for she was highly cultivated and "had no talent for the vulgarity the slick magazines required."

His sister, Alice, he wrote, "possessed considerable gifts as a painter and sculptor, with which she did next to nothing." Even his brother, the accomplished scientist Bernard, although he couldn't "draw for sour apples," as Vonnegut put it, late in his life experimented with creating interesting shapes by flattening blobs of paint between sheets of hard material.

"I am from a family of artists," he wrote.

> Here I am, making a living in the arts. It has not been a rebellion. It's as though I had taken over the family Esso station. My ancestors were all in the arts, so I'm simply making my living in the customary family way.

Vonnegut's first born, Mark, has written three books and publicly exhibited his watercolors. Mark's sisters, Edith and Nanette, are artists who have written text for books about their father's love letters and drawings, respectively. Steve Adams, one of the nephews he helped raise, has written movie and TV scripts and a book.

Vonnegut's adopted daughter, Lily, is an actor.

Besides writing and drawing to various degrees of acclaim, Vonnegut was an occasional sculptor—or at least a designer of sculpture. A joking remark at a neighborhood party led to a commission to build a long granite-and-metal piece for a cocktail lounge near Boston's Logan Airport in the late 1950s. Later, aluminum models based on some of his doodles were produced.

Also, he used to play the clarinet.

In his later years, Vonnegut was invigorated when hundreds of his drawings were converted into silkscreen prints by Kentucky artist Joe Petro III. The effect on Vonnegut was profound.

One of the best things that ever happened to me, a one-in-a-billion opportunity to enjoy myself in perfect innocence, was my meeting Joe...It seems quite possible in retrospect that Joe Petro III saved my life. I will not explain. I will let it go at that.

"God bless Rabo Karabekian!"

Other than the hack writer and morality messenger Kilgore Trout and the playwright/memoirist Howard W. Campbell Jr., Vonnegut's most significant fictional creator is the Abstract Expressionist painter named Rabo Karabekian.

He's in two of Vonnegut's novels. There's *Bluebeard*, the 1987 "hoax autobiography," as Vonnegut put it, narrated by Karabekian. Before that there was *Breakfast of Champions*, which in 1973 introduced the one-eyed Armenian as a supporting character with a prominent scene.

In the older novel, he delivers a stirring defense of modern nonrepresentational art—that is, of his own painting called *The Temptation of St. Anthony*, purchased by the Midland City, Ohio, arts committee for $50,000. Karabekian's work consists of a field of green wall paint and a single, vertical strip of "day-glo orange reflecting tape" on a huge canvas.

The community resents Karabekian and his painting. Then, in a Midland City cocktail lounge, he makes a wisecrack about the town's Olympic Gold Medal-winning swimmer. A young waitress fires back, voicing an opinion everyone shares: She has "seen better pictures done by a five-year-old."

Karabekian replies calmly but passionately.

"Listen...I have read the editorials against my painting in your wonderful newspaper. I have read every word of the hate mail you have been thoughtful enough to send to New York...

"The painting did not exist until I made it...Now that it does exist, nothing would make me happier than to have it reproduced again and again, and vastly improved upon, by all the five-year-olds in town. I would love for your children to find pleasantly and playfully what it took me many angry years to find.

"I now give you my word of honor...that the picture your city owns shows everything about life which truly matters, with nothing left out. It is a picture of the awareness of every animal. It is the immaterial core of every animal—the 'I am' to which all messages are sent. It is all that is alive in any of us—in a mouse, in a deer, in a cocktail waitress. It is unwavering and pure, no matter what preposterous adventure may befall us. A sacred picture of Saint Anthony alone is one vertical, unwavering band of light.

If a cockroach were near him, or a cocktail waitress, the picture would show two such bands of light. Our awareness is all that is alive and maybe sacred in any of us. Everything else about us is dead machinery....

"Citizens of Midland City, I salute you...You have given home to a masterpiece!"

You could say Karabekian sounds defensive and conceited and is full of baloney, claiming his work "shows everything about life which truly matters," calling it "a masterpiece." No one challenges whether his simple two-color pattern effectively communicates what he learned in his "many angry years" of effort. Perhaps no one in the cocktail lounge is capable of such a challenge.

But Karabekian's oration occurs during what the narrator/Vonnegut says is "the spiritual climax of this book." Within it is a declaration that *all* life possesses an "immaterial core."

"Our awareness," Karabekian says, "is all that is alive and maybe sacred in any of us."

Vonnegut, or a version of himself, sits in the lounge, observes the artist's oration, and unlike anyone else there is deeply affected. He compares the moment to an earthquake during which "spiritual continents began to shrug and heave."

The unnamed narrator reveals that, before hearing Karabekian's manifesto, he "had come to the conclusion that there was nothing sacred about myself or about any human being, that we were all machines, doomed to collide and collide and collide."

The speech in the lounge changes that.

"It is Rabo Karabekian who made me the serene Earthling which I am this day," the narrator says. "At the core of each person who reads this book is an unwavering band of light...God bless Rabo Karabekian!"

The Vonnegut character in the lounge, with his creation Kilgore Trout looking on, scrawls "$E=Mc^2$" on a tabletop even though he knows it's "a flawed equation...There should have been an 'A' in there somewhere for *Awareness*—without which the 'E' and the 'M' and 'c,' which was a mathematical constant, could not exist."

This concept of awareness as an illuminated band sounds like a pretty good, humanistic description of what some people call a soul. Trout called it exactly that in *Timequake*.

Fourteen years after the cocktail lounge scene in *Breakfast of Champions*, Karabekian has a whole book in which to explain his art. In *Bluebeard*, he expands upon his depiction of the soul as light, his view of people as "low-intensity neon tubes."

> I couldn't help seeing stories in my own compositions of strips of colored tape applied to vast, featureless fields of Sateen Dura-Luxe...Each strip of tape was the soul at the core of some sort of person or lower animal...If I watch two people talking on a street corner, I see not only their flesh and clothes, but narrow, vertical bands of color inside them.

In the lounge, narrator Vonnegut had admitted that he thought of human beings as machines until Karabekian persuaded him otherwise. Narrating his own story, Karabekian struggles to reconcile his lack of control over the tangible and intangible factors regulating his behavior.

He believes each human being is split between a sentient soul—to him, a flexible neon tube, a band of color—and an animated body, which he calls meat.

"My soul knows my meat is doing bad things, and is embarrassed," Karabekian confides to a fellow artist. "But my meat just keeps on doing bad, dumb things...All the tube could do was receive news about what was happening with the meat, over which it had no control."

Which raises the possibility that, even if we have souls, we lack free will. Vonnegut suggests that awareness, while essential, needs the meat—the machine, the body—to create.

Karabekian longs to make something that is informed by his awareness and that is brought into the world by his physical apparatus. He yearns to craft his personal statement, once he figures out what that is.

He is trying to use his talent to create meaningful art again, having long ago lost his status as a painter who had something worthwhile to say. His earlier attempts are objects of ridicule. They were composed of cheap paint that dried up and flaked off, leaving behind only blank canvases.

Much of *Bluebeard* concerns what artists and their work mean to society. The young Karabekian's mentor, Dan Gregory, who had gained popularity by painting ultrarealistic scenes frozen in time, sees artists as tastemaking arbiters. He challenges his protégé to decide, between a rifle and a human body, which represents good and which stands for evil.

> "And who renders the final decision on that?" he said.
> "God?" I said.
> "I mean here on Earth," he said.
> "I don't know," I said.
> "Painters—and storytellers, including poets and playwrights and historians," he said. "They are the justices of the Supreme Court of Good and Evil, of which I am now a member, and to which you may belong someday!"

How was that for delusions of moral grandeur?

Yes, and now that I think about it: maybe the most admirable thing about the Abstract Expressionist painters, since so much senseless bloodshed had been caused by cockeyed history lessons, was their refusal to serve on such a court.

Karabekian eventually joins the Abstract Expressionists. He acknowledges to a fortysomething widow who has become his muse that the incredibly detailed paintings of his earlier career, like those that made Gregory famous, lacked soul. They were the sort of art the then-new movement rebelled against.

He tells the widow, named Circe, "The whole magical thing about our painting [was that] it was pure *essence of human wonder.*"

But the masterwork locked up in a potato barn behind his house possesses its own pure essence in abundance. (A spoiler follows, so skip to the next section if you don't want to know any more about the painting in the barn.)

It's a far cry from an all-green canvas with orange tape stuck to it. It's a gigantic post-battle tableau across sixty-four feet of panels filled with precisely detailed human figures. World War II veteran Karabekian has depicted thousands of bands of light who gathered in a valley, bewildered, as the war in Europe concluded. For each figure, he's prepared to tell a story.

Along the bottom, the largest figure is the artist himself, his back to the viewer. "The crack between the fourth and fifth panels ran up my spine and parted my hair, and might be taken for the soul of Rabo Karabekian."

The fictional painting, according to real-life critic David Andrews, is a "humanistic masterpiece." (Karabekian, by the way, calls it *Now It's the Women's Turn.*)

In his moment of triumph, Karabekian unexpectedly gives credit not to his band of light but to his machinery.

"My soul didn't know what kind of picture to paint," he tells Circe, "but my meat sure did." Upon her prompting, he holds his hands up to his face and says, "Thank you, Meat."

His machinery has figured out how to portray in two dimensions what his vertical, unwavering band of light knows but cannot articulate.

To paraphrase Leonardo da Vinci, it's the spirit working with the hand.

Vonnegut labored for more than two decades to properly convey impressions about his own wartime recollections—including the very post-battle scene in Karabekian's painting—until meat and soul meshed at last and his masterwork, *Slaughterhouse-Five*, emerged.

Bridging the soul and the meat is the uncontrollable unconscious, a mysterious source of inspiration. In a 1982 essay about Jackson Pollock, the most famous Abstract Expressionist, Vonnegut elaborated on the concept of the unconscious. He called it "a part of the mind without ambition or information, which nonetheless is expert on what is beautiful."

Karabekian cannot explain how he created the painting in his barn. His soul alone—his awareness—was not enough.

His meat had to learn how to express his sense of wonder.

A way to make your soul grow

A note by Vonnegut prefacing *Bluebeard* provides a good idea of what he thought about art, or at least some of the attempts to place value on it. "Much of what I put into this book was inspired by the grotesque prices paid for works of art during the past century," he writes.

> Tremendous concentrations of paper wealth have made it possible for a few persons or institutions to endow certain sorts of human playfulness with inappropriate and hence distressing seriousness. I think not only of the mudpies of art, but of children's games as well—running, jumping, catching, throwing.
> Or dancing.
> Or singing songs.

Or telling stories, you could add.

At the time *Bluebeard* was published, the largest sum paid for a painting was the nearly $40 million exchanged for van Gogh's *Still Life: Vase with Fifteen Sunflowers*. That was more than three times the previous record-high transaction. A few weeks after *Bluebeard* came off the presses, somebody paid about $54 million for van Gogh's *Irises*.

Nowadays, a buyer who wants to set a record needs close to half a billion dollars.

The "tremendous concentrations of paper wealth," of course, are held by society's most powerful citizens. Vonnegut accused the elite of "endow[ing] certain sorts of human playfulness" with "distressing seriousness" not only as a way to show off their wealth but also as a means of staying at the top.

"They have to pretend to appreciate the arts in order to demonstrate their natural superiority," he told an audience of college graduates in 1972, "since they can scarcely demonstrate it in any other way."

To Vonnegut, the real value of art lay not in its commercial worth or its usefulness in corraling common folks. He marveled instead at its ability, as stated in the *Humanist*'s very description of humanism, to inspire. He urged young people, in particular, to make art—any kind of art—for their own good even without an audience.

> Practicing an art, no matter how well or badly, is a way to make your soul grow, for heaven's sake...Do it as well as you possibly can. You will get an enormous reward. You will have created something.

Just five months before he died, Vonnegut gave that very advice to a handful of high school students who had written to him, urging them to engage in any kind of art "to experience becoming, to find out what's inside you, to make your soul grow.

"Seriously! I mean starting right now, do art and do it for the rest of your lives."

Vonnegut's assignment for the students: Without telling anyone, write a six-line rhymed poem, making it as good as you possibly can. Then tear it "into teeny-weeny pieces" and throw them away.

> You will find that you have already been gloriously rewarded for your poem. You have experienced becoming, learned a lot more about what's inside you, and you have made your soul grow.

Vonnegut was declaring that internal rewards are the most meaningful. (A second option perhaps should have been offered: If you think the poem is good enough, show it to someone!)

Even the Creator of the Universe can grow by making things, Vonnegut showed in *The Sirens of Titan*. Winston Niles Rumfoord's revised Bible anticipates the insights of Rabo Karabekian: "In the beginning, God became the Heaven and the Earth...And God said, 'Let Me be light,' and He was light."

This is self-actualization. It is something individuals can do, even if they are not parts of nurturing extended families, even if they *can't* be.

Becoming is essential to living and is best achieved through individual effort, Vonnegut suggested to TV interviewer Charlie Rose in 1999:

> One thing I don't like about [having] computers in the home...is it cheats people out of the experience of becoming. Now, important life experiences are food, sex, but also becoming, and this involves reading, study, practicing an art, whatever. And what Bill Gates is saying is, "Hey, man, you don't have to become any more. Your computer's becoming."

Proof of God's existence

Imploring others to make art is a nearly evangelical mission of Vonnegut's writing and public speaking, along with urging people to be kind, to form familylike communities, and to laugh. Those things—even though "most people find life so hard and disappointing...that they don't care if life goes on or not"—could provide at least momentary relief, if not hope.

Music, in particular, made Vonnegut feel better. He called it sacred. "It makes practically everybody fonder of life than he or she would be without it," he wrote in 2005.

> Even military bands, although I am a pacifist, always cheer me up. And I really like Strauss and Mozart and all that. You must realize that the priceless gift that African Americans gave us musically is now almost the only reason many foreigners still tolerate us. That specific remedy for the worldwide epidemic of depression is "the blues."

One of many tombstone inscriptions Vonnegut wrote for himself was "THE ONLY PROOF HE NEEDED / FOR THE EXISTENCE OF GOD / WAS MUSIC." Asked about that in 2005, he confirmed for NPR's Liane Hansen his enthusiasm for music.

> Why this is so I don't know, and what music is I don't know, but it helps me so...Jazz—my goodness, what a wonderful, important discovery that is. And it's spiritually as important, or maybe even more important, than Beethoven's Ninth. Wow. So I really get off on jazz. And during the Great Depression, in Indianapolis, when I was in high school, I would go to jazz joints and listen to black guys playing, and, man, they could really do it. And I was really cheered up. It's still the case now.

"Music is the only art that's really worth a damn," Vonnegut wrote. Best of all, Vonnegut liked jazz, which he defined as "safe sex of the highest order." He was cheered by jazz, classical music, marches, the blues...and, it turns out, by the Statler Brothers and the Beatles.

The words to Lew DeWitt's "Flowers on the Wall" make up "yet another great contemporary poem by the Statler Brothers," Vonnegut wrote in *Palm Sunday*, which reprints the lyrics entirely. "It is a poem about the end of a man's usefulness."

Vonnegut gives John, Paul, George, and Ringo credit for fulfilling a crucial creative role. "The function of the artist is to make people like life better than they have before," he told *Rolling Stone*. "When I've been asked if I've ever seen that done, I say 'Yes, the Beatles did it.'"

The artistic function of music must have inspired Vonnegut when he conceived the wondrous, nearly spiritual creatures that dwell deep underground on Mercury in *The Sirens of Titan*. They certainly help twenty-three-year-old military commander Boaz to like life better than he did before.

For millennia, the diamond-shaped, paper-thin beings feed on vibrations. Then they consume music introduced to them by Boaz. They are nourished by severely dampened vibrations from recordings of the *1812 Overture,* say, or *Le Sacre du Printemps.*

These delicate, translucent membranes cannot commit or even conceive of harm. Clinging to subterranean walls, they communicate by touch and by transmitting weak but loving thoughts.

> They have only two possible messages. The first is an automatic response to the second, and the second is an automatic response to the first.
> The first is, "Here I am, here I am, here I am."
> The second is, "So glad you are, so glad you are, so glad you are."...

Though blind and indifferent to anyone's watching, they often arrange themselves so as to present a regular and dazzling pattern of jonquil-yellow and vivid aquamarine diamonds. The yellow comes from the bare cave walls. The aquamarine is the light of the walls filtered through the bodies of the creatures.

Because of their love for music and their willingness to deploy themselves in the service of beauty, the creatures are given a lovely name by Earthlings.

They are called *harmoniums.*

The most peaceful, most innocent creations of Vonnegut's career express themselves—express love—purely by acknowledging one another's existence. In art, especially music, Vonnegut found harmony.

When he found disharmony between words and music, an impulse to correct sometimes kicked in. At least twice, Vonnegut tried to improve musical productions by rewriting lyrics he considered terrible.

Two chapters ago, we saw what he did with the sixteenth-century text of Andrew Lloyd Webber's *Requiem.* Something similar happened when Vonnegut was commissioned by New York Philomusica to write new words for Stravinsky's *L'Histoire du Soldat (The Soldier's Story)* in 1993.

Based on a Russian folk tale, the original 1918 narration by C. F. Ramuz was "a piece of crap," Vonnegut had determined years earlier when he turned down an invitation to narrate a performance of Stravinsky's composition. He found the story to be an absurd relic of a time predating modern warfare, with a soldier toting a violin, presumably even in the rain.

> I thought it was just preposterous, and was somewhat troubled that this thing was premiered in 1918, during the most horrible war for soldiers in history...In 1918, to be a soldier was really something.

Vonnegut's new libretto put the focus on an actual soldier whose story he found tragically unjust: fellow World War II infantryman Eddie Slovik, a Polish American from Detroit who was court-martialed for desertion on November 11, 1944—Armistice Day, and coincidentally the day Vonnegut turned twenty-two.

"He was the only person to be executed for cowardice in the face of the enemy since the Civil War," Vonnegut explained, pointing out that the book *The Execution of Private Slovik* had gone out of print. "Slovik deserves to be kept alive. If his name had been McCoy or Johnson, I don't think he would have been shot."

So, besides Joe Crone and Michael Palaia, with their fictional counterparts in *Slaughterhouse-Five*, we can add Eddie Slovik to the roster of dead soldiers Vonnegut tried to keep alive.

In fact, Slovik gets a passing reference in that novel. In the waiting room of a facility where Billy Pilgrim is visiting his aged mother, he finds a copy of *The Execution of Private Slovik*.

> Billy read the opinion of a staff judge advocate who reviewed Slovik's case...*There was no recommendation for clemency in the case and none is here recommended.* So it goes.

Canaries in a coal mine

Before we finish exploring Vonnegut's views about art, we return to a point he made as far back as the early 1960s.

"Lies told for the sake of artistic effect," claims the so-called Editor's Note of *Mother Night*, "can be, in a higher sense, the most beguiling forms of truth."

As we saw in the chapter on his visits to Biafra and Mozambique, that's how Vonnegut felt about novels as opposed to New Journalism. Although he found something to like in both, it was clear which form of writing he favored.

He framed the difference in terms of music: "Fiction is melody, and journalism, new or old, is noise."

It isn't that lying through writing or other forms of art *is* truth. It's that lying through art, despite its apparent misdirection, can point us toward better comprehension of the world.

"We all know that art is not truth," Pablo Picasso stated in 1923. "Art is a lie that makes us realize truth, at least the truth that is given us to understand."

Artists feel the need to show us the truth as they see it. We can collect all the information we want, but it isn't enough. We seek meaning. Artists deliver meaning by increasing awareness and feeding our sense of wonder, as Rabo Karabekian learned to do.

"Works of art are just ways to pay attention to different things," multimedia artist Laurie Anderson said, "and to appreciate what is there."

And why should we pay attention?

Vonnegut had what he called "the canary-in-the-coal-mine theory of the arts." "Artists are useful to society because they are so sensitive," he said. "They are supersensitive." The theory places artists in the key role of early-warning agents who, Vonnegut felt, are ignored at society's peril.

> Coal miners used to take birds down into the mines with them to detect gas before men got sick. The artists certainly did that in the case of Vietnam. They chirped and keeled over. But it made no difference whatsoever. Nobody important cared. But I continue to think that artists—all artists—should be treasured as alarm systems.

Besides keeling over in times of war, artists help in other ways. Vonnegut recalled that his mentor at the University of Chicago taught that artists can find harmony within the noise of everyday life.

> Using the Socratic method, he asked his little class this: "What is it an artist does—a painter, a writer, a sculptor—?"
>
> ...His answer was this: "The artist says, 'I can do very little about the chaos around me, but at least I can reduce to perfect order this square of canvas, this piece of paper, this chunk of stone.'"
>
> Everybody knows that.

The benefits of this creativity are felt primarily by the creator—perhaps *only* by the creator.

"I believe art is foremost for the artist who creates it," Scottish painter Marion Boddy-Evans wrote. "You do it for your soul, and if the rest of the world gets something from it, that's a bonus."

Write a poem as well as you can write it, Vonnegut advised, then throw it away. It will make your soul grow.

But if the audience is secondary to the creator, what's the point of making art for others to experience?

Vonnegut said he wrote at least his early stories for his sister (and to make a living), but eventually he found a very large audience. His readers were hardly secondary.

Some of Vonnegut's thoughts about why to write for an audience can be applied to creating anything for others. His intent, as it was so often, was to connect.

> Still and all, why bother? Here's my answer: Many people need desperately to receive this message: "I feel and think much as you do, care about many of the things you care about, although most people don't care about them. You are not alone."

Chapter 12

Dignity

What could be more essential in a pluralistic society like ours than that every citizen see dignity in every other human being everywhere?

Kurt Vonnegut, January 27, 1980

Near the end of *Slaughterhouse-Five*, Kurt Vonnegut the writer again injects Kurt Vonnegut the man, and other real people, into his fiction. Vonnegut's friend Bernard V. O'Hare hands over a notebook into which he has printed facts gathered from myriad sources. He's struck by a projection he wants Vonnegut to read: The world's population will reach 7 billion people by the year 2000.

Vonnegut's reply: "I suppose they will all want dignity."

He's right, of course, even though—thanks to a declining birth rate—the prediction presumably made in 1945 and recalled in the 1969 novel was off by about a billion. People *do* want dignity.

Every protester holding a placard, every activist writing a letter to a Congressperson, every folk singer advocating for peace, every aggrieved loudmouth complaining about the War on Christmas is saying the same thing: "I demand dignity."

Vonnegut felt that "love is a rotten substitute for respect." Dignity goes well with respect and, in Vonnegut's estimation, is easier to give and receive. He cautioned, however, that conferring dignity leads down the slippery slope to kindness.

> Giving dignity, the sort of dignity that is of some earthly use, anyway, is something that only people do.

Dignity

Or fail to do... Be warned: If you allow yourself to see dignity in someone, you have doomed yourself to wanting to understand and help whoever it is.

If you see dignity in anything, in fact—it doesn't have to be human—you will still want to understand it and help it. Many people are now seeing dignity in the lower animals and the plant world and waterfalls and deserts—and even in the entire planet and its atmosphere. And now they are helpless not to want to understand and to help those things.

Poor souls!

That sort of kindness, come to think of it, sounds like a nice substitute for love.

Before all of that comes dignity. It can be a rare commodity on a planet with billions of people living on it, and so many of them poor.

Amnesty International's online call for worldwide governmental action to combat the effects of poverty is titled "Human Rights for Human Dignity." The statement is peppered with words like "rights," "respect," and "inclusion"—all markers of dignity that, as Vonnegut pointed out, is something people give...or fail to.

The absence of dignity, Amnesty implies, is an all-too-common trait of world leaders, worsening the plight of their people.

"Governments are simply unwilling to do something about" poverty, the Amnesty statement reads. "This is not an unfortunate reality of life, it is a shocking human rights scandal."

We're unshockable. There is so much unwillingness among governments to do something, we now regard entrenched poverty—a result of many factors, including insufficient dignity—as unfortunate but expected, not scandalous.

This happens because human beings practice denial so effortlessly. There is a "scheme for lasting world peace [that] is to be followed by individuals as well as great nations," according to Vonnegut.

The scheme keeps marginalizd people of all kinds in their place, from urban ghettos to Palestinian refugee camps. It is based, he wrote, on denial—of dignity, certainly, but of much more—with one simple precept:

Ignore agony.

The dignity of strangers

A descendant of freethinkers, Vonnegut called himself an agnostic and claimed that being an atheist in a foxhole gave him comfort. Those terms apply to his being unaffiliated with organized faith.

Humanist was Vonnegut's self-description when he talked about personal behavior. He said he "tried to behave decently" despite lacking belief in an afterlife. Such behavior partially defines humanism, he pointed out.

At times, Vonnegut sought to align with a religious community. "In order not to seem a spiritual quadriplegic to strangers trying to get a fix on me, I sometimes say I'm a Unitarian Universalist," he wrote.

Why did he like Unitarians? For one, he considered them "people who know pure baloney when they hear it." Waggishly ignoring the depth of their convictions, Vonnegut also once claimed, "Unitarians don't believe in anything. I am a Unitarian."

More seriously, he later called an audience of Unitarians "a congregation of people who have faith." He meant the belief that human beings are worthwhile and can solve their own problems. That's another definition of humanism.

The Unitarian sort of congregation appealed to the displaced Midwesterner. While helping commemorate the legacy of William Evering Channing, whose preaching helped found Unitarianism in the 1820s, Vonnegut returned to one of his favorite subjects: the folk society theorized by anthropologist Robert Redfield.

Vonnegut spoke admiringly about the folk society in which he assumed Channing was raised, "a relatively isolated community of like-thinking friends and relatives, a stable extended family of considerable size," as he put it to an audience of Unitarians in Cambridge, Massachusetts.

> I wish I had been born into a society like his—small and congenial and prosperous and self-sufficient. The people around here had ancestors in common then. They looked a lot like each other, dressed a lot like each other, enjoyed the same amusements and food. They were generally agreed as to what was good and what was evil—what God was like, who Jesus was.

In some ways Vonnegut was recalling the Indianapolis of his youth, where, he said, "I had uncles and aunts all over the place, and cousins, and family businesses that I could go into maybe, whole rows of cottages that were full of my relatives," where "there was always someone to talk with, to play with, to learn from."

Even though he left his hometown after high school, Vonnegut felt that his hometown never left him. It was his fundamental community, and it was essential to his identity.

"All my jokes are Indianapolis. All my attitudes are Indianapolis. My adenoids are Indianapolis," he told an audience of high school students in the Hoosier state in 1986. "If I ever severed myself from Indianapolis, I would be out of business. What people like about me is Indianapolis."

Still, Vonnegut realized that the kind of homogenous group to which Channing belonged is insufficient when it seeks to take a role in the larger society. Channing, he said, knew this even early in Unitarianism's development some twenty years into the nineteenth century.

> When Channing began preaching a new sort of sermon in this town, a sort of sermon we now perceive as Unitarian, he was urging his parishioners to credit with human dignity as great as their own persons not at all like their friends and relatives. The time to acknowledge the dignity of strangers, even black ones, had come.

Merely acknowledging the dignity of people with different skin color does not sound especially progressive nowadays—and Channing himself acknowledged even such a basic level of dignity imperfectly, as he did not embrace the abolition of slavery until late in his life—but in his day it was a significant, even radical, departure from folk society conventions that dominated mainstream thought.

Vonnegut's most pointed comments about race focus on our freedom-loving forefathers' creation of an inhumane system that left an entire group of people longing for dignity. He seldom misses a chance to bring that up.

Breakfast of Champions opens with grade-school-style lessons that expose the "evil nonsense" of American history.

Case in point: The claim that America was "discovered" in 1492, when in fact white "sea pirates" that year arrived at land on which millions of copper-colored people already were thriving and later devised a government that enslaved brown-skinned people it imported from overseas.

Instantly, this sounded right to me when I first encountered it as a middle-class white teenager. Maybe it wasn't the first time I had thought that way, but it was a reminder that I'd been taught a bunch of nonsense that offered this lesson above all: History is written by the winners.

That, of course, was old news to nonwhite people.

Spiritual companionship

Vonnegut the moralist wanted kindness. Vonnegut the amateur anthropologist believed that widespread dignity would lead kindness to grow throughout society. Mix in the Sermon on the Mount, and you have Vonnegutian humanism.

Somewhere along the way, Vonnegut must have heard about Ethical Culture. That movement began in New York City in 1876 when Felix

Adler, the German-born son of a prominent Reform rabbi, delivered a series of lectures that focused on the human rather than the divine. The New York Society for Ethical Culture since 1910 has maintained a building on Central Park West, about 24 minutes by subway from the Turtle Bay neighborhood where Vonnegut lived for most of his last 34 years.

I've been associating with Ethicals in Baltimore since 2013. Ethical Culture's unofficial motto—"Diversity in the creed, unanimity in the deed," Adler said in his founding address, simplified throughout the movement to "Deed before creed"—presumably would appeal to a freethinker who valued the merciful words and actions of a Jesus who was not the Son of God.

Vonnegut speculated that, if not for the self-induced "obliteration" of German culture in the United States between the two world wars,

> the mostly German-American Freethinker movement...might have become an extended family for the millions of good Americans who find all the big questions about life unanswered, save by ancient baloney of human manufacture...If there were Freethinker Societies today, lonely rationalists, children of the Enlightenment, wouldn't have to consider throwing away their brains, as though their heads were nothing but jack-o'-lanterns, in their desperate search for spiritual companionship.

As far as I know, Vonnegut did not think much, if at all, about Ethical Culture as a stop along that desperate search. By the time the New York Society hosted a posthumous tribute to Vonnegut in 2007, it was too late for ol' Kurt.

He would be pleased to know that freethinkers, German or otherwise, need not be left wandering in the desert, as it were.

Lonely rationalists today can find like-minded companions among Unitarians, of course, as Vonnegut occasionally did. They're probably the freethinkers who are easiest to find in America. Unitarian Universalism, its name the result of a 1961 merger, claims about a thousand congregations and 170,000 members in the United States, plus hundreds of thousands more who identify with UU.

It has deep roots and a canopy that covers multiple traditions, from liberal Christianity to atheism. Ministers of UU were instrumental in the civil rights movement of the 1960s and were major crafters of the Humanist Manifesto.

The much smaller Ethical Culture movement, unlike in the decades after it was formed, now largely aligns itself with humanism. The goals of both mesh well. I hope I've spelled out humanism's values well enough by now. Here are Ethical Culture's core values: treating people as if they have inherent worth, building relationships, and practicing social justice.

Eliot Rosewater would approve.

Besides Unitarianism and Ethical Culture, much newer nontheistic groups try to establish community, often oriented toward action. Some secular activity models itself on what takes place in churches, some on what happens in classrooms.

The Sunday Assembly, a worldwide movement that held its first meeting in London in 2013, resembles Ethical Culture in its dogma-free philosophy ("Live Better. Help Often. Wonder More.") and its approach to gathering as "a celebration of the one life we know we have."

Citizen University, founded by Eric Liu and Jená Cane in 2012, attempts to achieve change through political engagement in America. It asserts that citizenship "means bringing a sense of civic character to all that you do—and using your power for good." A Civic Saturday meeting is "a civic analogue to a faith gathering—a place to build faith in our democracy and one another."

Also dating to 2012, the values-based initiative called Oasis brings nonbelievers "together to celebrate the human experience" in a dozen US and Canadian chapters on Sunday mornings. Its core values line right up with those of Ethical Culture.

I'm sure well-behaved freethinkers would be allowed into most temples, synagogues, churches, mosques, revival tents, and converted storefronts too. Quakers and Taoists and Buddhists, with less rigid concepts of God, also might take in friendly skeptics.

At the risk of sounding unserious or unkind, I advise looking into the many parodies of fundamentalism if you consider comic relief to be essential. Vonnegut is an obvious inspiration, even when he's not credited as such.

For example, since 1979, followers of the Church of the SubGenius have revered a fake 1950s salesman as a living god. More recently they say some of their "Slack-filled young men and women of Yeti descent" created the virus that causes COVID-19. On the other hand, the Church of the Flying Spaghetti Monster, founded in 2005 to oppose the teaching of intelligent design in Kansas schools, issued exemptions for its members (Pastafarians) who did not want to work near people who were not vaccinated against the virus.

You'd be correct to question whether SubGenii or Pastafarians qualify as humanists, but at least consider how humor leads the former to mock conspiracy theories and the latter to challenge unfounded claims. They stand up for science!

From the sublime to the ridiculous, I have merely scratched the surface of the innumerable alternatives to traditional theistic belief systems.

Will these places and persons help imperfect mortals to connect and flourish through kindness, awareness, and good citizenship? Will they improve the lot of humankind?

Vonnegut judged believers on just such qualities. He told the Unitarians,

> You are like the early Christians in yearning for an era of peace and plenty and justice, which may never come. They thought Jesus would bring that about. You think human beings should be able to create such an era through their own efforts.

Vonnegut being Vonnegut, the endorsement comes with a catch: He doesn't think humanism is for everyone. In *Timequake* he says he received a letter from a man who had been incarcerated for many years as a juvenile and an adult—a jailbird, as it were. The man asked Vonnegut what he should do.

Vonnegut told him to join a church.

"I couldn't recommend Humanism for such a person," he tells us. "I wouldn't do so for the great majority of the planet's population... Humanists, by and large educated, comfortably middle-class persons with rewarding lives like mine, find rapture enough in secular knowledge and hope. Most people can't."

Humanist organizations across the world face this challenge. Many struggle to diversify their membership beyond middle-class white people. They seek to get their message to minorities and low-income individuals who otherwise would join a church, who might never be exposed to the idea that goodness need not rely on belief in a higher power.

Without a suitable tribe or an extended family to suggest to the letter writer, Vonnegut did not offer a freethinking alternative—not a Unitarian congregation, an Ethical Culture society, or a religion-neutral nonprofit. He missed the opportunity to prosyletize for humanism but not the chance to confer dignity.

It could be kind, he must have concluded, for a humanist to intentionally avoid recommending humanism to someone who asks for guidance in fashioning a meaningful life. (The letter is not even partially quoted, so for all we know the writer mentioned God, heaven, a divine Jesus, or something else indicating a theistic perspective to which Vonnegut responded.)

Vonnegut realized that, given accepted notions about religion and redemption, the American ex-offender is more likely to find the hope he needs in a church than in a secular setting. That was more important to Vonnegut than advancing the cause of his own spiritual beliefs, or lack of them.

"He honored the role of religion in the life of believers," wrote his Hoosier friend Dan Wakefield, whose return to Christianity in his fifties was the source of mild ribbing from Vonnegut but nothing more critical. Vonnegut did not seek to rob his friend of dignity.

When advising "Join a church," Vonnegut didn't specify which church, didn't say what to *do* there. Adults must figure out such details for themselves. Who knows? The former prisoner could have ended up with the Unitarians, sitting next to Kurt Vonnegut.

People like that jailbird long for an afterlife that's better than their current life, Vonnegut felt: "It seems to me that the most universal revolutionary wish now or ever is a wish for heaven, a wish by a human being to be honored by angels for something other than beauty or usefulness."

Is it nonsensical for a humanist to make such an observation?

Well, "in a lonely society, the main thing is not to make sense," Vonnegut said while addressing the Unitarians. "The main thing is to get rid of loneliness."

Conclusion

Balderdash

> *"Gentleness must replace violence everywhere, or we are doomed."*
>
> Dr. Woodly, *Happy Birthday, Wanda June*

Kurt Vonnegut did not recommend humanism for everyone, and I do not recommend Vonnegut for everyone. But there's at least one good reason to recommend Kurt Vonnegut to someone who's open to humanism:

The stories.

Like other kinds of art, they are examples of the "rich heritage of human culture" mentioned by the Humanist Manifesto.

Organized religions have that advantage over the various unsupernatural worldviews, at least when it comes to capturing an audience. "The balderdash is usually more beautiful," as Vonnegut put it for the Unitarians in 1980.

He was referring to "clearly invented" religious beliefs that science has found dubious or has flatly disproven. Those beliefs maintain a firm grip on American humans with help from ancient narratives and parables.

The Bible has a burning bush commanding an Egyptian Jew to lead his people out of slavery; a huge fish swallowing but not digesting a recalcitrant prophet; a kid with a slingshot felling an enemy warrior; and numerous other spectacles and feats of derring-do. And that's just in the Torah.

Everybody knows those stories, has read them or seen them on TV.

The life of Jesus—why, that's the Greatest Story Ever Told. Of course, Jesus himself is considered a master storyteller.

By extension, the New Testament begat plotlines that its writers could not have envisioned, for example in the novel and film *The Exorcist*, in all tales involving crucifix-averse vampires, even in *A Charlie Brown Christmas*. These entertainment options are just fine with me, and they would not be possible without the Gospels.

There is no one-volume secular equivalent to the Bible in the American public's consciousness—not even Shakespeare's collected works—but there is a lot of balderdash out there, some of it beautiful.

By *balderdash*, of course, I simply mean clearly invented stories. So much of it has in common with religion a reliance on the supernatural.

Shakespeare's plays often feature ghosts, witches, and fairies. Dickens' *A Christmas Carol* depends upon visits by a tormented soul and three otherworldly beings. Among the many tales told in Neil Gaiman's comic book saga *The Sandman* is an exploration of hell as a place, a realm, or perhaps a state of mind.

Nobody *believes* those chronicles the way many accept biblical tales as true, but we are happy to suspend disbelief so we can enjoy them.

We crave stories. Lessons and morals are simply easier to remember when put into narrative form, but it's more than that. Screenwriting instructor and consultant Robert McKee called storytelling "the most powerful way to put ideas into the world."

Vonnegut certainly felt that way. His novels, which are his greatest contribution to humanism, are about ideas—specifically *his* ideas. He knew that he shared with his writing idol an urge to communicate his principles ("Mark Twain was simply born to moralize. I think I was, too."), and he realized that fiction was the best way to convey those principles to the public.

"It's not easy to infect the brain of another person with an idea; it can be accomplished only by hitting the small exposed hole in the system," wrote neuroscientist and author David Eagleman. "For the brain, that hole is story-shaped. As anyone who teaches realizes, most information bounces off with little impression and no recollection. Good professors and statesmen know the indispensable potency of story."

I made the point a while back that Vonnegut would not be worth discussing if not for his books. My treatments of various topics in this book are based on what Vonnegut wrote and said in public. I can't claim firsthand knowledge about the man as opposed to the artist and spokesperson.

Readers who did not personally know Vonnegut can easily fall into a trap. Because he wrote about himself so much—even in his fiction—Vonnegut "consciously or unconsciously...created multiple and even contradictory identities," biographer Shields wrote.

He was a counterculture hero, a guru, and a leftist to his fans; a wealthy investor to his broker; a champion of family and community and yet a distant father; a man who had left his "child-centered" home to save his sanity, but then married a younger woman who was leading him into fatherhood again; a satirist of American life but feeding at the trough of celebrity up to his ears.

The longer Vonnegut remains dead, the less the disconnection between his public and private identities will matter to nonbiographers like you and me. He's no longer around to live up to his image, or fail to.

His books and stories are all we really need anyhow.

In some ways, perhaps he *is* still around. "Old storytellers never die," wrote Vera Nazarian, an author of speculative fiction. "They disappear into their own story."

Vonnegut did just that while he was still alive. Once deceased, he achieved an immortality through the novels he left behind. I've spent a lot of space in these pages on his nonfiction prose and comments because they support the moralistic perspective of his fiction so well.

At times, the personal takes and the narrative statements are a blur.

Taken all together, the fiction writer, the essayist, the character, the public speaker, and the interview subject constitute a persona we know as Kurt Vonnegut (Jr.). That persona is thoroughly humanistic and ought to be listened to and read, even if partly fabricated.

If Vonnegut is, as he said, a work of fiction—if we can believe he has disappeared into his own story—then he's a story worth telling.

Harmless untruths

Before wrapping up, here's some more balderdash. Remember those big questions I posed back in the Introduction? It's time to pretend that Vonnegut answered them.

The earnest pursuit of fake answers is a holy endeavor because you collect wisdom in the sometimes arduous journey. May these entirely inadequate responses bring you some respite.

- What's wrong with America? It replaced Armistice Day with Veterans Day.
- What's wrong with *people*? They love technology so much that they want to be replaced by machines.
- What's *right* with people? Saints are among us.
- Why do so many people need religion? It's a comfort that answers big questions.

- Why isn't religion enough for some people? It's a dubious promise.
- Is humor useful? Vonnegut thought so: "Jokes help a lot."
- What is life for? Being the eyes and ears and conscience of the Creator of the Universe.

An alternative to that last one, at least in part, is given by a character at the end of *The Sirens of Titan:* "A purpose of human life, no matter who is controlling it, is to love whoever is around to be loved." At least, *respect* whoever is around to be respected.

Which is similar to Mark Vonnegut's reply when his father asked him what life is all about: "Dad, we are here to help each other get through this thing, whatever it is."

When I presented the questions, I did not claim that Vonnegut provided answers. That would have been foolish. He "complained about and cared about" the subjects, is how I put it. I also used the word *lessons,* which might have been a stretch.

The answers, while they are lies, are useful. Most of them appear, in one way or another, in Vonnegut's fiction, where they can do more good than if they were intoned from a pulpit—because they tend to be more memorable.

I think of them a lot these days, both the ones above and others. The effect of technology on human beings would not bother me as much as it does if not for *Player Piano.* I have a better grasp of wartime atrocities committed by the good guys thanks to *Slaughterhouse-Five.* Also from that novel, the Tralfamadorian concept of time has helped me ponder the idea that human beings are a long way from grasping the basic nature of the universe.

Like Howard W. Campbell Jr., I wish we had a holiday dedicated to peace.

Like Eliot Rosewater, I believe we *have* to be kinder.

Surely, that's a conclusion that both humanists and nonhumanists can reach.

I think about my cousin who struggled with addictions for decades, joined an evangelical church, and there made friends who spoke lovingly and candidly about him after his death. I think how, because of those believers—with whom I would disagree strongly about many things—he must have felt a little less anguish, a little less regret, when he died.

I think about how humanism probably would not have worked for him.

Any lessons from Vonnegut, however insightful or personally applicable, do no more to solve the problems of human beings than Eliot Rosewater's dispensing of advice and small sums of money to his fellow townspeople. They might help, and at worst they do no harm.

"Rosewater's kindness imperative," says essayist David Andrews, "is an ethical lie, one unlikely to worsen humanity's plight." A fictional character expressed that imperative best: "God damn it, you've got to be kind."

The cumulative effect is worth it.

Calling the responses *balderdash* is a nod to my favorite prophet, Bokonon, who calls the religion he invented a pack of lies. Harmless untruths.

Reflecting Vonnegut, the responses above are better at getting you to think "Yes, right, that's a good way to put it" than to exclaim "My goodness, what an entirely new and brilliant way of seeing things!"

Vonnegut at his best is simple and meaningful. He helps you arrange the jumbled pieces of our existence a little better.

Bokonon intends his fabricated orthodoxy to provide some sense of hope for people and to combine with the rule of law to keep a teetering society relatively stable. At least, that's how it goes in the imaginary island nation in *Cat's Cradle*.

I intend my made-up answers to provide some sense that reading Vonnegut will help us feel better even if, as John Lennon put it, "there ain't no Jesus gonna come from the sky." Vonnegut's novels and their humanistic principles can keep a teetering believer or nonbeliever relatively sane for a while.

Vonnegut in effect tells Christians that they can have Jesus the divine miracle worker if Thomas Jefferson and everyone else can have Jesus the compassionate, mortal paragon of decency, and if both try to emulate the latter.

Either version is probably an unrealistic figment. But Jesus the divine has to be experienced internally—you might say spiritually—whereas wholly decent people are all around us.

You know at least one or two decent people, don't you? You might be one yourself! Truly decent people seem to be too good for this world, and yet they're in it. (Vonnegut's comments about them, a few of whom he called saints, are in Appendix B.)

Every Kurt Vonnegut fan I've met is a good person, as far as I can tell. Did reading Vonnegut make them good? I doubt it. Probably they already had goodness in them, already treated people with dignity. At least, they've tried.

We (and now I include myself as a fan who tries to be good) find in Vonnegut some validation that we see the world as it is. We don't flatter ourselves with the notion that we always know what's really going on— but we *know* we don't know. We find reason for delight and reason for despair. We find both comedy and tragedy in day-to-day life. Some of us find Jesus there too, while many do not.

Everyone has their own take. People of faith, people who find courage and hope in organized worship or in unaffiliated religion, can do great things. Once in a while they achieve a little justice. At their best, they can help lead some of us to peace.

Simply reading Vonnegut will not lead us there, but his messages about kindness, community, dignity, awareness, and art, I must finally admit, need not be balderdash if we put them to work against loneliness and corruption and greed.

John Figler knew as much. He was a mere high school student when Vonnegut quoted him in the prologue to *Jailbird*. Vonnegut called Figler's seven-word distillation of his more-than-quarter-century-old writing career "the single idea that lies at the heart of my work so far."

Figler had written that Vonnegut's message came down to this: "Love may fail, but courtesy will prevail."

So even a student still in high school—a great time to start reading Vonnegut, by the way—can be wise enough to derive an excellent lie from Vonnegut's balderdash.

Those of us far past high school can do the same.

Isn't that some nice balderdash?

Peace.

Appendix A
Timeline

The life of Kurt Vonnegut, condensed
Sources for the following include Vonnegut: Novels & Stories 1963–1973, Sidney Offit, editor; And So It Goes: Kurt Vonnegut, A Life *by* Charles J. Shields; The Brothers Vonnegut: Science and Fiction in the House of Magic *by* Ginger Strand; Critical Companion to Kurt Vonnegut *by* Susan Farrell; Conversations with Kurt Vonnegut, William Rodney Allen, editor; and Wikipedia. See bibliography for full publication details.

1922: Kurt Vonnegut Jr. born November 11 (then called Armistice Day) in Indianapolis to architect Kurt Vonnegut and brewery heiress Edith (nee Lieber) Vonnegut. He is the couple's third child, following Bernard (born August 29, 1914) and Alice (born November 18, 1917).

1927: Enters kindergarten at the private Orchard School.

1929: Family finances suffer after stock market crash on October 29 hastens Great Depression. Father's architectural commissions dry up for years.

1931: As family's financial situation worsens, Vonnegut is pulled from Orchard, begins fourth grade in public school.

1935 or thereabouts: Begins smoking Pall Mall cigarettes at age twelve.

1936–40: Attends Shortridge High School, Indianapolis. Writes for and edits its newspaper, *The Shortridge Daily Echo*.

1940–43: Attends Cornell University in Ithaca, New York, majoring in chemistry. Serves as assistant managing editor, associate editor, and columnist for its newspaper, *The Cornell Daily Sun*, and is a member of the Delta Upsilon fraternity. Enrolls in ROTC, is kicked out. Placed on academic probation. Develops pneumonia while on holiday break in Indianapolis (December 1942). Enlists in the United States Army (March 1943). Drops out of Cornell.

1943–44: Is sent to Carnegie Institute of Technology and the University of Tennessee to study mechanical engineering. The program is canceled due to a buildup of troops. Reassigned to the 106th "Golden Lion" Infantry Division, Second Battalion, 423rd Regiment. Reports for training as an intelligence scout to Camp Atterbury, near Edinburgh, Indiana, meets his longtime friend Bernard V. O'Hare Jr. of Shenandoah, Pennsylvania.

1944: At home with his parents and sister in Williams Creek, Indiana, on a three-day pass when his mother, age fifty-six, is found dead from an overdose of sleeping pills early in the morning of May 14, Mother's Day. Sent overseas with his unit, which is trained in England for three weeks before being deployed in the Ardennes. Captured by German troops at the Battle of the Bulge in December.

1945: Interned as a prisoner of war in Dresden, Germany. Survives the Allied firebombing of Dresden on February 13–15 while in underground slaughterhouse. Forced with other POWs to gather the bodies of bombing victims for mass burning. Liberated by Russian soldiers. He and O'Hare are shipped back to the United States. Promoted to corporal and honorably discharged. Marries Jane Marie Cox, an Indianapolis native and Swarthmore College graduate he had known since kindergarten, on September 14. Both are accepted into graduate programs at the University of Chicago (he in anthropology, she in Slavic languages) and move to an apartment near campus.

1946–47: Is impressed by the work of anthropology department chair Robert Redfield concerning folk societies. Works for Chicago City News Bureau.

1947: First child, son Mark, born on May 11. Thesis rejected, leaves graduate school without a degree. Moves to Alplaus, New York, to work across the river in Schenectady as a publicist for the General Electric Corporation, where brother Bernard has been an atmospheric scientist since 1945. Joins the Alplaus Volunteer Fire Department.

1949: *Collier's* accepts Vonnegut's short story "Report on the Barnhouse Effect," which becomes his first professionally published fiction (February 11, 1950, issue). The story is adapted for NBC's radio program *Dimension X*, broadcast April 22. Second child, daughter Edith, is born on December 29.

1951: Leaves his job at General Electric to write full time, having sold several short stories to magazines. Relocates with his family for a summer to Provincetown, Massachusetts, near the tip of Cape Cod. Then they move to Osterville, on the Cape's opposite end.

1952: *Player Piano,* his first novel, is published by Scribner's.

1954: Third child, daughter Nanette, is born on October 4. Bantam reissues *Player Piano* in paperback under the title *Utopia 14.*

1955: Vonneguts move to West Barnstable, Cape Cod.

1956: Kurt Vonnegut Sr. dies of lung cancer, age seventy-two.

1957: Vonnegut opens the second Saab auto dealership in the United States.

1958: Sister Alice's husband, James C. Adams, is killed when the commuter train on which he is a passenger plunges off a bridge in New Jersey on September 15. Alice, in the hospital and sick with breast cancer, dies the next day, age forty-one. Kurt and Jane take on Jim and Alice's four boys, raising three of them (Jim Jr., Steve, and Kurt, nicknamed "Tiger"). The youngest, twenty-one-month-old Peter, lives with them for about a year but then is raised by an Adams relative. TV adaptation of Vonnegut story "D.P." airs as "Auf Wiedersehen" on the CBS anthology *General Electric Theater.*

1959: *The Sirens of Titan* is published as a paperback original.

1960: Vonnegut's two-act play *Something Borrowed* premieres in an amateur theater on the Cape and later in the year is reworked as *Penelope.* The Saab dealership closes.

1961: *Canary in a Cat House,* a collection of twelve Vonnegut short stories that first appeared in magazines, is published. "Harrison Bergeron," which becomes Vonnegut's best-known short story, is published in *The Magazine of Fantasy and Science Fiction.* TV adaptation of Vonnegut story "Runaways" airs on ABC.

1962: *Mother Night* (publication date: 1961) is printed as a paperback original. Vonnegut teaches developmentally and emotionally challenged boys at the private Hopefields Riverview School in Cape Cod.

1963: *Cat's Cradle* is published.

1965: *God Bless You, Mr. Rosewater* is published, featuring the debut of a secondary character named Kilgore Trout. Vonnegut begins two-year residency at the University of Iowa Writers' Workshop.

1966: Signs three-book contract with Seymour "Sam" Lawrence. *Mother Night* is reprinted with a new introduction by Vonnegut.

1967: Travels with buddy O'Hare to Dresden on a Guggenheim Fellowship.

Appendix

1968: The collection *Welcome to the Monkey House*, with twenty-five short pieces from periodicals, mostly fiction, is published.

1969: *Slaughterhouse-Five* is published on March 31. It spends four months on the best-seller list, peaking at number four and vaulting Vonnegut into literary stardom.

1970: Travels to war-torn Biafra, writes about experience. Receives an Academy Award in Literature from the American Academy of Arts and Letters. Writes a further update of *Something Borrowed/Penelope*, which premieres off-Broadway as *Happy Birthday, Wanda June* in October, moves to Broadway in December, and lasts for 96 performances into March 1971. Lives alone in a friend's Greenwich Village penthouse during rehearsals. Meets and makes public appearances with photographer Jill Krementz. Moves to townhouse on East 51st Street in Manhattan near Krementz while commuting to Harvard to teach creative writing.

1971: Son Mark suffers a schizophrenic breakdown, later chronicled in his book *The Eden Express* (1975). Book version of *Happy Birthday, Wanda June* is published, film adaptation directed by Mark Robson is released. Awarded a master's degree in anthropology by the University of Chicago for *Cat's Cradle*.

1972: *Slaughterhouse-Five* film directed by George Roy Hill is released. *Between Time and Timbuktu*, an aggregation of scenes based on various Vonnegut works (although itself not written by him), is published in book form with the subtitle *Prometheus-5, a Space Fantasy*, and a teleplay version directed by Fred Barzyk is broadcast on National Educational Television. Vonnegut is elected a vice president of PEN American Center, which advocates for writers, literature, and free speech.

1973: *Breakfast of Champions* is published, becomes a number-one best seller. Vonnegut is elected to the American Academy of Arts and Letters. Begins one-year teaching term at City University of New York. Buys townhouse on East 48th Street, Manhattan, where he lives with Krementz.

1974: *Wampeters, Foma, & Granfalloons: Opinions*, a collection of nonfiction material, is published. Vonnegut begins four-year term as a National Institute of Arts and Letters vice president.

1975: Favorite uncle, Alex Vonnegut ("If this isn't nice, I don't know what is"), dies, age eighty-three.

1976: *Slapstick* is published.

1977: Buys a house with Krementz in Sagaponack, Long Island, a village in the Hamptons.

1979: *Jailbird* is published. Divorce from Jane becomes final. Marries Krementz on November 24. They live in Manhattan. Musical adaptation of *God Bless You, Mr. Rosewater* is produced off-off-Broadway and off-Broadway and lasts only 12 performances despite being created by future Disney hitmakers Howard Ashman and Alan Menken.

1980: *Sun Moon Star*, children's book collaboration between Vonnegut and illustrator Ivan Chermayeff, is published.

1981: *Palm Sunday,* second collection of nonfiction material, is published.

1982: *Deadeye Dick* is published. TV adaptation of short story "Who Am I This Time?" premieres on PBS. Vonnegut and Krementz adopt infant girl, Lily.

1984: Taken by ambulance to St. Vincent's Hospital after consuming pills and booze in apparent suicide attempt. *Slapstick (of Another Kind)*, film adaptation of *Slapstick* directed by Steven Paul, is released.

1985: *Galápagos* is published.

1986: Jane Vonnegut Yarmolinsky dies of cancer at home in Washington, DC. Vonnegut briefly appears as himself in *Back to School*, a film starring comedian Rodney Dangerfield.

1987: *Bluebeard* is published. TV adaptation of short story "Long Walk to Forever" premieres on A&E.

1988: Requiem Mass written by Vonnegut premieres in Buffalo, New York.

1990: Longtime friend Bernard O'Hare dies of throat cancer and tuberculosis. *Hocus Pocus* is published.

1991: *Fates Worse Than Death,* third collection of nonfiction material, is published. *Kurt Vonnegut's Welcome to the Monkey House,* TV anthology series of short story adaptations, premieres on cable network Showtime. Moves, alone, to Sagaponack.

1992: Named Humanist of the Year by the American Humanist Association and becomes AHA president, an honorary position that lasts the rest of his life.

1993: Stravinsky musical *L'Histoire du Soldat*, with new libretto by Vonnegut based on the execution of Private Edward Slovik for desertion during World War II, premieres at the Lincoln Center with a performance by the Philomusica Ensemble. Meets Kentucky printmaker Joe Petro III. They form Origami Express, which produces limited-edition silkscreen prints of Vonnegut drawings.

1994: Reconciles with Krementz, moves back from Sagaponack to Manhattan.

Appendix

1996: *Mother Night* film directed by Keith Gordon with a screenplay by Robert B. Weide is released. Vonnegut appears briefly but clearly in a slow-motion crowd shot.

1997: Brother Bernard dies, age eighty-three. Final novel, *Timequake*, is published.

1999: *Bagombo Snuff Box*, a collection of stories that first appeared in magazines, is published. *God Bless You, Dr. Kevorkian*, a collection of transcribed radio spots written for and read on NPR station WNYC, is published. *Like Shaking Hands With God*, the text of two conversations between Vonnegut and Lee Stringer about writing, one public and one private, is published. Has one line as a TV commercial director in *Breakfast of Champions* film directed by Alan Rudolph.

2000: Nearly dies from inhaling smoke in a fire in his Manhattan study. Temporarily moves to Northampton, MA, near daughter Nanny. Teaches creative writing at Smith College.

2004: Vonnegut family artwork exhibited at the Indianapolis Art Center, arranged by Petro.

2005: *A Man Without a Country*, a nonfiction collection based on his *In These Times* magazine columns and other material, is published.

2007: Suffers traumatic head injury in March after falling down steps outside his Manhattan brownstone. Dies on April 11.

Appendix B

Behaving Decently in an Indecent Society

Saints identified by Kurt Vonnegut

Oganized religions are not alone in canonizing people. Kurt Vonnegut did it a few times. Sure, he lacked true authority in these matters, but he bestowed high praise upon some of the individuals and organizations that he greatly admired. With a wink, the Christ-worshiping agnostic called them *saints*.

"I define a saint as a person who behaves decently in an indecent society," he wrote.

The honorees, including the sole cleric among them, were chosen for secular acts of selflessness. The saints he personally knew impressed Vonnegut because of their contributions to humankind rather than to himself alone. Even the one apparent exception—his second wife—made the list primarily for what she did before they met.

He left out his first wife. If anyone in his life deserved to be called a saint in the popular secular sense, it probably was Jane Marie Cox Vonnegut Yarmolinsky. As we've seen, however, his published words about her are nearly always tender and loving.

For that matter, Vonnegut did not call his dear friend Bernard V. O'Hare a saint, or his brother or his sister, or his favorite uncle. Or Ida Young, the African American cook his family employed when he was a boy. She taught young Vonnegut kindness and read to him from the Bible. He adored her.

Those individuals were in a different category. To Vonnegut, it seems, a saint was someone who more *publicly* "behaves decently in an indecent society." Still, he used the term arbitrarily.

Appendix

He considered Carl Sandburg and Eugene Debs to be "national treasures." He marveled over Lincoln's leadership and speeches, regarded George Orwell as "a man I admire almost more than any other man," and lauded the doomed germ theory pioneer Ignaz Semmelweis ("my hero"). Of all Americans throughout history, Vonnegut wrote, he "would most like to have been" Col. Joshua L. Chamberlain, under whose command a Maine brigade held the Union flank and helped turn the Battle of Gettysburg.

Vonnegut didn't call any of them saints.

Who else didn't make the cut? If you look for diversity, as most humanists do, you'll be disappointed in Vonnegut's choices. There are practically no women, and everyone's white. (One collective saint might increase the percentage of each a bit, as explained later.)

Sometimes, Vonnegut was transparently a man of his era and his place.

When these names are taken together—and Vonnegut never did collect them in one place, although he came close—the resulting list is decidedly incomplete. It's not just the limited range of gender and skin color. There are only eleven entries, after all. Almost all of them appear within a few pages of *Fates Worse Than Death*. There's one name in another nonfiction collection, *Palm Sunday*, and three more (including one repeat) in the novel/memoir hybrid *Timequake*.

Much like Vonnegut's views on socialism or atheism or economic systems, his declarations of sainthood should not be considered a fully formed, comprehensive statement. He probably put as much thought into a collective impression about saints as he put into a consistent portrayal of Kilgore Trout.

That is, not much.

OK, then why repeat the names of these people? Because the behavior of nearly each one is something for humanists to value. Figuratively canonizing them is a way to say, "Job very well done."

It's a nudge toward realizing that we too are capable of such behavior.

Because he didn't have to offer proof of three miracles per candidate, Vonnegut asserted, he was "more prompt than the Roman Catholic Church in announcing who is a saint."

> It is enough for me if a person (like a good anthropologist) easily finds all races and classes equally respectable and interesting, and doesn't keep score with money.

Here, then, are the Vonnegut-proclaimed saints, in more or less random order:

Mark Twain is the saint most closely associated with Vonnegut. They have similar places in literary history, as humorists who speak to American values. Both were freethinkers, although Twain confronted religion more directly in his brilliant, bitter *Letters from the Earth*.

Of course, for some years on the lecture circuit, Vonnegut *looked* like Twain, growing out his mustache and his unruly hair, wearing white suits. Another tangible measure of his devotion to Twain is that he and Jane named their first child after him.

Vonnegut expressed his gratitude and debt to his predecessor in a speech he gave at Twain's house in Hartford, Connecticut, in 1979.

> It seems clear to me, as an American writing one hundred years after this house was built, that we would not be known as a nation with a supple, amusing, and often beautiful language of our own, if it were not for the genius of Mark Twain...
>
> Imagine, if you will, the opinion we would now hold of ourselves and the opinions others would hold of us, if it were not for the myths about us created by Mark Twain. You can then begin to calculate our debt to this one man.

Someone who did not have Twain's and Vonnegut's religious skepticism was **Paul Moore Jr.** (1919–2003), the thirteenth Episcopal bishop of the Diocese of New York. Vonnegut's second wife, Jill Krementz, had known Moore since she was a child. The Vonneguts and Moore and his wife traveled to Galápagos together. Moore baptized the couple's daughter, although Vonnegut did not attend the ceremony.

Moore was long associated with the Cathedral of St. John the Divine, where Vonnegut was among several speakers who gave anti-nuclear-weapons addresses in 1983. The bishop took on many liberal political causes. His courage in ordaining a gay woman, opening a homeless shelter on church grounds, and performing other acts of progressivism and kindness made him the sort of religious leader whom Vonnegut longed for.

> He is a very good man, always on the side of the powerless when they are abused or scorned or cheated by the powerful (mostly subscribers to The Wall Street Journal). A pregnant woman asked me one time if I thought it was wrong to bring a child into such an awful world. I replied that what made living almost worthwhile for me was all the saints I met, and I named Bishop Moore.

Concern about marginalized people was a trait that drew Vonnegut to Jesus, to Bishop Moore, and to certain persons who were not known primarily as religious figures. One of the latter was **Robert Maslansky** (1930–2017), who began his medical career in Minnesota, where he pioneered substance abuse treatment. Vonnegut met Maslansky during the doctor's thirty-year tenure at Bellevue–NYU.

Maslansky "treats every sort of addict at Bellevue Hospital in New York City, and in the jails, too...(When we take walks together many homeless people greet him by name.)"

Like Moore, Maslansky was a military veteran, part of an important community for Vonnegut. Maslansky was in the army, Moore was a marine.

Wartime service of another kind was a factor in adding Vonnegut's wife's name to those of Moore, Maslansky, and Twain. While acknowledging the effect **Jill Krementz** had on his life ("If it weren't for her I think I probably would have died of too much sleep long ago."), it's her wartime photographs that qualified the second Mrs. Vonnegut for her husband's unofficial pantheon.

Vonnegut notes that Krementz "photographed the Vietnamese people rather than the war stuff long before I met her." He quotes extensively from a letter written to her by Dean Brelis, who had supplied the text for a 1968 book collecting what Vonnegut called Krementz's "humane and beautiful pictures" of Vietnamese people ravaged by conflict.

"Your actions and behavior in Vietnam, like your photographs, wanted a better world," Brelis wrote.

"So," Vonnegut added, Krementz "is yet another saint."

In the same passage, Vonnegut repeatedly calls her Xanthippe. That's a little curious. Xanthippe, the wife of Socrates, is known for being long suffering—but also for being a shrew.

Before moving on to the saint that Vonnegut wrote about the most, here are some folks he mentioned briefly:

> Tris Coffin and his wife Margaret, who get out a four-page weekly called *The Washington Spectator*, are saints...Morris Dees, the southern lawyer who takes on the likes of the Ku Klux Klan in court (thus putting his life on the line) on his own initiative, is a saint...Sure, and former Peace Corps people (now middle-aged) whom I met in Mozambique, who were working for the relief agency CARE there, are saints. They not only lived in friendly and shrewd harmony with the human beings they found there but taught them shipping and warehousing and accountancy (hard-edge business practices), so that starving to death might still be kept to a minimum after CARE went elsewhere (possibly to Leningrad).

Tristram Coffin (1912–1997) grew up in Indianapolis and like Vonnegut attended Shortridge High School. He had a long career in politics and journalism before starting the newsletter then called *Washington Watch*, in 1968. Vonnegut, to his credit, includes Tristram's wife of sixty-four years, **Margaret Coffin** (1911–1995), as co-publisher. She is not mentioned in 1997 obituaries of her husband that were published in, for example, *The New York Times* and *The Indianapolis Star*.

The **Peace Corps people** in Mozambique are still at it. The organization's presence there began in the early 1990s. At this writing more than one hundred Peace Corps volunteers serve in the African republic, successor to the dying socialist state that Vonnegut wrote about. Some of these volunteers undoubtedly have been and are nonwhites or women or both, so there's more diversity among Vonnegut's saints than meets the eye, although the Peace Corps members are honored collectively.

Most problematic of the saints is **Morris Dees**, co-founder of the Southern Poverty Law Center in 1971. It's little wonder Vonnegut singled him out twenty years later. Dees, after all, was the SPLC's public face for three decades. He touted high-profile projects such as lawsuits that financially crippled the Ku Klux Klan and annual lists that exposed the reach of hate groups in America.

Dees, however, was dismissed by the SPLC in 2019 for unspecified workplace transgressions. Complaints about a poor work environment under Dees had circulated over the years. After Dees was fired, former SPLC staffer Bob Moser publicly detailed allegations that Dees mistreated minority employees and harassed female workers.

Impressed by the SPLC's worthy efforts and the public image Dees projected, it seems Vonnegut was duped along with the rest of us.

Or maybe the point is that even saints, like mythical heroes and celebrated modern personalities, are flawed.

A clowning genius

Humorists such as performers Bob Elliott and Ray Goulding, Hoosier cartoonist/writer Kin Hubbard, and of course Twain had impressed Vonnegut throughout his life. Once, he made a passing reference to his favorite comedians, **Stanley Laurel** and **Oliver Hardy**, as saints.

But one man in particular embodied activism and attitude for Vonnegut, by using humor to place attention where he felt it belonged. This was **Abbie Hoffman** (1936–1989), a co-founder of the Youth International Party (the Yippies), a member of the Chicago Seven, a subject of FBI observation, a conservationist—and, by the way, the author of ten books. Hoffman was arrested a few times, and for a while he was a fugitive from justice.

Appendix

Vonnegut appreciated how Hoffman's "frenzied sense of humor [was] the sanest thing in this country during the Vietnam War." That sense of the absurd informed several outlandish acts of defiance.

There were two well-known such provocations in 1967. Hoffman led a group of protesters who tossed real and fake money onto the floor of the New York Stock Exchange. Several weeks later, he led tens of thousands in the March on the Pentagon. As tension mounted, Hoffman pledged to levitate the building with psychic energy.

About two years after Hoffman's death—he OD'd on barbiturates and booze—Vonnegut called him "a clowning genius" who was

> high on [his] list of saints, of exceptionally courageous, unarmed, unsponsored, unpaid souls who have tried to slow down even a little bit state crimes against those Jesus Christ said should inherit the Earth someday.
>
> He did this with truth, anger, and ridicule.

"I was utterly in sympathy with his clowning," Vonnegut said. "It seemed to me that it was the only way to respond to brutality with any effectiveness."

And yet, ultimately Hoffman was ineffective, Vonnegut admitted, the same as any artist who attempts to halt conflict between nations: "Abbie in fact was defeated. He was not a success in even slowing down the Vietnam War...Humor is powerless except to make us proud of human beings even in times of great shame."

Pride in times of shame. Decency in an indecent society. Defeat in the hopeless pursuit of peace. To Vonnegut, contrariness in favor of kindness and sanity was worthy of sainthood.

The admiration—maybe even envy—that Vonnegut felt for Hoffman is unmistakable. He grasped that taking chances on the printed page cannot compare to risking one's personal liberty.

> During the Vietnam War, as a personality I wasn't much in evidence. It was all simply my books that circulated. And I went to some really huge rallies, in Washington, mainly, but was just part of the crowd and was not a speaker. And Abbie recognized me as a kindred spirit, and I was certainly much honored and terribly pleased, as he was a celebrity and I was not.

Vonnegut became a celebrity soon after *Slaughterhouse-Five* was published and hailed as an essential antiwar statement and its author praised as a sort of, well, clowning genius.

BEHAVING DECENTLY

Through humor and the tweaking of establishment values, Vonnegut aimed to report what was really going on. He could say the same of the original Yippie.

> Abbie Hoffman was a very good writer...If he had been a crude writer, it wouldn't have mattered much because he was saying things that hadn't been heard for a long time and people were dying for somebody to say...I myself have found that, speaking to university audiences, they go almost crazy with gratitude when you are candid with them and tell them something they already know that is supposed to go unspoken. And of course Abbie did that and told the truth, that our government was behaving in a criminal way.

Appendix C

Humanism and Its Aspirations: Humanist Manifesto III (2003)

A successor to the Humanist Manifesto of 1933
The first Humanist Manifesto (1933) was the result of collaboration between thirty-four humanist leaders, including philosopher and psychologist John Dewey. It has been revised twice, in 1973 and 2003, to reflect shifts in focus and changes from the original patriarchal language. It is not a creed but a declaration of principles. Signatories of Humanist Manifesto III, titled "Humanism and Its Aspirations," include 21 Nobel laureates and Kurt Vonnegut. Besides "Humanism and its Aspirations," which is a statement of the American Humanist Association, worthwhile documents are the Secular Humanist Declaration (1980), compiled by former Humanist magazine editor Paul Kurtz, and the Amsterdam Declaration (2002), endorsed by the International Humanist and Ethical Union, a collection of organizations that includes the AHA.

Humanism is a progressive philosophy of life that, without supernaturalism, affirms our ability and responsibility to lead ethical lives of personal fulfillment that aspire to the greater good of humanity.

The lifestance of Humanism—guided by reason, inspired by compassion, and informed by experience—encourages us to live life well and fully. It evolved through the ages and continues to develop through the efforts of thoughtful people who recognize that values and ideals, however carefully wrought, are subject to change as our knowledge and understandings advance.

This document is part of an ongoing effort to manifest in clear and positive terms the conceptual boundaries of Humanism, not what we must believe but a consensus of what we do believe. It is in this sense that we affirm the following:

Knowledge of the world is derived by observation, experimentation, and rational analysis. Humanists find that science is the best method for determining this knowledge as well as for solving problems and developing beneficial technologies. We also recognize the value of new departures in thought, the arts, and inner experience—each subject to analysis by critical intelligence.

Humans are an integral part of nature, the result of unguided evolutionary change. Humanists recognize nature as self-existing. We accept our life as all and enough, distinguishing things as they are from things as we might wish or imagine them to be. We welcome the challenges of the future, and are drawn to and undaunted by the yet to be known.

Ethical values are derived from human need and interest as tested by experience. Humanists ground values in human welfare shaped by human circumstances, interests, and concerns and extended to the global ecosystem and beyond. We are committed to treating each person as having inherent worth and dignity, and to making informed choices in a context of freedom consonant with responsibility.

Life's fulfillment emerges from individual participation in the service of humane ideals. We aim for our fullest possible development and animate our lives with a deep sense of purpose, finding wonder and awe in the joys and beauties of human existence, its challenges and tragedies, and even in the inevitability and finality of death. Humanists rely on the rich heritage of human culture and the lifestance of Humanism to provide comfort in times of want and encouragement in times of plenty.

Humans are social by nature and find meaning in relationships. Humanists long for and strive toward a world of mutual care and concern, free of cruelty and its consequences, where differences are resolved cooperatively without resorting to violence. The joining of individuality with interdependence enriches our lives, encourages us to enrich the lives of others, and inspires hope of attaining peace, justice, and opportunity for all.

Working to benefit society maximizes individual happiness. Progressive cultures have worked to free humanity from the brutalities of mere survival and to reduce suffering, improve society, and develop global community. We seek to minimize the inequities of circumstance and ability, and we support a just distribution of nature's resources and the fruits of human effort so that as many as possible can enjoy a good life.

Humanists are concerned for the well being of all, are committed to diversity, and respect those of differing yet humane views. We work to uphold the equal enjoyment of human rights and civil liberties in an open, secular society and maintain it is a civic duty to participate in the democratic process and a planetary duty to protect nature's integrity, diversity, and beauty in a secure, sustainable manner.

Thus engaged in the flow of life, we aspire to this vision with the informed conviction that humanity has the ability to progress toward its highest ideals. The responsibility for our lives and the kind of world in which we live is ours and ours alone.

Humanist Manifesto is a trademark of the American Humanist Association. © 2003 American Humanist Association

Notes

Titles that lack complete publication details in this section refer to works that appear fully cited in the bibliography.

Epigraphs
"Time, have mercy": *Fates Worse Than Death*, chap. VI, 227 (from a Requiem Mass that Vonnegut wrote in 1985).
"Don't be a fool!": *Cat's Cradle*, chap. 118, 188.

Introduction: Who is Kurt Vonnegut?
Epigraph "I myself am a work of fiction": *Wampeters, Foma & Granfalloons*, Preface, xxi.
"glib Philosopher": *Wampeters, Foma & Granfalloons*, Preface, xvi.
"Oh, it's just so damn cheap": *Mother Night*, chap. 23, 100.
"When I was a boy, all the people of all the nations": *Breakfast of Champions*, Preface, 6.
"On Armistice Day": *Fates Worse Than Death*, chap. XV, 150.
"not going to put on" *Breakfast of Champions*, Preface, 5.
"I loved him, and I was afraid of him": Comment by Steve Adams made on January 20, 2022, during a Kurt Vonnegut Museum and Library online event, "Welcome to Earth Babies: Vonnegut @ 100," via Zoom.
"had next to no interest": Mark Vonnegut, quoted in Charlie Jane Anders, "Kurt Vonnegut died a bitter man [UPDATED]," December 5, 2011, https://io9.gizmodo.com/5865297/kurt-vonnegut-died-a-bitter-man-who-kept-thinking-he-was-a-failure.

Why pay attention to Kurt Vonnegut?
"God damn it, you've got to be kind": *God Bless You, Mr. Rosewater*, chap. 7, 93.

Notes

"farting around": Vonnegut's full quote, from *A Man Without a Country*, chap. 6, 62, is "How beautiful it is to get up and go out and do something. We are here on Earth to fart around. Don't let anybody tell you any different."

"I apologize because": "How I Learned From an Artist What Teachers Do," *If This Isn't Nice, What Is?* (Second Edition), 85.

"body of work reveals": *Complete Stories*, Foreword, xii.

Chaplin's speech: "The Final Speech from *The Great Dictator*," transcript at https://www.charliechaplin.com/en/articles/29-The-Final-Speechfrom-The-Great-Dictator, quotes Jesus saying in the Gospel of Luke that "the Kingdom of God is within man."

Chapter 1: He's Up in Heaven Now

Epigraph "I am a humanist": *God Bless You, Dr. Kevorkian*, Introduction, 9.

"that greatest and most humane": *A Man Without a Country*, chap. 9, 95.

"as having inherent worth": See Appendix C, "Humanism and Its Aspirations."

"largely a product of the Renaissance": Fred Edwords, "What is Humanism?," American Humanist Association, 1989 and 2008, https://americanhumanist.org/what-is-humanism/edwords-what-is-humanism/.

"religionless Christianity that begins": Arthur G. Broadhurst, in description of his book *The Possibility of Christian Humanism*, home page of http://www.christian-humanist.net/background-and-history.html.

Philosopher Chris Sunami: "History of Humanism," August 11, 2016 (repost of 2004 essay), http://popculturephilosopher.com/history-of-humanism/.

a label that "charmed" him: "Address to the American Physical Society," New York City, 1969, *Wampeters, Foma & Granfalloons*, 92 ("I am charmed that you should call me in your program notes here a humanist").

"We are talking about a society": Speech, "Address to the Women of America," July 10, 1971, excerpted in an audio clip at https://vimeo.com/23513858.

"I have made my peace" and "It seems to me": Hurston, "Religion," *Dust Tracks on a Road* (New York: Harper Perennial Modern Classics, 1995), 226.

"I would be the last to condemn" and "Man by his own power": King, *Strength to Love* (Minneapolis: Fortress Press, 2010. Text © 1963 Martin Luther King Jr. First published in 1977 by Collins + World, Cleveland), chap. 13, 136.

"the informed conviction": See Appendix C, "Humanism and Its Aspirations."

"man at last is becoming": "Humanist Manifesto I," American Humanist Association, https://americanhumanist.org/what-is-humanism/manifesto1/.

"To be anti-humanist": "A Bridge Supreme: Connecting Humanism to a Liberal, Loving Christianity," American Humanist Association, October 25, 2016, https://thehumanist.com/magazine/november-december-2016/features/

bridge-supreme-connecting-humanism-liberal-loving-christianity.

"The task of the Christian church": "A Bridge Supreme: Connecting Humanism to a Liberal, Loving Christianity."

"The idolatry of Western man": *Worlds Aflame* (Garden City, NY: Doubleday, 1965), 127, https://b-ok.cc/book/2038060/6b67ad.

"Humanism is satanic" and "Young people accepted": "Humanism — Man as Master," Christian Philosophy, http://www.diovive.com/english/Filosofia/man_master.htm (originally appeared in *New Wine* magazine, February 1979.

"isn't an either-or proposition" and "Humanism is yours": "What is Humanism?"

Tremendously interested in human beings

"You have called me a humanist": "Address to the American Physical Society," *Wampeters, Foma & Granfalloons*, 94.

"readers are human beings": "Address to the American Physical Society," *Wampeters, Foma & Granfalloons*, 95.

"About belief or lack of belief": *God Bless You, Dr. Kevorkian*, Introduction, 9–11. Some of the same material appears in *A Man Without a Country*, chap. 8, and *If This Isn't Nice, What Is?* (Second Edition), chap. 2, and derives from Vonnegut's commencement address at Agnes Scott College on May 15, 1999. Video of that speech is at http://www.c-span.org/video/?123554-1/agnes-scott-college-commencement-address.

"Whereas formal religions": *God Bless You, Dr. Kevorkian*, Introduction, 12. By the way, Vonnegut did capitalize *Humanism* sometimes, as shown elsewhere—including just two years earlier, in *Timequake*. (See chapter 12 of this book.)

"Humanism is a progressive lifestance": American Humanist Association, https://americanhumanist.org/what-is-humanism/definition-of-humanism/.

"The goal of maximizing": Pinker, *Enlightenment Now: The Case for Reason, Science, Humanism, and Progress* (New York: Viking, 2018), 410.

"acts and policies" and "The consequences needn't": *Enlightenment Now*, 416.

"I urge you to please notice": *A Man Without a Country*, 132.

Chapter 2: About Five Dollars for Each Corpse

Epigraph "It was the largest massacre": *Mother Night*, Introduction, vi. (Also see note under "Children's Crusade" subheading below.)

several dozen fellow American prisoners: Biographer Charles J. Shields wrote that "150 POWs from the 106th" were sent to Dresden (*And So It Goes: Kurt Vonnegut, A Life*, 62), a number that also appears in Vonnegut's May 29, 1945, letter home (*Armageddon in Retrospect*, 11) and in his 1946 essay "Wailing Shall Be in All Streets" (*Armageddon in Retrospect*, 35). But, during his National Air and Space Museum speech in May 1990, Vonnegut said he was with ninety-nine fellow POWs in the Dresden labor detail (*Fates Worse Than Death*, chap. X, 101). Of course, it's possible that 150 American POWs were taken to Dresden and that only 100 of them were in the slaughterhouse during the Dresden bombing.

"our six guards": *Mother Night*, Introduction, vi. Uncited details about Vonnegut's wartime experience in this chapter also come from *Mother Night*'s 1966 introduction and from other sources, primarily History.com, Wikipedia, *Among the Dead Cities: The History and Moral Legacy of the WWII Bombing of Civilians in Germany and Japan* by British humanist and philosophy professor A. C. Grayling (New York: Walker and Company, 2006), and the Shields biography, *And So It Goes*.

tens of thousands of inhabitants had been incinerated: Estimates of deaths during the February 13–15 air raids on Dresden have ranged over the years from 8,000 to more than 200,000, due to varying agendas and the indeterminate number of refugees who had flowed into the city from the eastern front with Russia. *Slaughterhouse-Five*, chapter 8, claims that one hundred and thirty thousand died. Vonnegut in his May 1990 speech at the National Air and Space Museum said a death total of 135,000 "sounds right to me" (*Fates Worse Than Death*, chap. X, 101), and he used that figure as late as 2005 (*A Man Without a Country*, chap. 2, 17). Vonnegut and many standard reference volumes apparently got the figure from *The Destruction of Dresden*, David Irving's 1963 book from which Vonnegut quotes in chapter 9 of *Slaughterhouse-Five*. Vonnegut's novel contains excerpts from two forewords to Irving's book, written by retired military commanders who both cite the 135,000 figure. (Irving, by the way, later was convicted in Austria of being a Holocaust denier.) But many other sources cite a much lower Dresden death total. Irving himself, in later editions of his book, restated the number of dead to as few as 50,000 (https://en.wikipedia.org/wiki/David_Irving). Back in 1966 Irving had acknowledged in a letter to *The Times* (London) that the total was likely closer to twenty-five thousand, citing an area police chief's March 1945 report to which he gained access after his book was first published. That same report is cited in British historian Frederick Taylor's *Dresden: Tuesday, February 13, 1945* (New York: Harper Perennial, 2005), 351–352. Taylor thoroughly reviews propaganda efforts that inflated the total and ultimately concludes that, taking into account the imprecise tally of buried corpses, "the fairest estimate seems...to lie between twenty-five thousand and forty thousand" (448). Grayling's *Among the Dead Cities* includes in the appendix a "schedule of RAF bombing attacks on Germany" (page 325) that shows "More than 30,000 dead/250,000 bombed out" in Dresden on February 13–14, 1945. In the book itself Grayling says "The firestorm... killed somewhere in the region of 25,000 people" (page 72), which he calls "the most conservative figure, though the number of unrecognizable bodies, and the number of refugees, probably means that the figure should be higher" (page 333). The uncredited article "Bombing of Dresden" at History.com finds it "improbable that only 35,000 of the million or so people in Dresden at the time were killed. Cellars and other shelters would have been meager protection against a firestorm that blew poisonous air heated to hundreds of degrees Fahrenheit across the city at hurricane-like speeds" (https://www.history.com/topics/world-war-ii/battle-of-dresden). A group of historians commissioned by the city of Dresden produced a report, published in March 2010, on the death total from the February 1945 air raid. The report (available at: https://www.dresden.de/media/pdf/stadtarchiv/Historikerkommission_Dresden1945_Abschlussbericht_V1_14a.pdf) is in German, but Jan-Christian Petersen, founder of the Humanist Initiative in Schleswig-Holstein, Germany, wrote this to me (September 3, 2021, email): "In that report the historians came to an elaborate but slightly differentiated conclusion. The official death toll is 18,000–20,000. That is mentioned in bold letters in the PDF at the bottom of page 49. Viewing the occurrences from another perspective, it is also correct to conclude that 'up to 25,000 people were killed in the air raids on Dresden.' That is mentioned in bold letters at the end of page 67. However, the whole report clearly shows that a higher death toll is false and misleading."

"We heard the bombs walking around": *Mother Night*, Introduction, vi.

"Now and then there would be": *Mother Night*, Introduction, vi-vii.

"But not me": "Letter from PFC Kurt Vonnegut, Jr., to his family, May 29, 1945," *Armageddon in Retrospect*, 12.

"The importance of Dresden": David Standish, "*Playboy* Interview: Kurt Vonnegut, Jr." (*Playboy*, July 1973), 70. The interview is reprinted in *Conversations with Kurt Vonnegut*, ed. William Rodney Allen (Jackson, MS: University Press of Mississippi, 1988), and in *Wampeters, Foma & Granfalloons*. Vonnegut edited the interview and wrote, "It is what I *should* have said, not what I *really* said" (*Wampeters*, Preface, xxii).

"During the question-and-answer": *Fates Worse Than Death*, chap. XVI, 156. The National Air and Space Museum speech was presented on May 3, 1990, according to Jerome Klinkowitz, *Vonnegut in Fact: The Public Spokesmanship of Personal Fiction* (Columbia, SC: University of South Carolina Press, 1998), 24.

his mother overdosed on sleeping pills and died: Vonnegut later referred to his mother's death as a suicide. There is no definitive evidence. In *Pity the Reader: On Writing with Style* (New York: Seven Stories Press, 2019), his friend Suzanne McConnell wrote this: "Kurt's brother and father weren't certain. She was a writer and left no note. But she was a very absent, depressed mother, locking herself in her room for long periods. Mark [his son] thinks Kurt may have lumped all that absence together as 'suicide.'"

Justifiable homicide?

"the Dresden atrocity": Introduction, *Slaughterhouse-Five* (Franklin Center, Pennsylvania: Franklin Library, 1978), reprinted in *Palm Sunday*, chap. XVII, 301.

"World War II was a good one": Robert Scholes, "A Talk with Kurt Vonnegut, Jr." (1966 interview), in *The Vonnegut Statement: Original Essays on the Life and Work of Kurt Vonnegut, Jr.*, Jerome Klinkowitz and John Somer, eds. (New York: Dell Publishing, 1973), 118.

"about as sinister": National Air and Space Museum speech, *Fates Worse Than Death*, chap. X, 100.

Notes

"How the hell do I feel": Richard Todd, "The Masks of Kurt Vonnegut, Jr.," *New York Times Magazine*, January 24, 1971, reprinted in *Conversations with Kurt Vonnegut*, 34.

"If it's always wrong": Undated paper at http://docplayer.net/43734073-A-humanist-discussion-of-war.html.

"I was flunking": David Hayman, David Michaelis, George Plimpton, and Richard Rhodes, "Kurt Vonnegut, The Art of Fiction No. LXIV," *Paris Review*, No. 69, Spring 1977, reprinted in *Conversations with Kurt Vonnegut*, 181.

"self-interview": *Conversations with Kurt Vonnegut* (see previous note) reprints the *Paris Review* introduction, which explains that the interview had been stitched together from four sessions between the mid–1960s and 1976 and had "gone through an extensive working over by the subject himself" (page 168), and Vonnegut's admission that "with uptmost tenderness, I interviewed myself" (194). Vonnegut eliminated that last quote in the *Palm Sunday* chapter containing the piece, but he added, "This interview is purely written. Not a word of it was spoken aloud" (chap. V, 83).

"World War II made war reputable": Douglas Brinkley, "Vonnegut's Apocalypse," *Rolling Stone*, August 24, 2006, 78.

"thought it was not only a duty": This is in Vonnegut's comment following "What My Son Mark Wanted Me to Tell the Psychiatrists in Philadelphia, Which was Also the Afterword to a New Edition of His Book *The Eden Express*," *Fates Worse Than Death*, 208.

"near-Holy motives": "Wailing Shall Be in All Streets," *Armageddon in Retrospect*, 44.

"Especially from the point of view": A. C. Graymling, interview on Philosophy Bites podcast (beginning just past the two-minute mark), November 9, 2008, http://philosophybites.com/2008/11/anthony-graylin.html.

"This isn't to say": Speckhardt, *Creating Change Through Humanism* (Washington, DC: Humanist Press, 2015), 119.

"a war crime": Victor Gregg, "I survived the bombing of Dresden and continue to believe it was a war crime," *The Guardian*, February 15, 2013, https://www.theguardian.com/commentisfree/2013/feb/15/bombing-dresden-war-crime. Gregg goes on to cite air raids in Bosnia, Benghazi, and elsewhere in Europe long after Dresden and "the manner in which as a nation we still tend to be sympathetic to the use of superior aircraft strength to bomb overcrowded refugee centres" as reasons for his continued anger.

"there is nothing intelligent": *Slaughterhouse-Five*, chap. 1, 19.

"to say something," "dropped an atom bomb" and "Jesus—I dunno": *Happy Birthday, Wanda June*, Act 1, Scene 1, 2.

"It was a bitch": *Happy Birthday, Wanda June*, Act 1, Scene 1, 3.

"Certainly enemy military": "Wailing Shall Be in All Streets," *Armageddon in Retrospect*, 43.

"pure nonsense, pointless destruction": *A Man Without a Country,* chap. 2, 17.

"The whole city was burned down": *A Man Without a Country,* chap. 2, 17–18.

"American civilians and ground troops": "Kurt Vonnegut: The Art of Fiction LXIV," *Paris Review,* reprinted in *Conversations with Kurt Vonnegut,* 174.

"It wasn't as though the bombardiers": *Fates Worse Than Death,* chap. X, 101.

"was a work of art": Speech, National Air and Space Museum, May 1990, *Fates Worse Than Death,* 103. The next few quotes, through "That is how crazy we had all become," are from the same source and page.

Poo-tee-weet?

"no important differences": *Slaughterhouse-Five,* chap. 2, 34.

"look at all the different moments": *Slaughterhouse-Five,* chap. 2, 27.

"Well, here we are": *Slaughterhouse-Five,* chap. 4, 77.

"is just fine in plenty": *Slaughterhouse-Five,* chap. 2, 27.

"not about time travel": "'I Was There': On Kurt Vonnegut," *The Nation,* May 16, 2012, https://www.thenation.com/article/i-was-there-kurt-vonnegut/.

"a movie about American bombers": This and the next three quotes are from *Slaughterhouse-Five,* chap. 4, 74–75.

Children's Crusade

"amid the smashed masonry": *Armageddon in Retrospect,* 75.

"a number of human beings": *Armageddon in Retrospect,* 110.

"over one hundred thousand": *Armageddon in Retrospect,* 37.

"Wailing Shall Be in All Streets"…was turned down repeatedly: Strand, *The Brothers Vonnegut: Science and Fiction in the House of Magic,* chap. 3, 54–55.

"It is with some regret": and "we surely created": *Armageddon in Retrospect,* 40.

"The death of Dresden": *Armageddon in Retrospect,* 43.

"but I felt then": *Armageddon in Retrospect,* 45.

"I thought it would be easy": *Slaughterhouse-Five,* chap. 1, 2.

"He was astonished": *God Bless You, Mr. Rosewater,* chap. 13, 175.

"Eliot, rising from his seat": *God Bless You, Mr. Rosewater,* chap. 13, 176.

"was the largest massacre": *Mother Night,* Introduction, vi. This is almost certainly an exaggeration that uses an inaccurate death count for Dresden (see earlier note for first section of this chapter). The Battle of Hamburg (aka Operation Gomorrah, July 24 to August 3, 1943), for example, resulted in 42,600 deaths, according to Wikipedia, https://en.wikipedia.org/wiki/Bombing_of_Hamburg_in_World_War_II, citing Noble Frankland and Charles Webster, *The Strategic Air Offensive Against Germany, 1939–1945, Volume II: Endeavour, Part 4,* London: Her Majesty's Stationery Office (1961, no publisher given), 260–261.

Notes

Vonnegut intends "massacre" to mean "something that happens suddenly," he told NPR interviewer Terry Gross when he repeated the "largest massacre in European history" claim in May 1986, https://www.npr.org/templates/story/story.php?storyId=9567370, so he might not have considered the longer duration of the Hamburg bombings to qualify even had he acknowledged a higher death count there than for Dresden's two days of raids.

"If I'd been born in Germany": *Mother Night*, Introduction vii.

"You were just babies": *Slaughterhouse-Five*, chap. 1, 14.

"there won't be a part": *Slaughterhouse-Five*, chap. 1, 15.

"lousy little book": *Slaughterhouse-Five*, chap. 1, 2.

"The war parts": *Slaughterhouse-Five*, chap. 1, 1.

"the loveliest city": *Slaughterhouse-Five*, chap. 6, 148.

"That was I": *Slaughterhouse-Five*, chap. 5, 125.

Poor Edgar Derby…is modeled after: Shields, *And So It Goes*, 75–76.

"on a hospital cart of starvation and despair": from "Unknown Soldier" by Joe Reinan, *Democrat and Chronicle* of Rochester, NY, May 3, 1995, reprinted in *Shadows of Slaughterhouse Five: Recollections and Reflections of the American Ex-POWs of Schlachthof Funf, Dresden, Germany* by Ervin E. Szpek Jr. and Frank J. Idzikowski (Bloomington, IN: iUniverse, 2008), chap. 13, "The Death of Edward Crone—Giving Up on Life," 374–379, https://books.google.com/books?id=nkLvXopZLRwC&printsec=frontcover&hl=en#v=onepage&q=Crone&f=false. Vonnegut wrote that Crone "let himself starve to death before the firestorm" (*Fates Worse Than Death*, 107), leaving slightly unclear whether Crone died or simply *decided* to die prior to the deadly air raids. Some accounts suggest Crone did not succumb until after the bombing. Reinan in his *Democrat and Chronicle* article writes that Crone "witnessed the firebombing of Dresden in February 1945," and Shields (*And So It Goes*, 76–77) describes Crone dying in April 1945, based on an interview with a man who was in the same unit.

"Joe was deeply religious": Reinan, "Unknown Soldier."

"Billy wouldn't do anything": *Slaughterhouse-Five*, chap. 2, 34.

well over thirty thousand: The figure is based on information at https://www.archives.gov/research/military/vietnam-war/casualty-statistics showing 36,956 American fatal casualties in Vietnam through 1968; the *Life* magazine issue of June 27, 1969, noting 36,000 American deaths by that time (http://time.com/3485726/faces-of-the-american-dead-in-vietnam-one-weeks-toll-june-1969/); and the Public Broadcasting System website stating that the Korean War's US casualty count of 33,629 was passed in Vietnam in April 1969 http://www.pbs.org/battlefieldvietnam/timeline/index3.html.

on best-seller lists for months, peaking at number four: https://en.wikipedia.org/wiki/Slaughterhouse-Five.

"doing quite well": *Slaughterhouse-Five*, chap. 1, 4.

"living in easy circumstances": *Slaughterhouse-Five*, title page.

"Being present at the destruction": *Palm Sunday*, chap. XVII, 301.

"I...learned only that people": Introduction, *Slaughterhouse-Five*, Franklin Library, reprinted in *Palm Sunday*, chap. XVII, 301–302.

"about five dollars for each corpse": *Fates Worse Than Death*, chap. X, 100.

A Reading from the First Book of Bokonon

"In the beginning": *Cat's Cradle*, chap. 118, 188.

Chapter 3: Comforting Lies

Epigraph "Live by the foma": Epigraph, *Cat's Cradle*.

"Only in superstition": "Up is Better Than Down," *Vogue*, August 1, 1970, reprinted as "Address to Graduating Class of Bennington College, 1970" in *Wampeters, Foma & Granfalloons*, 163–164.

In fact, it ended up being: The accounts of Vonnegut's thesis submissions are from Shields, *And So It Goes.*, 276.

"similarities between the Cubist": *Bagombo Snuff Box*, Introduction, 7.

"It confirmed my atheism": Hayman, et al., "Kurt Vonnegut, The Art of Fiction No. LXIV," *Paris Review*, reprinted in *Conversations with Kurt Vonnegut*, 181.

the actual historical group of Lakotans: The accounts of the new Lakotan religion and the events at Wounded Knee are from fold3.com, at https://www.fold3.com/page/1296_lakotathe_massacre_at_wounded_knee#description, and Indian Country Today, https://indiancountrymedianetwork.com/history/events/wounded-knee-healing-the-wounds-of-the-past/. The Sioux death count sometimes is given as lower, if casualties subsequent to the massacre itself are not included.

A useful religion

"don't say anything": Standish, "*Playboy* Interview," 59.

"'Thou shalt not kill'": Standish, "*Playboy* Interview," 59.

"the information that they need" and "Well, I'm giving them": "Kurt Vonnegut," from transcript of September 15, 1970, *60 Minutes* segment, *Conversations with Kurt Vonnegut*, 19.

"Anyone unable to understand": *Cat's Cradle*, chap. 4, 4.

"cynically and playfully": *Cat's Cradle*, chap. 78, 121.

"I wanted all things": *Cat's Cradle*, chap. 58, 90–91.

"became the one real instrument": *Cat's Cradle*, chap. 78, 121.

"Truth was the enemy": *Cat's Cradle*, chap. 78, 121–122.

"So I said good-bye": *Cat's Cradle*, chap. 78, 122.

"The truth was that life" and "both became": *Cat's Cradle*, chap. 79, 123.
"a whopping lie": *Cat's Cradle*, chap. 65, 101.
"strikingly Bokononist": *Cat's Cradle*, chap. 114, 180.
"a very un-ambassadorial thing": *Cat's Cradle*, chap. 114, 180.
"We are gathered here": *Cat's Cradle*, chap. 114, 180–181.
"Not even God": *Cat's Cradle*, chap. 94, 149.

Plausible new religions
"has a congregation": "Report on the Barnhouse Effect," *Welcome to the Monkey House*, 162.
"all the different kinds": *The Sirens of Titan*, chap. 1, 9.
"That Earth's glorious victory": *The Sirens of Titan*, chap. 7, 177.
"Any man who would": *The Sirens of Titan*, chap. 7, 176.
"Rumfoord's humanistic anti-faith": *Unstuck in Time*, New York: Seven Stories Press (2011), 51.
"Puny man can do nothing," "Take Care of the People" and "Why should you believe": *The Sirens of Titan*, chap. 7, 183.
"the weakest and the meekest": *The Sirens of Titan*, chap. 10, 224.
"During my next visit": *The Sirens of Titan*, chap. 7, 184.
"the most popular American religion": *Slapstick*, chap. 38, 210.
"We must drop" and "I marvelled": *Slapstick*, chap. 38, 212.
"I'm not averse": "Humanism and Its Discontents," adapted from June 8, 2007, speech and question-and-answer session for TheHumanist.com, https://thehumanist.com/magazine/november-december-2007/features/humanism-and-its-discontents.

Pretend to be good always
"merely ludicrous" and "so many people": *Mother Night*, chap. 29, 122.
"I would fool": *Mother Night*, chap. 9, 31.
"No matter what I was": *Mother Night*, chap. 10, 33–34.
"This war isn't going to let": *Mother Night*, chap. 9, 30.
"I became what I am": *Mother Night*, chap. 10, 34.
"Tell them the things": *Mother Night*, chap. 3, 9.
"We are what we pretend": *Mother Night*, Introduction, v.
"a man who served evil": *Mother Night*, Editor's Note, xii.
"the man who perceived": *Mother Night*, chap. 43, 185.
"absolutely pure evil": *Mother Night*, chap. 43, 188.

"There are plenty of good reasons": *Mother Night*, chap. 43, 190.

"Pretend to be good always": *God Bless You, Mr. Rosewater*, chap. 14, 177.

"Belief is nearly": *Bluebeard*, chap. 19, 152.

Different kinds of truth

"intolerable balancing...true feelings" and "I felt and still feel": *Happy Birthday, Wanda June*, preface, ix.

"many people find": *Fates Worse Than Death*, chap. X, 104.

"where all the different": *The Sirens of Titan*, chap. 1, 9.

"the fourteenth edition": *The Sirens of Titan*, chap. 1, 8.

"There is room enough": *The Sirens of Titan*, chap. 1, 8.

"there are so many different": *The Sirens of Titan*, chap. 1, 9.

"they would get into": *The Sirens of Titan*, chap. 1, 8.

"where each Daddy could finally": *The Sirens of Titan*, chap. 1, 9.

"a first-grader should" and "but it's more than fashionable": Standish, "*Playboy* Interview," 74.

"People will believe": Standish, "*Playboy* Interview," 216.

"accept our life as all" and "the rich heritage": See Appendix C, "Humanism and Its Aspirations."

"hobgoblins": *Galápagos*, Book One, chap. 4, 17.

Chapter 4: Thanks a Lot, Big Brain

Epigraph "Nothing ever happens": Leon Trout (narrator), *Galápagos*, Book Two, chap. 8, 259.

"bacterium which eats": *Galápagos*, Book One, chap. 33, 186.

"Human beings had": *Galápagos*, Book One, chap. 1, 3.

"Nobody believed anybody": *Galápagos*, Book One, chap. 14, 70.

"When I was alive": *Galápagos*, Book One, chap. 6, 29.

"the hobgoblins of opinions": *Galápagos*, Book One, chap. 4, 17.

"Take it from somebody": *Galápagos*, Book One, chap. 32, 77.

"The best book I ever wrote": *Fates Worse Than Death*, chap. XIV, 131.

he told radio show host Terry Gross: NPR's *Fresh Air*, May 13, 1986, rebroadcast April 13, 2007, http://www.npr.org/templates/story/story.php?storyId=9567370.

He had previously given grades: *Palm Sunday*, chap. 18, 311–312. Vonnegut was not ranking his books within all of world literature but was, he said, "comparing myself to myself."

Notes

"That's an A+": Kevin P. Simonson, "Kurt Vonnegut Visits a Strip Club," *Hustler*, December 2016.

"I'm not very grateful for Darwin"
"the most broadly influential" and "did more to stabilize": *Galápagos*, Book One, chap. 3, 13.

"I'm not very grateful": Standish, "*Playboy* Interview," 59.

"would become the mothers": *Galápagos*, Book One, chap. 27, 153.

"It is not the fittest": Lorrie Moore, "How Humans Got Flippers and Beaks," *New York Times*, October 6, 1985, https://www.nytimes.com/1985/10/06/books/how-humans-got-flippers-and-beaks.html.

"Evolution can go to hell": *A Man Without a Country*, chap. 2, 9.

In memory of Hollis L. Howie and "and he told us the names": *Galápagos*, Dedication.

"I have seen those birds": *Fates Worse Than Death*, chap. XV, 142.

"This was a very innocent planet": *Galápagos*, Book One, chap. 2, 9.

"There is no stopping us": From "Light at the End of the Tunnel?," *Lear's* magazine, November/December 1988, reprinted in *Fates Worse Than Death*, chap. XI, 116.

"a sort of old poop": From *Lear's*, in *Fates Worse Than Death*, chap. XI, 113.

"Almost none of the ancient wise men": From *Lear's*, in *Fates Worse Than Death*, chap. XI, 116.

"The good Earth": *A Man Without a Country*, chap. 11, 122.

"a planetary duty": See Appendix C, "Humanism and Its Aspirations."

Hope for humankind
"In spite of everything": *Galápagos*, Epigraph. The quote is from Anne Frank's *Diary of a Young Girl*.

"You'll learn, you'll learn": *Galápagos*, Book Two, chap. 13, 295.

"You believe that human beings": *Galápagos*, Book Two, chap. 7, 257.

"looked back at the tunnel" and "I have now completed": *Galápagos*, Book Two, chap. 8, 259.

Life: Half Full or Half Empty?
"Hey, Corporal Vonnegut": "Address to Graduating Class of Bennington College, 1970," *Wampeters, Foma & Granfalloons*, 162. Vonnegut most often referred to himself as a private in the army, but upon returning stateside after the war he was promoted and assigned to Fort Riley, Kansas (Shields, *And So It Goes*, 79).

"Everything is going to become": "Address to Graduating Class of Bennington

College, 1970," *Wampeters, Foma & Granfalloons*, 162.

"I couldn't survive my own pessimism": Standish, "*Playboy* Interview," 60.

"For two thirds of my life": Address to Hobart and William Smith Colleges, May 26, 1974, *Palm Sunday*, chap. XI, 209–210.

"I'm really quite optimistic": Interview on *Reader's Almanac*, WNYC, January 2, 1983, http://www.wnyc.org/story/vonnegut-deadeye-dick .

"I think the human situation": Speech at Chautauqua Institution, 1989, https://vimeo.com/261003598/e7d003a6dc?blm_aid=6320310 .

"I'm pessimistic just 'cause": *Across Indiana*, 1991, at 5:42, https://www.youtube.com/watch?v=9X8fT3_fdZc .

"It seems to me that it's no more": From *An Unsentimental Education: Writers and Chicago*, University of Chicago Press, 1995, published as "How I Got My First Job as a Reporter and Learned to Write in a Simple, Direct Way, While Not Getting a Degree in Anthropology" in *If This Isn't Nice, What Is?* (Second Edition), 157.

"I believe in original sin": *Timequake*, chap. 61, 202.

"I know now that there is": *A Man Without a Country*, chap. 7, 71.

"I have to have been": *A Man Without a Country*, Author's Note, 142.

"There is nothing": Brinkley, "Vonnegut's Apocalypse," 78.

"My country is in ruins": From "God Bless You, Mr. Vonnegut," interview by J. Rentilly, *U.S. Airways Magazine*, June 2007 (© Project 13 Productions), reprinted in *Kurt Vonnegut: The Last Interview and Other Conversations*, Tom McCartan, ed. (Brooklyn, NY: Melville House, 2011), 161.

Chapter 5: A Great Time for Comedians

Epigraph "Jokes can be noble": From Vonnegut's Palm Sunday speech at St. Clement's Episcopal Church, *Palm Sunday*, chap. XIX, 327–328.

"I had to laugh like hell": Jack Patton, the *Hocus Pocus* character, is shot to death by a sniper in Vietnam (chap. 6, 52).

"We aim for our fullest": See Appendix C, "Humanism and Its Aspirationns."

"Affirmations of Humanism: A Statement of its Principles": Paul Kurtz, *Free Inquiry*, https://www.secularhumanism.org/index.php/12.

Researchers report laughter-like reactions: There are innumerable studies about animal laughter, but see the article "Do animals have a sense of humour?" by Peter Mcgraw and Joel Warner, Slate, March 27, 2014, https://www.newscientist.com/article/dn25312-do-animals-have-a-sense-of-humour/.

"Laughter is...not simply": "Did laughter make the mind?," Aeon, February 11, 2019, https://aeon.co/essays/does-laughter-hold-the-key-to-human-consciousness.

Notes

The soul seeking some relief

"scientific truth was going": "Address to Graduating Class at Bennington College, 1970," *Wampeters, Foma & Granfalloons*, 161.

"I have been a consistent pessimist": "Address to Graduating Class at Bennington College, 1970," *Wampeters, Foma & Granfalloons*, 162.

"earned optimism": Comments by Dan Simon in this paragraph were made on January 20, 2022, during a Kurt Vonnegut Museum and Library online event, "Welcome to Earth Babies: Vonnegut @ 100," via Zoom.

"He had an odd kind of optimism": Mark Vonnegut during "Welcome to Earth Babies: Vonnegut @ 100," January 20, 2022.

"Even in the darkest times": *Galápagos*, Book Two, chap. 8, 259.

"You'll learn, you'll learn": *Galápagos*, Book Two, chap. 13, 295.

"Oh, happy Meat": *Bluebeard*, chap. 37, 300.

"We are still in the Dark Ages": *Deadeye Dick*, Epilogue, 240.

"a sardonic fable in a bed of gloom": *Fates Worse Than Death*, 184. Vonnegut attributes the phrase to William Keough in *Punchlines: The Violence of American Humor* (New York: Paragon House, 1990).

comedy is tragedy plus time: The first verified appearance of the phrase (in the form "Tragedy plus time equals comedy") was by Steve Allen in *Cosmopolitan* magazine in 1957, according to Quote Investigator, https://quoteinvestigator.com/2013/06/25/comedy-plus/.

"A laughing prophet of doom." Larry L. King, *New York Times Book Review*, September 1, 1968. Special thanks to Quote Investigator for tracking this down. Its entry about the quote is at https://quoteinvestigator.com/2019/11/25/laugh-prophet/.

"Some things aren't funny": *A Man Without a Country*, chap. 1, 2–3.

"Do you think a literary agent" and "For book club": *Mother Night*, chap. 29, 128.

"There would be Jews": *Mother Night*, chap. 5, 14.

"the banality of evil": Arendt, *Eichmann in Jerusalem: A Report on the Banality of Evil* (New York: Viking Press, 1963).

Only one way to get anybody's attention

"way of dealing with": Standish, "*Playboy* Interview," 66.

"Well, I try": Standish, "*Playboy* Interview," 66.

"It is my serious belief": *Fates Worse Than Death*, chap. XX, 194.

"An exaggeration of the truth": Chatalogical Humor, April 24, 2017, https://live.washingtonpost.com/chatological-humor-20170424.html?hpid=hp_chat-schedule-desktop_no-name%3Ahomepage%2Fchat-schedule.

"Humor is one of the most serious": From Jong's letter published in *The New York Times Book Review*, July 29, 1984, page BR27, column 2. Special thanks to quoteinvestigator.com for tracking this down. Its entry about the Jung quote is at https://quoteinvestigator.com/2019/11/23/humor.

"a satirist with a heart": "Still Asking the Embarrassing Questions," *New York Times*, September 9, 1990, http://movies2.nytimes.com/books/97/09/28/lifetimes/vonnegut-hocuspocus.html.

"All I really wanted to do": *A Man Without a Country*, chap. 12, 130.

"We are here on Earth": *A Man Without a Country*, illustration, 54. The line first appeared in *Timequake*, chap. 57, 191, published when Vonnegut was seventy-four.

"The telling of jokes is an art": J. Rentilly, "The Best Jokes Are Dangerous," McSweeney's, September 2002, https://www.mcsweeneys.net/articles/the-best-jokes-are-dangerous-an-interview-with-kurt-vonnegut-part-three.

"often as brilliant" "they have probably": *Between Time and Timbuktu, or Prometheus-5* (New York: Delta, 1972), Preface, xvii.

"screamingly adorable" and "did their best": *Slapstick*, Prologue, 1. The novel is dedicated to Laurel and Hardy.

"I used to laugh and laugh": *A Man Without a Country*, chap. 1, 4.

"People still laugh": *Galápagos*, Book One, chap. 36, 204.

"was a great time": Scholes, "A Talk with Kurt Vonnegut, Jr.," *The Vonnegut Statement*, 109. The interview took place in October 1966.

"When I was the littlest kid": Hayman, et al., "Kurt Vonnegut, The Art of Fiction No. LXIV," *Paris Review*, reprinted in *Conversations with Kurt Vonnegut*, 192.

An air of defeat

the person for whom he said he wrote: *Bagombo Snuff Box* introduction, 13.

"'Soap opera!' ": *Slapstick*, Prologue, 12.

"Exhaustion, yes": *Slapstick*, Prologue, 14.

"full retreat from life" and "an air of defeat": *Jailbird*, Prologue, 13.

"I'm damned if I'll pass": Standish, "*Playboy* Interview," 216.

"Until recently, every twenty days": Standish, "*Playboy* Interview," 62.

"But for me": Standish, "*Playboy* Interview," 66.

"But any sadness": Standish, "*Playboy* Interview," 66.

"Gallows humor is nothing much": Vance Bourjaily, "What Kurt Vonnegut Is and Isn't," *The New York Times*, August 13, 1972, http://www.nytimes.com/1972/08/13/archives/what-vonnegut-is-and-isnt-vonnegut.html?_r=0.

"people laughing in the middle": Standish, "*Playboy* Interview," 66.

"It's humor about weak": Standish, "*Playboy* Interview," 68.

"My fascination with it": Standish, "*Playboy* Interview," 216.

"Sons of suicide," "blew his brains out" and "Characteristically, they find": *God Bless You, Mr. Rosewater*, chap. 8, 103.

"monopolar depressive": *Timequake*, chap. 26, 89.

"Suicide is at the heart": Standish, "*Playboy* Interview," 214–216.

"This is a very bad book": *Breakfast of Champions*, chap. 18, 193.

"unconscious from a combination": Shields, 362.

"I had tried to kill myself": *Fates Worse Than Death*, chap. XVIII, 181.

An optimist posing as a pessimist

"There was a bizarre," "Of all the medications" and "He didn't want to be happy": *Armageddon in Retrospect*, Introduction, 7.

"He was more angry than depressed": Mark Vonnegut, email message to author, February 13, 2019.

"As he aged": Nanette Vonnegut, email message to author, March 1, 2019.

"It wasn't until the Iraq War": *Armageddon in Retrospect*, Introduction, 7.

"Many years ago I was so innocent": *A Man Without a Country*, chap. 7, 71.

No tomorrow

"Religious skeptics often become": *Palm Sunday*, chap. VIII, 168.

"For whatever reason": "Notes From My Bed of Gloom: Or, Why the Joking Had to Stop," *The New York Times*, April 22, 1990, section 7, page 14, https://www.nytimes.com/1990/04/22/books/notes-from-my-bed-of-gloom-or-why-the-joking-had-to-stop.html.

"But jokesters are all through": *Fates Worse Than Death*, chap. XIX, 185.

"We have squandered": *A Man Without a Country*, chap. 4, 44–45.

"The biggest truth to face now": *A Man Without a Country*, chap. 7, 70.

"It may be that I am": *A Man Without a Country*, chap. 12, 129–130.

Highest ideals

"It would be a mistake to think": Clay Farris Naff, "Enlightenment Wow: The *Humanist* Interview with Steven Pinker," *The Humanist*, March/April 2018, 13.

"Certainly, if anyone were": Naff, 16.

"unduly simplistic": Nick Spencer, "Enlightenment and Progress, or why Steven Pinker is wrong," Theos Think Tank, February 20, 2018, https://www.theosthinktank.co.uk/comment/2018/02/20/enlightenment-and-progress-or-why-steven-pinker-is-wrong.

"profoundly maddening" and "has little patience for": Jennifer Szalai, "Steven Pinker Wants You to Know Humanity Is Doing Fine. Just Don't Ask About Individual Humans," *The New York Times*, February 28, 2018, https://www.nytimes.com/2018/02/28/books/review-enlightenment-now-steven-pinker.html.

"Humanism and Its Aspirations" excerpts: See Appendix C.

An aspirin tablet

"During the years of his friendship": Offit, Foreword, *Look at the Birdie* (New York: Dial Press Trade Paperback, 2009), vii.

"He looked really morose": From "Morley Safer Remembers Kurt Vonnegut," interview by David Meyer recorded January 20, 2011, https://www.youtube.com/watch?v=xZD4fKnyXzg.

"He was one of the most": Shawn E. Milnes, "How Kurt Vonnegut's First and Only Opera Was Completed," *The Daily Beast*, September 14, 2016, http://www.thedailybeast.com/articles/2016/09/14/how-kurt-vonnegut-s-first-and-only-opera-was-completed.html.

"Like my distinct betters": *A Man Without a Country*, chap. 8, 88.

"How beautiful it is": *A Man Without a Country*, chap. 6, 62.

"Humor can be a relief": *A Man Without a Country*, chap. 12, 130.

"I think he always had the seeds": Nanette Vonnegut, email message to author, March 1, 2019.

Chapter 6: A Man Within a Country

Epigraph "The aborigines didn't know": *Fates Worse Than Death*, chap. XVII, 175.

His occasional occupation: Vonnegut volunteered with the Alplaus, NY, fire station while he was working for General Electric in Schenectady (Strand, *The Brothers Vonnegut*, 108), and after his death he was saluted by that firehouse's tolling bell (Gregory Sumner, "Vonnegut's Firefighters," September 11, 2011, https://www.vonnegutlibrary.org/vonnegut's-firefighters/).

"Populists screaming in pain": "A Political Disease," *Wampeters, Foma & Granfalloons*, 234.

"Am I a New Journalist?": *Wampeters, Foma & Granfalloons*, Preface, xix-xx.

"In either case, the principal issue": *Wampeters, Foma & Granfalloons*, Preface, xx.

"stories and features": This definition of humanistic journalism is from the Department of Journalism and Media Studies at the Univerity of Florida—St. Petersburg, https://www.usf.edu/arts-sciences/departments/journalism/robert-dardenne-award.aspx.

Notes

An admirable nation

Details about the Nigerian civil war not attributed to Vonnegut in this chapter are from the Encyclopaedia Brittanica, https://www.britannica.com/place/Biafra.

"a committee of one": "Biafra: A People Betrayed," *McCall's*, April 1970, reprinted in *Wampeters, Foma & Granfalloons*, 142.

"I flew in from Gabon": *Wampeters, Foma & Granfalloons*, 140.

"move readers to voluptuous tears" and "an admirable nation": *Wampeters, Foma & Granfalloons*, 142.

"about one-third of all": *Wampeters, Foma & Granfalloons*, 146.

"It was embarrassing": *Wampeters, Foma & Granfalloons*, 155.

"I did it three days": *Wampeters, Foma & Granfalloons*, 153.

"It was like a free trip": *Wampeters, Foma & Granfalloons*, 142.

"They all had" and "We were taken to a training camp": *Wampeters, Foma & Granfalloons*, 147.

"His humor was superb": *Wampeters, Foma & Granfalloons*, 145.

"and that goddam Vonnegut": Bourjaily, "What Vonnegut Is and Isn't."

"You won't open your mouth" and "It was true": *Wampeters, Foma & Granfalloons*, 146.

"he finally found a country": Gary McMahon, *Kurt Vonnegut and the Centrifugal Force of Fate* (Jefferson, NC: McFarland & Company, 2009), 44.

A particularly maddening catastrophe

Details about Mozambique not otherwise attributed in this chapter are from William Finnegan's two-part article, "The Emergency," in the May 22 and 29, 1989, issues of *The New Yorker*, http://archives.newyorker.com/?i=1989-05-22#folio=044 and http://archives.newyorker.com/?i=1989-05-29#folio=068. Vonnegut refers to the articles in *Fates Worse Than Death* and presumably learned much background about Mozambique from them.

"This is a particularly maddening catastrophe" and "It should be a paradise": *The Dick Cavett Show*, October 25, 1989, https://www.shoutfactorytv.com/the-dick-cavett-show/the-dick-cavett-show-authors-kurt-vonnegut-october-25-1989/5632559369702d04dd964200.

perhaps forty-five thousand bandits: Part 1 of Finnegan's article (May 22, 1989, page 70), printed about eight months before Vonnegut's account, states that "estimates of the number of full-time Renamo soldiers range from eight thousand to twenty-five thousand." Finnegan includes an analysis of RENAMO forces that contains more nuance than the term "bandits" suggests. Some of the group's units were more organized than others. In fact, Finnegan writes, "the nature of the war is so different from region to region that it may be misleading to write about 'Renamo' " (page 71).

"had been raping and murdering" and "Our own State Department estimates": "My Visit to Hell," *Parade*, January 7, 1990, excerpted in *Fates Worse Than Death*, chap. XVII, 169 and 170.

"that most awful of things" and "very close to the Sermon on the Mount": *The Dick Cavett Show*, October 25, 1989.

"They let their Government choose evil": "Slaughter in Mozambique," *New York Times*, November 14, 1989, https://www.nytimes.com/1989/11/14/opinion/slaughter-in-mozambique.html?searchResultPosition=1.

"[W]hat is new": *The Dick Cavett Show*, October 25, 1989.

"I confessed that something": *Fates Worse Than Death*, chap. XVII, 174.

Chapter 7: Science Certainly Tried

Epigraph "In all of history": *Kurt Vonnegut: Letters*, 405. During the 2007 memorial service for Vonnegut at the New York Society for Ethical Culture, historian Howard Zinn referred to what might have been the same unpublished Vonnegut letter. But he said it read simply, "I know of only one country that has dropped a nuclear bomb on innocent people" (the 41:25 mark at https://www.youtube.com/watch?v=7-BhShNUS2s). "*The New York Times* did not print that letter," Zinn said. "So much for freedom of the press."

"I marveled at all the epitaphs": *Happy Birthday, Wanda June*, preface, ix.

"I hold a master's degree in anthropology": *Fates Worse Than Death*, chap. II, 31.

"The most racist": "Kurt Vonnegut Interview" by David Barsamian, *The Progressive*, June 12, 2003, https://progressive.org/magazine/kurt-vonnegut-interview-barsamian/.

Good ways to kill more efficiently

Details about the bombings of Hiroshima and Nagasaki in this chapter primarily are from the Wikipedia entry, https://en.wikipedia.org/wiki/Atomic_bombings_of_Hiroshima_and_Nagasaki.

"If they do not now accept": Text of Truman's speech is available at https://millercenter.org/the-presidency/presidential-speeches/august-6-1945-statement-president-announcing-use-bomb.

"Ask all of those": *Fates Worse Than Death*, chap. X, 104.

Hiroshima was bombed: Options that Truman considered are summarized in "Harry S Truman's Decision to Use the Atomic Bomb" at https://www.nps.gov/articles/trumanatomicbomb.htm. A 1946 letter to *The Atlantic* and Truman's reply are at https://www.theatlantic.com/international/archive/2013/08/less-costly-struggle-and-bloodshed-i-the-atlantic-i-defends-hiroshima-in-1946/278407/. Pew Research Center's 2015 study that showed fifty-six percent of Americans still approved of the two Japan bombings is at http://www.pewglobal.org/2015/04/07/americans-japanese-mutual-respect-70-years-after-the-end-of-wwii/.

the only other defendable bombing: *Fates Worse Than Death*, chap. X, 104.

"During the '30s": Robert Musil, "There Must Be More to Love than Death: A Conversation with Kurt Vonnegut," *The Nation*, August 2–9, 1980, reprinted in *Conversation with Kurt Vonnegut*, 236–237.

"But for me it was terrible": Musil, "There Must Be More . . .," *The Nation*, reprinted in *Conversation with Kurt Vonnegut*, 232.

A much different sort of world order. Information in the next few paragraphs about German efforts to make an atomic bomb is from various sources, notably "German Atomic Bomb Project," October 18, 2016, at the Atomic Heritage Foundation website, https://www.atomicheritage.org/history/german-atomic-bomb-project, which is a good starting point for further exploration of this topic. Also consulted was Nicholas Dawidoff, *The Catcher Was a Spy* (New York: Pantheon Books, 1994), especially pages 156–158.

"Langmuir was absolutely indifferent": Musil, "There Must Be More...," *The Nation*, reprinted in *Conversation with Kurt Vonnegut*, 233–234.

"I'm no scientist": Hayman, et al., "Kurt Vonnegut, The Art of Fiction No. LXIV," *Paris Review*, reprinted in *Conversations with Kurt Vonnegut*, 183.

"His research had intended": Strand, *The Brothers Vonnegut*, 208.

"It can make quite a difference": *Fates Worse Than Death*, chap. XII, 117.

"A virtuous physicist": "Address to the American Physical Society," *Wampeters, Foma & Granfalloons*, 95–96.

"were afraid that careers in science" and "I tell them not to take more": "Address to the American Physical Society," *Wampeters, Foma & Granfalloons*, 100.

the self-described Luddite: Vonnegut applied the word to himself often. One example is that he continued using a typewriter long after word processors and then computer software became common tools for writers.

"I am a very bad scientist": *Cat's Cradle*, chap. 98, 155.

"space boondoggle": National Air and Space Museum speech, *Fates Worse Than Death*, chap. XI, 109.

"Our children have inherited technologies": *A Man Without a Country*, chap. 7, 70.

"Awareness without corresponding": Sandra Steingraber, "Despair Not," June 2011 *In These Times*, https://inthesetimes.com/article/despair-not.

"Action is the antidote to despair." Steingraber, "Despair Not."

"Science alone did not": Steingraber, "How we banned fracking in New York," EcoWatch.com, January 22, 2015, https://www.ecowatch.com/how-we-banned-fracking-in-new-york-1882001710.html#toggle-gdpr. (These are prepared remarks Steingraber gave during a victory party the previous day after a rally outside Cuomo's State of the State address.)

"I would not be interested": Frank McLaughlin, "An Interview with Kurt Vonnegut, Jr.," *Media and Methods*, May 1973, reprinted in *Conversations with Kurt Vonnegut*, 72.

"Writing and art": Simmons B. Buntin, "Speaking Truth to Power: An Interview with Sandra Steingraber," September 22, 2007, Terrain.org, https://www.terrain.org/2007/interviews/sandra-steingraber/.

"I used to think that science would save us": "Address to Graduating Class of Bennington College, 1970," *Wampeters, Foma & Granfalloons*, 163.

Something we started to do to ourselves

"It isn't knowledge" *Player Piano*, chap. Nine, 82.

"I think the trouble with Dresden": Musil, "There Must Be More . . .," *The Nation*, reprinted in *Conversation with Kurt Vonnegut*, 234.

"Science had given humanity": *Bagombo Snuff Box* (New York: Berkley Publishing Group, 2000), 29.

"rising to the top ... creatures from Pluto": "Why Social Justice Does More Than Art to Nourish the American Dream," speech at The State University of New York at Albany, May 20, 1972, in *If This Isn't Nice, What Is?* (Second Edition), 104.

"My guess is that": "Why Social Justice Does More Than Art to Nourish the American Dream," *If This Isn't Nice, What Is?* (Second Edition), 105.

"broken our hearts. It prolonged something": Standish, "*Playboy* Interview," 72.

"had become more and more": *Breakfast of Champions*, chap. 19, 209.

"made our leadership": *A Man Without a Country*, chap. 2, 20.

"taught us to resent": Standish, "*Playboy* Interview," 74.

"C-Students from Yale": *A Man Without a Country*, chap. 9, 99. Vonnegut offered the phrase as the title "for a really scary reality TV show."

"psychopathic personalities": *A Man Without a Country*, chap. 9, 88.

"haters of information," "unelected leaders," and "as the result": *A Man Without a Country*, chap. 9, 86–87.

"Our leaders are sick": Brinkley, "Vonnegut's Apocalypse," 78.

"This borders on the outrageous"

"any ill will towards": Excerpts are from Nason's "Darkness visible—an interview with Kurt Vonnegut," *The Australian*, November 19, 2005. Among the sites that quote extensively from the article and include comments about Vonnegut are https://www.crikey.com.au/2005/11/21/the-oz-takes-the-machete-to-kurt-vonnegut/ and http://forums.pelicanparts.com/off-topic-discussions/251995-darkness-visible-interview-kurt-vonnegut.html.

"Kurt Vonnegut Lauds Suicide Bombers": The post, by Daniel Pipes, is at https://www.danielpipes.org/blog/2005/11/kurt-vonnegut-lauds-suicide-bombers.

"Kurt, every so often": Mark Vonnegut, "Twisting Vonnegut's views on terrorism," *Boston Globe*, December 27, 2005, http://archive.boston.com/news/globe/editorial_opinion/oped/articles/2005/12/27/twisting_vonneguts_views_on_terrorism/.

"If I'd been born in Germany": *Mother Night*, Introduction, vii.

"The opposite of humanism": *A Thousand Small Sanities: The Moral Adventure of Liberalism* (New York: Basic Books, 2019), 81.

"The only difference between Bush and Hitler": Harvey Wasserman, "Kurt Vonnegut's 'Stardust Memory,' " *Free Press*, March 4, 2006, http://freepress.org/columns/display/7/2006/1326.

"Our president is a Christian?": *A Man Without a Country*, chap. 8, 88.

While Nazis did collect: The rise of the Nazis and Hitler to power is chronicled at the Holocaust Encyclopedia, https://encyclopedia.ushmm.org/content/en/article/the-nazi-rise-to-power.

"Hitler clearly thought": Weikart's comment, from his book *Hitler's Religion: The Twisted Beliefs that Drove the Third Reich* (Washington, DC: Regnery History, 2016), is taken from an excerpt at https://www.historyonthenet.com/hitlers-religion.

So dependable and efficient and tireless

"We may feel": "David Simon Unravels the Moral Twists of *Paths of Glory*," Criterion Collection video essay, May 9, 2018, https://www.criterion.com/current/posts/5636-david-simon-unravels-the-moral-twists-of-paths-of-glory.

"Are taking the halfway decent": *Bagombo Snuff Box*, Introduction, 8.

"You can't fight progress": *Bagombo Snuff Box*, Introduction, 10.

"To have a little clicking box": Standish, "*Playboy* Interview," 68.

"was the miracle": *Player Piano*, chap. One, 1.

"Replacement is not": *Player Piano*, chap. Thirty, 270.

"radical proposals" and "I propose that men and women": *Player Piano*, chap. Thirty, 271.

"poor and powerless": *Hocus Pocus*, chap. 8, 67.

"are already eager": *Player Piano*, chap. 35, 305.

"I was raised": McLaughlin, "An Interview with Kurt Vonnegut, Jr." *Media and Methods*, May 1973, reprinted in *Conversation with Kurt Vonnegut*, 72.

Chapter 8: Good for the Common Man

Epigraph "My politics in a nutshell": "What the 'Ghost Dance' of the Native Americans and the French Painters Who Led the Cubist Movement Have in Common," from February 17, 1994, address at the University of Chicago in *If This Isn't Nice, What Is?* (Second Edition), 77.

"change the World in a significant way": *The Sirens of Titan*, chap. 7, 176.

"on behalf of the people": *Jailbird*, Epilogue, 272.

"one plausible romantic theory": "What the 'Ghost Dance' of the Native Americans…," 77.

"Dr. Redfield's theory": "What the 'Ghost Dance' of the Native Americans…," 77–78.

"might be regarded as petri dishes": "What the 'Ghost Dance' of the Native Americans…," 79.

"For want of a better word": "What the 'Ghost Dance' of the Native Americans…," 79.

"We must become a family": "Why Social Justice Does More Than Art to Nourish the American Dream," from May 20, 1972, speech at The State University of New York at Albany in *If This Isn't Nice, What Is?* (Second Edition), 110–111.

Simple enough and reasonable enough

"a typical Hoosier idealist": *A Man Without a Country*, chap. 2, 13.

"Socialism is idealistic": *A Man Without a Country*, chap. 2, 13.

"I imagined that I was a socialist": *Jailbird*, Prologue, 11.

"Most Americans don't know": *A Man Without a Country*, chap. 2, 10–11.

Historical facts about American socialism and presidential elections are from various sources, notably *The American Labor Year Book 1917–1918*, http://bitly.ws/oAmY, and Dexter Perkins, "The Constitution in Retrospect," *The Constitution of the United States*, 1787–1962, ed. Putnam F. Jones (Pittsburgh: University of Pittsburgh Press, 1962), http://bitly.ws/oBF9, and Wikipedia, https://en.wikipedia.org/wiki/United_States_presidential_election,_1912.

"tales of labor's sufferings" and "labor history was pornography": *Jailbird*, Prologue, 19.

"The laws that say," "never attended a lecture," and "How else could he ever": *Jailbird*, chap. 18, 210.

"I don't believe government": From Sanders' November 19, 2015, speech at Georgetown University, https://www.c-span.org/video/?400961-1/senator-bernie-sanders-address-democratic-socialism (quote begins at 53:07).

"believed in free enterprise" and "It had made his forebearers rich": Shields, *And So It Goes*, 298.

"personally invested heavily" and "a strip mining company": Shields, *And So It Goes*, 299.

"What he objected to": Shields, *And So It Goes*, 298.

"I made a lot of money": "Imagine the Worst," *Mother Jones*, October 1, 1983, http://www.motherjones.com/politics/1983/10/imagine-worst.

Notes

"work for a socialist" and "Free Enterprise is much too hard": "Address to Graduating Class of Bennington College, 1970," *Wampeters, Foma & Granfalloons*, 168.

"I think any form of government": *Hocus Pocus*, chap. 32, 227.

"was a middle-class person": *A Man Without a Country*, chap. 2, 13.

"heartfelt moral code" and "We sure need such a thing": From the May 26, 1974, address to Hobart and William Smith Colleges, *Palm Sunday*, chap. XI, 202.

"How can we help you?"

"a man who is that *kind*": Joe David Bellamy and John Casey, "Kurt Vonnegut, Jr.," *The New Fiction: Interviews with Innovative American Writers* (Urbana, IL: University of Illinois Press, 1974), reprinted in *Conversations*, ed. Allen, 160.

"I could hear him comforting": Bellamy and Casey, "Kurt Vonnegut, Jr.," *The New Fiction*, reprinted in *Conversations*, 160.

"the maggots in the slime": *God Bless You, Mr. Rosewater*, chap. 3, 36.

"he calmly lay down": *God Bless You, Mr. Rosewater*, chap. 6, 64.

"She was a wise": *God Bless You, Mr. Rosewater*, chap. 1, 14.

"this Utopia gone bust" and "every grotesquely rich American": *God Bless You, Mr. Rosewater*, chap. 1, 13.

"rapacious citizens": *God Bless You, Mr. Rosewater*, chap. 1, 12.

"'Oh, I have what a lot' ": *God Bless You, Mr. Rosewater*, chap. 7, 87–89.

Swimmers and sinkers

"do-gooders" and "I see two alternatives": *God Bless You, Mr. Rosewater*, chap. 2, 27.

"I just know that": Standish, "*Playboy* Interview," 66.

"the free enterprise system": *God Bless You, Mr. Rosewater*, chap. 10, 118.

"to buy decent food": *God Bless You, Mr. Rosewater*, chap. 10, 119.

"Giving away a fortune": *God Bless You, Mr. Rosewater*, chap. 10, 120–121.

"on the path of conservativism": *God Bless You, Mr. Rosewater*, chap. 10, 119.

"I will be grateful": *God Bless You, Mr. Rosewater*, chap. 11, 133.

"America is the wealthiest nation": *Slaughterhouse-Five*, chap. 5, 128–129.

"Ortiz's brain was so big": *Galápagos*, chap. 15, 75–76.

"Uncover the steaks": *Galápagos*, chap. 16, page 80.

"opinion of himself": *Galápagos*, chap. 16, page 82.

"We must find a cure"

"that there should be upper limits": Robeyns, "What, if Anything, is Wrong with Extreme Wealth?," *Journal of Human Development and Capabilities*,

Volume 20, 2019, Issue 3, 251–266, https://doi.org/10.1080/19452829.20 19.1633734. One contrasting view is "Rejecting Ingrid Robeyns' Defense of Limitarianism" by Thomas J. Nickles (*University of Pennsylvania Journal of Philosophy, Politics, and Economics*, Volume 16 (2021), Issue 1, abstract at https://repository.upenn.edu/spice/vol16/iss1/5/).

Patriotic Millionaires: https://patrioticmillionaires.org.

"Working to benefit society": See Appendix C, "Humanism and Its Aspirations."

"I'm going to love": *God Bless You, Mr. Rosewater*, chap. 3, 36.

"Hello, babies": *God Bless You, Mr. Rosewater*, chap. 7, 93.

"You're my *only* friend": *God Bless You, Mr. Rosewater*, chap. 13, 172.

"if we can't find reasons": *God Bless You, Mr. Rosewater*, chap. 14, 183.

"Poverty is a relatively mild": *God Bless You, Mr. Rosewater*, chap. 14, 184.

"It seems to me": *God Bless You, Mr. Rosewater*, chap. 14, 186–187.

"Let their names": *God Bless You, Mr. Rosewater*, chap. 14, page 190.

Lonesome no more!

"You're not happy": Standish, "*Playboy* Interview," 74.

"I spoke of American loneliness": *Slapstick*, chap. 33, 183.

"Utopian scheme": *Slapstick*, chap. 32, 177.

"We said it was possible" and "The framers had not noticed": *Slapstick*, chap. 6, 57.

"proposed that the Constitution": *Slapstick*, chap. 6, 58.

"bad sorts of extended families" and "nearly insane to outsiders": *Slapstick*, chap. 32, 178.

"a seeming team that was meaningless": *Cat's Cradle*, chap. 42, 65.

"An ideal extended family": *Slapstick*, chap. 32, 178.

"My longer-range schemes": *Wampeters, Foma & Granfalloons*, Preface, xxiv.

"Only connect!": E. M. Forster, *Howards End* (New York: Everyman's Library, Alfred A. Knopf, 1991), chap. 22, 195, https://archive.org/stream/howard-send002321mbp#page/n233/mode/2up.

"Tolerance": Forster, "What I Believe" in *Two Cheers for Democracy* (1951), http://spichtinger.net/otexts/believe.html.

"There's nothing I'd rather do" and "scolded by several speakers": *Slapstick*, chap. 45, 243.

"I saw several people killed": *Slapstick*, chap. 47, 250.

"there's no such thing as a battle": *Slapstick*, chap. 47, 249.

"Because we're just families": *Slapstick*, chap. 47, 250.

People wishing to imitate Christ

"Socialism is, in fact": Barsamian, "Kurt Vonnegut Interview," *The Progressive*.

"had chosen to endure": Gregory D. Sumner, *Unstuck in Time* (New York: Seven Stories Press, 2011), 192.

"'Mr. Hapgood,' he said": *Jailbird*, Prologue, 19. Vonnegut uses a similar anecdote at the end of the novel, replacing Hapgood with narrator Walter Starbuck and the judge with Congressman Richard Nixon.

The Sermon on the Mount

Epigraph "The Sermon on the Mount suggests": *Palm Sunday*, chap. XIX, 329.

The Gospel passage is from the New King James Version of the Bible at https://www.biblegateway.com/passage/?search=matthew+5&version=NKJV.

Chapter 9: Christ Worshiper

Epigraph "I say with all my American ancestors": "Advice to Graduating Women (That All Men Should Know)," from May 15, 1999, commencement address at Agnes Scott College, Decatur, Georgia, *If This Isn't Nice, What Is?* (Second Edition), 20.

"a Christ-worshiping agnostic": *Palm Sunday*, chap. XIX, 327. Vonnegut used the word *agnostic* here. Elsewhere, he called himself an atheist, a freethinker, a Unitarian Universalist, and so on. Broadly, *agnosticism* is noncommittal, believing God unknowable, while *atheism* is disbelief in God.

"My family has been" and "And so if I declare": Interview on June 8, 1976, by Robert Short, *Something to Believe In: Is Kurt Vonnegut the Exorcist of Jesus Christ Superstar?* (New York: Harper & Row, Publishers, 1978), 285 and 289.

"I am enchanted": *Palm Sunday*, chap. XIX, 325.

"What, exactly, was the Sermon on the Mount?": *Jailbird*, Prologue, 19–20.

opiate for the masses: Vonnegut points out that Karl Marx's well-known comment about religion was made at a time (1844) "when opium and opium derivatives were the only painkillers...He might as well have said, 'Religion is the aspirin of the people.'" (Barsamian, "Kurt Vonnegut Interview," *The Progressive*.)

"I do not believe": *Sceptical Essays* (London: Unwin Paperbacks, 1988), chap. 12, 113. The book was first published in 1928.

"*Religion poisons everything*": Christopher Hitchens, *God is Not Great* (New York: Twelve/Hachette Book Group USA, 2007), chap. 2, 25 (italics in original).

"In America, it's easy to form": Standish, "*Playboy* Interview," 60.

"I believe that religion" and "It doesn't matter what you believe": Craig Ferguson, *Riding the Elephant: A Memoir of Altercations, Humiliations, Hallucinations & Observations* (New York: Blue Rider Press, 2019), 105 and 107. The Bible passage in James to which Ferguson refers ("Thus also faith by itself, if it does not have works, is dead") can be found at https://www.biblegateway.com/passage/?search=-

James+2%3A14-26&version=NKJV.

"For some reason": *A Man Without a Country*, chap. 9, 98.

"I don't think they've ever paid": *Real Time with Bill Maher*, September 9, 2005, https://www.youtube.com/watch?v=yUh8FdKuWIg.

"a phony Christian": Brinkley, "Vonnegut's Apocalypse," *Rolling Stone*, August 24, 2006, 80.

"was nothing but a poor people's religion": *Fates Worse Than Death*, chap. XVI, 163.

"Now what is it, do you think": *Fates Worse Than Death*, chap. XVI, 158–160.

"I had hoped": *Mother Night*, chap. 29, 122.

"a Truth that may yet be": Email from Sullivan to Harris, January 17, 2007, "Is Religion Built Upon Lies?," https://samharris.org/sam-harris-vs-andrew-sullivan/.

"You ask legitimately": Email from Sullivan to Harris, January 25, 2007.

"We must be vigilant": From Barr's speech at the University of Notre Dame, October 11, 2019, https://www.justice.gov/opa/speech/attorney-general-william-p-barr-delivers-remarks-law-school-and-de-nicola-center-ethics.

"Why argue somebody": *Hocus Pocus*, chap. 1, 16.

"And of course, this enriched": *Hocus Pocus*, chap. 9, 74–75.

Full of white magic

"the substance of things hoped for": The New King James Version of Hebrews 11:1 is at https://www.biblegateway.com/passage/?search=Hebrews+11&version=NKJV#en-NKJV-30174.

Scholars probe: Studies of Hebrews 11:1's meaning are extensive. Two sites that were consulted for this book are Bible Hub, https://biblehub.com/commentaries/hebrews/11-1.htm, and BibleTools, https://www.bibletools.org/index.cfm/fuseaction/bible.show/sVerseID/30174/eVerseID/30174.

"Without…hope of paradise" and "I love sleep": Short, *Something to Believe In*, 307–308.

"The certainty that something": From *Disturbing the Peace* at the Václev Havel Library Foundation site, https://www.vhlf.org/havel-quotes/disturbing-the-peace/.

"Are we enemies": *Timequake*, chap. 21, 72–73.

"are good because": "Address to Graduating Class of Bennington College, 1970," *Wampeters, Foma & Granfalloons*, 164.

"What is so comical": *Palm Sunday*, chap. XI, 215.

"Living alone and far from home": *Palm Sunday*, chap. XI, 216.

"painful" and "alliances with the supernatural": *Palm Sunday*, chap. X, 192.

"working white magic": *Palm Sunday*, ch. XIII, 235.

Notes

"it was mainly religion": *Palm Sunday*, chap. XI, 192.

"Jane could believe": *Timequake*, chap. 34, 117.

"His sort of divinity is attainable by us"
"like a General Electric engineer": "Yes, We Have No Nirvanas," *Esquire*, June 1968, reprinted in *Wampeters, Foma & Granfalloons*, 39.

"Maharishi was asked": *Wampeters, Foma & Granfalloons*, 39–40.

"religious persuasion": *Fates Worse Than Death*, chap. XVI, 165.

"Jesus is particularly stimulating": "My Reply to a Letter from the Dean of the Chapel at Transylvania University About a Speech I Gave There," *Fates Worse Than Death*, Appendix, 238–239.

"When Jesus Christ was nailed": "Advice to Graduating Women (That All Men Should Know)," from May 15, 1999, commencement address at Agnes Scott College, Decatur, Georgia, *If This Isn't Nice, What Is?* (Second Edition), 19.

"He was another human being": Short, *Something to Believe In*, 295.

"Then Mary took a pound": This and subsequent quotes from John, chapter 12, use the New King James Version at https://www.biblegateway.com/passage/?search=John+12&version=NKJV. A similar account is in the Gospels according to Matthew and Mark with much the same response from Jesus, but John names names.

"Whenever anybody out that way": *Palm Sunday*, chap. XIX, 327.

"This line has self-pity": From interview with Walter Miller during his *Reader's Almanac* series, available on the Caedmon compact disc *Essential Vonnegut* (1981, New York: HarperCollins, 2006), track 4, 6:23 mark.

Selective editing

"to the corruptions of Christianity": The April 21, 1803, letter from Jefferson to Rush is at https://founders.archives.gov/documents/Jefferson/01-40-02-0178-0001.

"In general,...passages that reflect violence": *A Jefferson Bible for the Twenty-first Century*, Luis Granados and Roy Speckhardt, eds. (Washington, DC: Humanist Press, 2014), Introduction, 6.

These would include Jesus: Cited passages are from the New King James Version at https://www.biblegateway.com.

"the least of these": This and other passages from Matthew 25 are from the New King James Version at https://www.biblegateway.com/passage/?search=Matthew+25&version=NKJV.

"These words appalled me": *Jailbird*, chap. 3, 81.

Is behaving decently enough?

"sadistic and masochistic" and "promising a Paradise": *Fates Worse Than*

Death, chap. VI, 71.

"A day of wrath" (original version): "English Translation of the Latin Mass Promulgated by Pope St. Pius V in 1570 by Decree of the Council of Trent," *Fates Worse Than Death*, Appendix, 223–224.

"A day of wrath" (Vonnegut version): "Mass Promulgated by Me in 1985," *Fates Worse Than Death* Appendix, 227–228.

Clemens, a co-founder: "Minutes of the First Meeting for the Founding of a Free Congregation (Part 1)," IUPUI University Library, https://ulib.iupui.edu/static/exhibits/circle/freethinker/engminutes_1.html.

"He who believes in Him": The New King James Version of John 3:18 is at https://www.biblegateway.com/passage/?search=John+3%3A18+&version=NKJV.

But some scholars interpret the passage differently: The Greek word *krino*, some scholars point out, is the root of words in the Bible that are translated to variations of *condemn* and *judge*. (Examinations of this word in the Gospel according to John abound. Among those consulted for this book are http://www.exploringgodsword.co/egw/Vocab/judge.htm and the Panda's Vineyard blog, http://xiongmaoputao.blogspot.com/2013/04/the-greek-words-for-condemn-and.html.) In that sense, *condemn* in John 3:18 refers to one's Earthly state, to sealing one's fate in the present by not believing. John concludes the third chapter of his Gospel with, "He who believes in the Son has everlasting life; and he who does not believe the Son shall not see life, but the wrath of God abides on him." (The New King James Version of John 3:36 is at https://www.biblegateway.com/passage/?search=John+3%3A36&version=NKJV.) While there's no mention of hell for unbelievers, there's no life at all for them after death. Note "the wrath of God," though. The Greek word *orgé*, translated as *wrath*, means "settled anger," a steadfast opposition. Not lightning bolts or fiery imprisonment, but rather God's perpetual displeasure, if you will, leaving the unbeliever subject to judgment that already has been reached. (Interpretations of the meaning of *orgé* can be found on the page discussing John 3:36 at https://biblehub.com/commentaries/john/3-36.htm.) Speaking of judgment, the Bible's concluding book of Revelation—possibly written by the Gospel author John, or a disciple of his, or someone else entirely—is heavy with a more vengeful-sounding wrath. In one of its fevered visions of the Day of the Lord, "anyone not found written in the Book of Life was cast into the lake of fire." (The New King James Version of the book of Revelation's chapter 20, featuring this quote and references to Hades, the realm of the dead, can be found at https://www.biblegateway.com/passage/?search=Revelation+20&version=NKJV.) But even the United States Conference of Catholic Bishops regards the apocalyptic accounts in Revelation to be "symbolic descriptions [that] are not to be taken as literal descriptions." (See the USCCB's introduction to the book of Revelation at http://www.usccb.org/bible/revelation/0.) Pope Francis has described hell as the result of using free will to make a terrible choice: "This is hell: It is telling God, 'You take care of yourself because I'll take care of myself.' They don't send you to hell, you go there because you choose to be there. Hell is wanting to be distant from God because I do not want God's love." (Quoted in "Vatican:

Claim that pope denied hell's existence is unreliable" by Junno Arocho Esteves, Catholic News Service, March 29, 2018, https://www.americamagazine.org/faith/2018/03/29/vatican-claim-pope-denied-hells-existence-unreliable.) Christian writer C. S. Lewis wrote that "the doors of hell are locked on the inside… [The damned] enjoy forever the horrible freedom they have demanded, and are therefore self-enslaved: just as the blessed, forever submitting to obedience, become through all eternity more and more free." (*The Problem of Pain*, chapter 8, HarperCollins, 2001 paperback edition. First published in 1940.)

"more bad things instead of good things": *Slaughterhouse-Five*, 172.

Pew Research poll: "Views on the afterlife: Majorities of U.S. adults say they believe in heaven, hell," Pew Research Center, November 23, 2021, https://www.pewforum.org/2021/11/23/views-on-the-afterlife/. Polling numbers are available at the Methodology link there. Similar percentages were found with more than thirty-five thousand respondents to Pew's 2014 Religious Landscape Study, https://www.pewforum.org/2015/11/03/u-s-public-becoming-less-religious/. The earlier study's definition of hell ("where people who have led bad lives and die without being sorry are eternally punished") appears in researcher Caryle Murphy's November 10, 2015, article "Most Americans believe in heaven… and hell," available at http://www.pewresearch.org/fact-tank/2015/11/10/most-americans-believe-in-heaven-and-hell/. More recent Gallup and Harris polls put belief in hell among American adults even higher, but without defining hell.

"a reality that exists": Short, *Something to Believe In*, 38.

To be taken seriously

Vonnegut had some idea: He put his own spin on the belief that hell does not exist in the afterlife while revisiting "a naïve sermon" he gave at St. John the Divine in New York City in 1983: "What I should have said from the pulpit was that we weren't *going* to Hell. We were *in* Hell, thanks to technology which was telling us what to do, instead of the other way around." (*Fates Worse Than Death*, chap. XV, 150.) Earlier he recalled the words of a minister at a Unitarian church: "No matter what we did in life, he said, we wouldn't burn throughout eternity in hell. We wouldn't even fry for ten or fifteen minutes. He was just guessing, of course." (From the May 26, 1974, address to Hobart and William Smith Colleges, *Palm Sunday*, chap. XI, 204.)

"I still quote": *Timequake*, chap. 36, 122.

"I will dream of a baby": The untitled poem by Vonnegut is one of the "Carols for Christmas 1969," *New York Times Magazine*, December 21, 1969, page 5. Accessed via Times Machine search tool.

"Those who would kill Him" and "one hell of a story": November 30, 1988, letter to Foss, *Kurt Vonnegut: Letters*, 324.

Christ for kids

"The Very First Christmas Morning" by Kurt Vonnegut Jr. was published in *Better Homes and Gardens*, December 1962, and is available at http://merryandbright.blogspot.com/2016/11/a-literary-treat-from-1962.html.

Sun Moon Star: Vonnegut reads the whole thing in about 10 minutes at https://www.youtube.com/watch?v=LCRknMLu2q8.

"more than anything": Standish, "*Playboy* Interview," 60.

Leaving Vonnegut's company: Specifically, Shields asked the question on his way out the door on March 14, 2007, according to a talk he gave at the University of Mary Washington on January 24, 2012 (49:45 mark at https://www.umw.edu/greatlives/2012/02/24/kurt-vonnegut/).

"I don't know": Shields, *And So It Goes*, 415.

Chapter 10: The Eyes and Ears and Conscience of the Creator of the Universe

Epigraph "His prose was frightful": *Slaughterhouse-Five*, chap. 5, 110.

The first few representations of Kilgore Trout are from (one source novel per paragraph), respectively, *Breakfast of Champions*, *Timequake*, *Galápagos*, and *Jailbird*.

"Vonnegut's chief avatar": Kathryn Hume, "The Hericlitean Cosmos of Kurt Vonnegut," *Critical Essays on Kurt Vonnegut*, ed. Robert Merrill (Boston: G. K. Hall & Company, 1990), 220–221. From *Papers on Language and Literature* 18, no. 2, Spring 1982.

"any conscious intent" and "Well, no, only a perversity": Bellamy and Casey, "Kurt Vonnegut, Jr.," *Conversations with Kurt Vonnegut*, 160.

"'If I'd wasted my time'": *Timequake*, chap. 18, 63.

Other similarities (all from *Timequake*): army scout (chap. 3, 9), hard to know (chap. 8, 28), born November 11 (chap. 13, 46), died age eighty-four (chap. 13, 46).

How to love people who have no use

"Kilgore Trout is the lonesome": From "Ask Them Yourself," *Family Week*, June 28, 1973, page 3, as cited in Jerome Klinkowitz and Douglas L. Lawler, eds., *Vonnegut in America: An Introduction to the Life and Work of Kurt Vonnegut*, Delacorte Press/S. Lawrence, 1977, 20.

"I have been a soreheaded occupant": "Science Fiction," *Wampeters, Foma & Granfalloons*, 1. First published in the *The New York Times Book Review*, September 5, 1965, section BR, page 2.

Then there's the related matter of sales: Shields in *And Go It Goes*, citing private letters and other sources, reports that *Player Piano* sold 3,600 copies of its initial printing by Scribner's (page 127), *The Sirens of Titan* "sold...miserably" (162), *Mother Night* "was a flop" (173), and "*Cat's Cradle* didn't outsell its initial printing of six thousand copies" (180).

"I love you sons of bitches": *God Bless You, Mr. Rosewater*, chap. 2, 18.

Notes

"The only hero of our time": *God Bless You, Mr. Rosewater*, chap. 2, 19.

"You said Trout could explain": *God Bless You, Mr. Rosewater*, chap. 14, 182.

"a rascal who could rationalize": *God Bless You, Mr. Rosewater*, chap. 14, 186.

"What you did in Rosewater": *God Bless You, Mr. Rosewater*, chap. 14, 183.

"Please, would you ask": *Player Piano*, chap. 33, 287.

"What in hell are people *for*?": *God Bless You, Mr. Rosewater*, chap. 2, 21.

"will kill strong and weak" and "There we have people": *God Bless You, Mr. Rosewater*, chap. 14, 184.

Why Christians find it so easy to be cruel

"unpopularity was deserved" and "His prose": *Slaughterhouse-Five*, chap. 5, 110.

"a bitter man": *Slaughterhouse-Five*, chap. 8, 166.

"I could go to jail": *Slaughterhouse-Five*, chap. 8, 171.

"Poor Maggie turned gray": *Slaughterhouse-Five*, chap. 8, 172.

"a cross to be used": *Slaughterhouse-Five*, chap. 9, 202.

"slipshod storytelling" and "why Christians found it": *Slaughterhouse-Five*, chap. 5, 108.

"*From this moment on*": *Slaughterhouse-Five*, chap. 5, 110 (italics in original).

"a passion play": This and subsequent quotes to the end of this section are from Vonnegut's January 27, 1980, address at the First Parish Unitarian Church in Cambridge, Massachusetts, *Palm Sunday*, chap. XI, 217–218.

"The message, please"

"a nobody at the time" and "one of the most beloved": *Breakfast of Champions*, chap. 1, 7.

"What is the purpose," "what [Trout] would have," and "*To be / the eyes*": *Breakfast of Champions*, chap. 7, 67.

"a dialogue between": *Breakfast of Champions*, chap. 19, 208.

"a planet where the natives": *Breakfast of Champions*, chap. 5, 58.

"Give me the message": *Breakfast of Champions*, chap. 22, 252.

"doing their best to live": *Breakfast of Champions*, chap. 19, 209–210.

"You are an experiment": *Breakfast of Champions*, chap. 22, 253.

"became a pioneer": *Breakfast of Champions*, chap. 1, 15.

"recognized as a great artist" and "We are healthy": *Breakfast of Champions*, chap. 1, 16.

"that humanity is at the center": "Address to Graduating Class of Bennington College, 1970," *Wampeters, Foma & Granfaloons*, 163.

He's back, more or less

"I am going to set at liberty": *Breakfast of Champions*, Epilogue, 293.

"Arise, Mr. Trout": *Breakfast of Champions*, Epilogue, 294.

"Make me young": *Breakfast of Champions*, Epilogue, 295 (italics in original).

"Yes—Kilgore Trout is back again": *Jailbird*, Prologue, 9.

"the only American": *Jailbird,* chap. 4, 81.

"tall and big-boned": *Jailbird,* chap. 5, 97.

"The 2 prime movers": *Hocus Pocus,* chap. 3, 30.

"Sally in the garden": *Jailbird,* chap. 6, 102. Vonnegut is tweaking or perhaps simply excerpting the lyrics of an old folk song that has several variations, many of them bawdy. For details about the song's history, see http://pancocojams.blogspot.com/2014/06/sally-in-garden-siftin-sand-lyrics.html.

"silent awarenesses": *Jailbird,* chap. 5, 98.

"all the money he made": *Jailbird,* chap. 6, 106.

Fender's appropriation: In the preface to later editions of *Venus on the Half-Shell* (1988 and 2013, Titan Books), Farmer wrestles with the inconsistencies of Trout's first few appearances and revises his biography of the character to include events in *Breakfast of Champions*. The preface insists that Trout is real. Farmer also notes that in *Jailbird* "Mr. Vonnegut claims that it was not Trout but another man who wrote the works which Vonnegut hitherto had claimed to be Trout's. Nobody believes this disclaimer." Reducing Trout to a pen name in *Jailbird* might have been Vonnegut's way of exacting some revenge.

"intelligent threads of energy": *Hocus Pocus,* chap. 25, 188.

"It appeared to the Elders": *Hocus Pocus,* chap. 26, 191.

"I wish I knew his name": *Hocus Pocus,* chap. 26, 192.

"The story was very likely pirated": *Hocus Pocus,* chap. 26, 194.

Nature's experiment with cynicism

"Truth be told" and "The moral of the story": *Galápagos* , Book One, chap. 33, 184.

"Nature's experiments": *Galápagos* , Book One, chap. 16, 83.

"He made a fortune": *Galápagos* , Book One, chap. 14, 71.

"The craze...for having machines": *Galápagos* , Book One, chap. 14, 70.

"about what life is really like": *Galápagos* , Book Two, chap. 7, 253.

"The more you learn": *Galápagos* , Book Two, chap. 7, 254.

"that human beings are good": *Galápagos* , Book Two, chap. 7, 257.

"Nature's experiment with cynicism": *Galápagos* , Book One, chap. 16, 82.

Notes

Kilgore's Creed

"Wake up! Wake up!": *Timequake*, chap. 46, 155.

"The old science fiction writer" and "You were sick": *Timequake*, chap. 50, 167.

"I was a victim": *The Sirens of Titan*, chap. 10, 232.

"the fulfillment of an ancient dream": *Timequake*, chap. 61, 202.

"And yet—let us believe": *Timequake*, chap. 61, 202.

"the greatest President," "was a major event" and "Who is there left": *Timequake*, chap. 58, 194.

"As the curtain descended": *Timequake*, chap. 61, 203.

"Being alive is a crock of shit": *Timequake*, chap. 1, 3.

"All that good people": *God Bless You, Dr. Kevorkian*, 73.

"the planet is trying": *A Man Without a Country*, chap. 11, 122. In the original version of the "interview," published in the October 15, 2004, edition of *In These Times*, Trout has a bit more to say for himself. But the important takeaway is an "editor's note," presumably written by Vonnegut, that offers another biographical alteration: "Trout committed suicide by drinking Drano at midnight on October 15 in Cohoes, New York, after a female psychic using tarot cards predicted that the environmental calamity George W. Bush would once again be elected president of the most powerful nation on the planet by a five-to-four decision of the Supreme Court, which included '100 per-cent of the black vote.'" http://inthesetimes.com/article/1351/requiem_for_a_dreamer

"transcendent humanism" and "Kilgore's Creed, Vonnegut suggests": Taylor, "Fictional Humans and Humanist Fictions," The Vonnegut Review, September 2013, http://www.vonnegutreview.com/2013/09/timequake.html.

"There on the beach": *Timequake*, chap. 63, 212.

"look precisely": *Timequake*, chap. 63, 213.

"Your awareness": *Timequake*, chap. 63, 213–214 (italics in original).

Chapter 11: Becoming

Epigraph "I now believe": *Wampeters, Foma & Granfalloons*, Preface, xxvii.

"a rational philosophy": The *Humanist* magazine. While the magazine is published by the American Humanist Association, the AHA Board of Directors-approved definition of humanism is slightly different: "a progressive philosophy of life that, without theism or other supernatural beliefs, affirms our ability and responsibility to lead ethical lives of personal fulfillment that aspire to the greater good." https://americanhumanist.org/what-is-humanism/definition-of-humanism/

"a plausible mission of artists": *Timequake*, chap. 1, 1.

"The arts are not a way": *A Man Without a Country*, chap. 3, 24.

"where the practice of the arts": *Palm Sunday*, chap. II, 43–44.

"He was asked what the trouble was": *Palm Sunday*, chap. II, 43.

"had no talent for the vulgarity": *Palm Sunday*, chap. V, 96–97.

"possessed considerable gifts": *Fates Worse Than Death*, chap. III, 37. The essay was first published in *Architectural Digest*.

"draw for sour apples": *Timequake*, chap. 43, 142.

"I am from a family of artists": *A Man without a Country*, chap. 2, 14–15.

Vonnegut was an occasional sculptor: Details about the Logan Airport sculpture can be found in the Shields biography *And So It Goes*, Nanette Vonnegut's introduction to *Kurt Vonnegut Drawings* (The Monacelli Press, 2014), and Jerome Klinkowitz's introduction to his book *The Vonnegut Effect* (Columbia, SC: University of South Carolina Press, 2004). The accounts differ as to when the sculpture was made (1957, the late 1950s, or the early 1960s), its name ("New England Enters the Space Age" or "Comet"), its length (eighteen or thirty feet), and how much Vonnegut was paid ($1,100 or $600). Vonnegut had considerable help from a welder, a carpenter, and a friend with a boat trailer, according to Klinkowitz. His piece, by far the most detailed, is available at https://books.google.com/books?id=3nwMCAAAQBAJ&pg=PT12&lpg=PT12&dq=vonnegut+sculpture+Comet+logan+airport&source=bl&ots=3Y-W8nX25Ff&sig=ACfU3U1agAjd_ES-aSow-bZC0vhS7RDe1w&hl=en&sa=X-&ved=2ahUKEwjZnYXc-dTrAhUCgnIEHSPcBWAQ6AEwCXoECAoQAQ#v=onepage&q=vonnegut%20sculpture%20Comet%20logan%20airport&f=false. Rebecca Rego Barry at the Fine Books & Collections blog (August 9, 2018) remarked upon a Vonnegut-made "aluminum silhouette... clearly reminiscent of his famous felt-tipped drawings" that sold for $5,040 (https://www.finebooksmagazine.com/blog/kurt-vonnegut-sculptor).

"One of the best things": *A Man Without a Country*, Author's Note, 142–143.

"God bless Rabo Karabekian!"

"hoax autobiography": *Bluebeard*, Author's Note.

"day-glo orange": *Breakfast of Champions*, chap. 19, 208.

"seen better pictures" and "Listen— ... I have read": *Breakfast of Champions*, chap. 19, 220.

"the spiritual climax": *Breakfast of Champions*, chap. 19, 218.

"spiritual continents" and "had come to the conclusion": *Breakfast of Champions*, chap. 19, 219.

"It is Rabo Karabekian": *Breakfast of Champions*, chap. 19, 220.

"At the core of each person": *Breakfast of Champions*, chap. 19, 225.

"a flawed equation": *Breakfast of Champions*, chap. 19, 241.

"low-intensity neon tubes": *Bluebeard*, chap. 26, 212.

"I couldn't help seeing": *Bluebeard*, chap. 26, 211–212.

"My soul knows": *Bluebeard*, chap. 32, 258.

"And who renders": *Bluebeard*, chap. 17, 140–141.

"The whole magical thing": *Bluebeard*, chap. 36, 294 (italics in original).

"The crack between": *Bluebeard*, chap. 35, 284.

"humanistic masterpiece": "Vonnegut and Aesthetic Humanism," *At Millennium's End: New Essays on the Work of Kurt Vonnegut*, ed. Kevin Alexander Boon (Albany, NY: State University of New York Press, 2001), 20.

"My soul didn't know" and "Thank you, Meat": *Bluebeard*, chap. 37, 300.

"a part of the mind": *Fates Worse Than Death*, chap. III, 44. The essay was first published in *Esquire*, December 1983, and according to Vonnegut inspired him to write *Bluebeard*.

A way to make your soul grow

"Much of what I put": *Bluebeard*, Author's Note.

At the time *Bluebeard* was published: A running list of top prices paid for paintings, including a conversion to today's US currency value, is at https://en.wikipedia.org/wiki/List_of_most_expensive_paintings.

"They have to pretend": "Why Socialism Does More Than Art to Nourish the American Dream," speech at State University of New York at Albany, May 20, 1972, *If This Isn't Nice, What Is?* (Second Edition), 101.

"Practicing an art": *A Man Without a Country*, chap. 3, 24.

"to experience becoming," "into teeny-weeny pieces," and "You will find that you": November 5, 2006, letter to Xavier High School students, http://www.lettersofnote.com/2013/10/make-your-soul-grow.html.

"In the beginning": *The Sirens of Titan*, chap. 9, 199.

"One thing I don't like" *The Charlie Rose Show*, 1999, https://www.youtube.com/watch?v=ROyr83rib3Q. Vonnegut might not have been aware that Microsoft founder Gates and other technology leaders limited their children's use of computers. (See the August 30, 2018, post "Did Bill Gates, Steve Jobs, and Other Tech Billionaire Parents Advocate Limiting Children's Technology Use?" at https://www.snopes.com/fact-check/tech-billionaire-parents-limit/.) Gates may well have agreed that learning—and by inference becoming—should involve "reading, studying, practicing an art." His then-wife and fellow philanthropist, Melinda Gates, wrote this in an op-ed for *The Washington Post* published August 24, 2017: "Phones and apps aren't good or bad by themselves, but for adolescents who don't yet have the emotional tools to navigate life's complications and confusions, they can exacerbate the difficulties of growing up: learning how to be kind, coping with feelings of exclusion, taking advantage of freedom while exercising self-control. It's more important than ever to teach empathy from the very beginning, because our kids are going to need it." https://wapo.st/3NmutW2

Proof of God's existence

"most people find life so hard": *Fates Worse Than Death*, chap. XI, 109–110.

He called it sacred: After expressing his preference for Armistice Day over Veterans Day, Vonnegut wrote, "What else is sacred? Oh, *Romeo and Juliet*, for instance. And all music is" (Preface, *Breakfast of Champions*).

"It makes practically everybody": *A Man Without a Country*, chap. 7, 67.

"THE ONLY PROOF HE NEEDED": *A Man Without a Country*, chap. 7, 66.

"Why this is so": "Kurt Vonnegut: 'A Man Without a Country,'" Weekend Edition Sunday, NPR, posted September 11, 2005, https://www.npr.org/transcripts/4839818.

"Music is the only art": *Letters*, 231. Vonnegut had written on January 7, 1976, to the band Ambrosia, which had released a *Cat's Cradle*-inspired song, "Nice, Nice, Very Nice."

"Safe sex of the highest order": *Armageddon in Retrospect*, 25.

"yet another great contemporary poem": *Palm Sunday*, chap. XVIII, 305. The lyrics begin there too.

"It is a poem": *Palm Sunday*, chap. XVIII, 307.

"The function of the artist": Brinkley, "Vonnegut's Apocalypse," 110.

"They have only two": *The Sirens of Titan*, chap. 8, 189–190.

"a piece of crap" and "I thought it was just preposterous": from "Life During Wartime" by Alicia Zuckerman, *New York*, March 23, 2006, http://nymag.com/arts/classicaldance/classical/features/16514/.

Private Eddie Slovik: The Official Military Personnel File for Edward Slovik can be viewed at https://catalog.archives.gov/id/74881321. Links to several more online records concerning Slovik are at https://historyhub.history.gov/thread/7585S.

"He was the only person": from Zuckerman, "Life During Wartime."

"Billy read the opinion": *Slaughterhouse-Five*, chap. 2, 45 (italics in original).

Canaries in a coal mine

"Lies told for the sake": *Mother Night*, ix.

"Fiction is melody": *Wampeters, Foma & Granfalloons*, Preface, xx.

"We all know that art is not truth": "Picasso Speaks: A Statement by the Artist," *The Arts: An Illustrated Monthly Magazine Covering All Phases of Ancient and Modern Art*, Volume 3, Number 5, May 1923 (New York: The Arts Publishing Corporation), 315, https://babel.hathitrust.org/cgi/pt?id=mdp.39015020076041&view=1up&seq=1. The provenance of the quote and variants attributed to Picasso and others is laid out with a timeline at https://quoteinvestigator.com/2019/10/29/lie-truth/.

"Works of art are just ways": Amanda Stern, "An Interview With Laurie

Anderson," *The Believer*, January 2012, https://believermag.com/an-interview-with-laurie-anderson/.

"Artists are useful to society": "Address to the American Physical Society," *Wampeters, Foma & Granfalloons*, 92.

"Coal miners used to take birds": Standish, "*Playboy* Interview," 59.

"Using the Socratic method": *Palm Sunday*, chap. XIX, 321. Vonnegut did not name his mentor in *Palm Sunday* but referred to him as someone "so brilliant, who could not find anyone to publish his most audacious work, and who committed suicide" (319).

"I believe art is foremost": The quote is attributed to Marion Boddy-Evans without further citation at http://www.art-quotes.com/auth_search.php?authid=6101#.X3-7ki3My8o. Boddy-Evans confirmed the quote's accuracy (email message to author, October 8, 2020) but could not specify in which of her numerous articles about painting it appeared.

Vonnegut said he wrote at least his early stories for his sister: "I knew it was my sister Allie I had been writing for" (*Bagombo Snuff Box*, Introduction, 13). He explained further in his introduction to *Slapstick* (14–15) "I had never told [Alice] so, but she was the person I had always written for…Yes, and she was nice enough, or Nature was nice enough, to allow me to feel her presence for a number of years after she died—to let me go on writing for her." Vonnegut might not have come to this realization until after Alice died in 1958 or his first marriage dissolved a decade later. Perhaps he'd forgotten what he wrote to Jane Cox when he was wooing her (circa October/November 1943): "You are the one person in this world to whom I like to write. If ever I do write anything of length—good or bad—it will be written with you in mind" (*Love, Kurt: The Vonnegut Love Letters, 1941–1945*, 67).

"Still and all, why bother?": *Timequake*, chap. 58, 193.

Chapter 12: Dignity

Epigraph "What could be more essential": From address at First Parish Unitarian Church in Cambridge, Massachusetts, *Palm Sunday*, chap. XI, 213.

"I suppose they": *Slaughterhouse-Five*, chap. 10, 212.

The world's population: Information Please cites United Nations Department of Economic and Social Affairs reports that put the population at 6.1 billion in 2000, https://www.infoplease.com/world/population/total-population-world-decade-1950-2050. It cites a United Nations Population Division report saying world population first reached 7 billion in 2011, https://www.infoplease.com/world/population/world-population-milestones.

"love is a rotten substitute": Address at First Parish Unitarian, *Palm Sunday*, 216.

"Giving dignity": *Palm Sunday*, 214.

"Governments are simply unwilling": "Human Rights for Human Dignity,"

Amnesty International statement, https://www.amnesty.org/en/what-we-do/living-in-dignity/.

"scheme for lasting world peace": "In a Manner That Must Shame God Himself," *Wampeters, Foma & Granfalloons*, 203.

Ignore agony: "In a Manner That Must Shame God Himself," *Wampeters, Foma & Granfalloons*, 204 (italics in original).

The dignity of strangers

"In order to seem": *Fates Worse Than Death*, chap. XVI, 157.

"people who know": June 1986 speech in Rochester, New York, *Fates Worse Than Death*, chap. XVI, 163.

"Unitarians don't believe": "Yes, We Have No Nirvanas," *Wampeters, Foma & Granfalloons*, 31.

"a congregation of people": June 1986 speech, *Fates Worse Than Death*, chap. XVI, 157–158.

"a relatively isolated community" and "I wish I had been born": Address at First Parish Unitarian, *Palm Sunday*, chap. XI, 211.

"I had uncles and aunts" and "there was always someone": J. Rentilly, "God Bless You, Mr. Vonnegut," *U.S. Airways Magazine*, June 2007, reprinted in *Kurt Vonnegut: The Last Interview*, 160.

"All my jokes are Indianapolis": Speech at North Central High School, Indianapolis, in 1986. https://bookmarkindy.com/locations/kurt-vonnegut-mural/.

"When Channing began": Address at First Parish Unitarian, *Palm Sunday*, 213.

Spiritual companionship

about 24 minutes by subway: Google Maps estimate for trip from Vonnegut's home on East 48th Street to the NYSEC building at 2 West 64th Street.

"Diversity in the creed": New York Society for Ethical Culture, https://ethical.nyc/about/.

"obliteration" and "the mostly German-American": *Fates Worse Than Death*, chap. XXI, 200.

the New York Society hosted a posthumous tribute: The event can be viewed at https://www.youtube.com/watch?v=7-BhShNUS2s.

Unitarian Universalism: Details about UU and its link to humanism are from "Humanist Common Ground: Unitarian Universalism" at https://americanhumanist.org/paths/unitarianism/.

"a celebration of the one": Sunday Assembly, https://sundayassembly.online/about-sunday-assembly/.

"means bringing a sense": Citizen University, https://citizenuniversity.us/about/.

Notes

"a civic analogue": Civic Saturday, https://www.youtube.com/playlist?list=PLO-9e9xShjTo4S7qv9UpajtuADxH_dFlZR.

"together to celebrate": Oasis, https://www.oasisnetwork.com/about-us.

"Slack-filled young men and women": http://www.subgenius.com.

Church of the Flying Spaghetti Monster: https://www.spaghettimonster.org.

"You are like the early Christians": June 1986 speech, *Fates Worse Than Death*, chap. XVI, 162.

"I couldn't recommend Humanism": *Timequake*, chap. 21, 74.

"He honored the role": Dan Wakefield, "Kurt Vonnegut, Christ-Loving Atheist," *Image* Issue 82, https://imagejournal.org/article/kurt-vonnegut/?fbclid=IwAR3XO47-9KCgOcv5Xel28zxtX2IoqP8Q5obBX4rG0BnhDhlCJmL-JLJ2jyvU.

"It seems to me": *Palm Sunday*, chap. XVIII, 308.

"in a lonely society:" *Palm Sunday*, chap. XI, 216.

Conclusion: Balderdash

Epigraph "Gentleness must replace violence": *Happy Birthday, Wanda June*, Act One, Scene One, 2.

"The balderdash" and "clearly invented": Address at First Parish Unitarian, *Palm Sunday*, chap. XI, 215.

Bible stories for further reading: Moses is in Exodus 3: 1–10, Jonah is in Jonah 1:17, and David and Goliath are in 1 Samuel 17: 49, https://www.biblegateway.com/versions/New-King-James-Version-NKJV-Bible/#booklist.

"the most powerful": Quoted on McKee's website, https://mckeestory.com/is-it-possible-to-bring-storytelling-into-marketing/.

"Mark Twain was simply": Foreword, *At Millennium's End: New Essays on the Work of Kurt Vonnegut*, vii-viii.

"It's not easy to infect the brain": Eagleman, "The Moral of the Story," *The New York Times*, Aug. 3, 2012 (review of *The Storytelling Animal: How Stories Make Us Human* by Jonathan Gottschall), https://www.nytimes.com/2012/08/05/books/review/the-storytelling-animal-by-jonathan-gottschall.html.

"consciously or unconsciously" and "He was a counterculture hero": *And So It Goes*, 351.

"Old storytellers never die": *The Perpetual Calendar of Inspiration: Old Wisdom for a New World* (Highgate Center, VT: Norilana Books, 2011), Kindle https://www.amazon.com/dp/B005R2IQGQ.

Harmless untruths

"Jokes help a lot": "Kurt Vonnegut at Clowes Hall, Indianapolis, April 27, 2007" (delivered by Mark Vonnegut), *Armageddon in Retrospect*, 31.

"A purpose of human life": *The Sirens of Titan*, Epilogue, 317.

"Dad, we are here to help each other": "Kurt Vonnegut at Clowes Hall," *Armageddon in Retrospect*, 30.

"Rosewater's kindness imperative": Andrews, "Vonnegut and Aesthetic Humanism," 18.

"There ain't no Jesus gonna come from the sky": Lennon, "I Found Out," track 3, *Plastic Ono Band*, Parlophone CDP 7 46770 2, compact disc. Originally released in 1970.

"The single idea": *Jailbird*, Prologue, 9. Figler attended Lake Central High School in St. John, IN, at the time he wrote to Vonnegut (Associated Press item, December 24, 1979, https://news.google.com/newspapers?nid=2519&dat=19791224&id=jPRdAAAAIBAJ&sjid=lF8NAAAAIBAJ&pg=5111,3656662&hl=en). He died in Chicago on November 8, 2015, age fifty-three (obituary, http://www.legacy.com/obituaries/nwitimes/obituary.aspx?pid=176858854).

"Love may fail": *Jailbird*, Prologue, 10.

Appendix B: Behaving Decently in an Indecent Society

Names in **bold** *are followed by where Vonnegut cited them as saints.*

"I define a saint": *Timequake*, chap. 42, 141.

He adored her [Ida Young]: *Wampeters, Foma & Granfalloons*, Preface, xiv-xv.

"national treasures": *A Man Without a Country*, chap. 2, 13.

"a man I admire": *Wampeters, Foma & Granfalloons*, 94.

"my hero": *A Man Without a Country*, chap. 8, 89.

"would most like": *Fates Worse Than Death*, chap. XVI, 165.

"more prompt than the Roman Catholic Church" and "It is enough for me": *Fates Worse Than Death*, chap. XIX, 191.

Mark Twain. *Palm Sunday*, chap. II, 31.

"It seems clear to me": *Palm Sunday*, chap. VIII, 171.

"Imagine, if you will": *Palm Sunday*, chap. VIII, 172.

Paul Moore Jr. *Fates Worse Than Death*, chap. XV, 152. His *New York Times* obituary is at https://www.nytimes.com/2003/05/02/nyregion/episcopal-bishop-paul-moore-jr-83-dies-strong-voice-social-political-issues.html.

Vonnegut did not attend [daughter Lily's baptism]: *Fates Worse Than Death*, chap. XVI, 157. ("There is a sound reason for hating me right there, but I think the main reason is cigarettes.")

"He is a very good man": *Fates Worse Than Death*, chap. XV, 152.

Robert Maslansky. *Fates Worse Than Death*, chap. XIX, 191. His *New York Times* obituary is at https://www.legacy.com/obituaries/nytimes/obituary.aspx-

?n=robert-maslansky&pid=185838004. Maslansky also fits the description of an unnamed "longtime friend, a physician who treats every sort of addict at Bellevue Hospital," whom Vonnegut calls "a saint" in *Timequake*, chap. 42, 141.

"treats every sort of addict": *Fates Worse Than Death*, chap. XIX, 191.

Jill Krementz. *Fates Worse Than Death*, chap. XIX, 191.

"If it weren't for her," "photographed the Vietnamese people," and "humane and beautiful pictures": *Fates Worse Than Death*, chap. XIX, 190.

"Your actions and behavior," and "So...is yet another saint": *Fates Worse Than Death*, chap. XIX, 191.

"Tris Coffin and his wife Margaret": *Fates Worse Than Death*, chap. XIX, 191.

Tristram and Margaret Coffin: *Fates Worse Than Death*, chap. XIX, 191. Tristram's *New York Times* and *Indianapolis Star* obituaries, respectively, are at https://www.nytimes.com/1997/06/16/us/tristram-coffin-is-dead-at-84-created-washington-spectator.html and https://www.newspapers.com/image/107645378/.

Peace Corps people: *Fates Worse Than Death*, chap. XIX, 191.

still at it: Information about the Peace Corps in Mozambique is at https://www.peacecorps.gov/mozambique/about/.

Morris Dees: *Fates Worse Than Death*, chap. XIX, 191.

allegations that Dees mistreated: The *New Yorker* article by Bob Moser is at https://www.newyorker.com/news/news-desk/the-reckoning-of-morris-dees-and-the-southern-poverty-law-center.

A clowning genius

Stanley Laurel and Oliver Hardy: *Timequake*, chap. 63, 209.

Abbie Hoffman: *Fates Worse Than Death*, chap. XIX, 189.

"frenzied sense of humor": *Fates Worse Than Death*, chap. XIX, 187.

"a clowning genius...high on": *Fates Worse Than Death*, chap. XIX, 189.

"I was utterly in sympathy" and subsequent quotes in this appendix: From "Dear Abbie" radio broadcast (1989) at Brandeis University Archives, https://ensemble.brandeis.edu/hapi/v1/contents/permalinks/t2CEw65S/view.

Bibliography

Books by Kurt Vonnegut

In order by date of original publication. The edition consulted for this book, when not the original, is cited.

Player Piano. New York: Charles Scribner's Sons, 1952. From Delacorte Press/Seymour Lawrence edition.

The Sirens of Titan. New York: Dell, 1959. From Dial Press paperback edition, New York, 2006.

Mother Night. Greenwich, CT: Fawcett, 1961. From 1966 edition, Harper & Row, New York.

Cat's Cradle. New York: Holt, Rinehart & Winston, 1963. From Delacorte Press/Seymour Lawrence edition.

God Bless You, Mr. Rosewater. New York: Holt, Rinehart & Winston, 1965. From Dell paperback edition, New York, 1974.

Welcome to the Monkey House. New York: Delacorte Press/Seymour Lawrence, 1968. From Dell paperback edition, New York, 1970.

Slaughterhouse-Five. New York: Delacorte Press/Seymour Lawrence, 1969. From Dell paperback edition, New York, 1979.

Happy Birthday, Wanda June. New York: Delacorte Press/Seymour Lawrence, 1970. From Dell paperback edition, New York, 1971.

Between Time and Timbuktu, or Prometheus 5. New York: Delacorte Press/Seymour Lawrence, 1972. From Dell paperback edition, New York, 1972.

Breakfast of Champions. New York: Delacorte Press/Seymour Lawrence, 1973. From Dell paperback edition, New York, 1976.

Bibliography

Wampeters, Foma & Granfalloons: Opinions. New York: Delacorte Press/Seymour Lawrence, 1974. From Dell paperback edition, New York, 1976.

Slapstick. New York: Delacorte Press/Seymour Lawrence, 1976. From Dial Press paperback edition, New York, 2010.

Jailbird. New York: Delacorte Press/Seymour Lawrence, 1979. From Dell paperback edition, New York, 1980.

Sun Moon Star with Ivan Chermayeff, illustrator. New York: Harper & Row, 1980.

Palm Sunday. New York: Delacorte Press, 1981.

Deadeye Dick. New York: Delacorte Press/Seymour Lawrence, 1982.

Galápagos. New York: Delacorte Press/Seymour Lawrence, 1985.

Bluebeard. New York: Delacorte Press, 1987.

Hocus Pocus. New York: Putnam's, 1990. From paperback edition, 1990.

Fates Worse Than Death: An Autobiographical Collage. New York: Putnam's, 1991. From Berkley paperback edition, New York, 1992.

Timequake. New York: Putnam's, 1997. From paperback edition, 1997.

Bagombo Snuff Box: Uncollected Short Fiction. New York, Putnam's, 1999. From Berkley paperback edition, New York, 2000.

God Bless You, Dr. Kevorkian. New York: Seven Stories Press, 1999. From Washington Square Press paperback edition, New York, 2001.

Like Shaking Hands with God with Lee Stringer. New York: Seven Stories Press, 1999.

A Man Without a Country. New York: Seven Stories Press, 2005. From Random House paperback edition, New York, 2007.

Armageddon in Retrospect and Other New and Unpublished Writings on War and Peace. New York: Putnam's, 2008.

Look at the Birdie: Unpublished Short Fiction. New York: Delacorte Press, 2009. From Dial Press paperback edition, New York, 2010,

Kurt Vonnegut: Letters, Dan Wakefield, ed. New York: Delacorte Press, 2012.

We Are What We Pretend to Be: The First and Last Works. New York: Vanguard Press, 2012.

If This Isn't Nice, What Is? Advice to the Young. New York: Seven Stories Press, 2013. From second edition, 2016.

Kurt Vonnegut Drawings. New York: Monacelli Press, 2014.

Kurt Vonnegut Complete Stories. New York: Seven Stories Press, 2017.

Pity the Reader: On Writing with Style with Suzanne McConnell. New York: Seven Stories Press, 2019. From paperback edition, 2020.

Love, Kurt: The Vonnegut Love Letters, 1941–1945, Edith Vonnegut, ed. New York: Random House, 2020.

Shorter works by Kurt Vonnegut

"Biafra: A People Betrayed," *McCall's,* April 1970. Reprinted in *Wampeters, Foma & Granfalloons,* 139-158.

"My Visit to Hell," *Parade,* January 7, 1990, 16–17. Excerpted in *Fates Worse Than Death,* chap. XVII, 168–173.

"The Very First Christmas Morning," *Better Homes & Gardens,* December 1962, pages 14, 19, 20, 24.

Untitled poem, *The New York Times Magazine,* December 21, 1969, page 5.

"Vonnegut On Trout," letter, *The Magazine of Fantasy and Science Fiction,* April 1975, 158.

Other Kurt Vonnegut sources

Cosmos Cantata. Music by Seymour Barab, text by Kurt Vonnegut. Manhattan Chamber Orchestra, Richard Auldon Clark, conductor. Kleos Classics compact disc. Pleasantville, NY: Helicon Records, 2001.

Essential Vonnegut: Interviews Conducted by Walter Miller. Caedmon Essentials compact disc. New York: HarperCollins, 2006.

Books about Kurt Vonnegut

Allen, William Rodney, ed. *Conversations with Kurt Vonnegut.* Jackson, MS: University Press of Mississippi, 1988.

Allen, William Rodney. *Understanding Kurt Vonnegut.* Columbia, SC: University of South Carolina Press, 1991.

Boon, Kevin Alexander, ed. *At Millennium's End: New Essays on the Work of Kurt Vonnegut.* Albany, NY: State University of New York Press, 2001.

Broer, Lawrence R. *Sanity Plea: Schizophrenia in the Novels of Kurt Vonnegut.* Ann Arbor, MI: UMI Research Press, 1989.

_____. *Vonnegut and Hemingway: Writers at War.* Columbia, SC: University of South Carolina Press, 2011.

Davis, Todd F. *Kurt Vonnegut's Crusade: Or, How a Postmodern Harlequin Preached a New Kind of Humanism.* Albany, NY: State University of New York Press, 2006.

Failey, Majie Alford and Those Who Knew Him. *We Never Danced Cheek to Cheek: The Young Kurt Vonnegut in Indianapolis and Beyond.* Carmel, IN: Hawthorne, 2010.

Farrell, Susan. *Critical Companion to Kurt Vonnegut: A Literary Reference to His Life and Work.* New York: Facts on File, 2008.

Handyside, Sarah. *Renovating Vonnegut: How a Black Sheep Opened the Side Door to High Society for a Band of Modern Misfits.* Self-published.

Klinkowitz, Jerome. *Vonnegut in Fact: The Public Spokesmanship of Personal Fiction.* Columbia, SC: University of South Carolina Press, 1998.

Klinkowitz, Jerome and John Somer, eds. *The Vonnegut Statement: Original Essays on the Life and Work of Kurt Vonnegut, Jr.* New York: Dell Publishing, 1973.

Leeds, Marc. *The Vonnegut Encyclopedia* (Revised and Updated Edition). New York: Delacorte Press, 2016.

McCartan, Tom, ed. *Kurt Vonnegut: The Last Interview and Other Conversations.* Brooklyn, NY: Melville House, 2011.

McMahon, Gary. *Kurt Vonnegut and the Centrifugal Force of Fate.* Jefferson, NC: McFarland, 2009.

Rackstraw, Loree. *Love as Always, Kurt: Vonnegut as I Knew Him.* Cambridge, MA: Da Capo Press, 2009.

Reed, Peter J. *The Short Fiction of Kurt Vonnegut.* Westport, CT: Greenwood Press, 1997.

Roston, Tom. *The Writer's Crusade: Kurt Vonnegut and the Many Lives of Slaughterhouse-Five.* New York: Abrams Press, 2021.

Shields, Charles J. *And So It Goes: Kurt Vonnegut, A Life.* New York: Henry Holt, 2011.

Short, Robert. *Something to Believe In: Is Kurt Vonnegut the Exorcist of Jesus Christ Superstar?* New York: Harper & Row, 1978.

Simmons, David, ed. *New Critical Essays on Kurt Vonnegut.* New York: Palgrave Macmillan, 2009.

Strand, Ginger. *The Brothers Vonnegut: Science and Fiction in the House of Magic*. New York: Farrar, Straus and Giroux, 2015.

Sumner, Gregory D. *Unstuck in Time: A Journey Through Kurt Vonnegut's Life and Novels*. New York: Seven Stories Press, 2011.

Whitehead, Julia A. *Breaking Down Vonnegut*. Hoboken, NJ: Jossey-Bass, 2022.

Yarmolinsky, Jane Vonnegut. *Angels Without Wings: How Tragedy Created a Remarkable Family*. Boston: Houghton Mifflin, 1987.

Other sources

Farmer, Philip José (as Kilgore Trout). *Venus on the Half-Shell*. New York: Dell, 1975.

Granados, Luis and Roy Speckhardt, eds. *A Jefferson Bible for the Twenty-first Century*. Washington, DC: Humanist Press, 2014.

Grayling, A. C. *Among the Dead Cities: The History and Moral Legacy of the WWII Bombing of Civilians in Germany and Japan*. New York: Walker & Company, 2006.

Hitchens, Christopher. *God is Not Great: How Religion Poisons Everything*. New York: New York: Twelve, Hatchette Group USA, 2007.

Hurston, Zora Neale. "Religion," *Dust Tracks on a Road* (New York: Harper Perennial Modern Classics, 1995), 215–226.

Jefferson, Thomas. *The Jefferson Bible*. Washington, DC: Smithsonian Books, 2011.

King, Martin Luther Jr. *Strength to Love*. Minneapolis: Fortress Press, 2010. Text © 1963 Martin Luther King Jr. First published in 1977 by Collins + World, Cleveland.

Musil, Robert. "There Must Be More to Love than Death: A Conversation with Kurt Vonnegut," *The Nation*, August 2–9, 1980. Used by permission.

Offit, Sidney, ed. "Chronology," *Vonnegut: Novels & Stories 1963–1973*, 811–832. New York: The Library of America, 2011.

Pinker, Steven. *Enlightenment Now: The Case for Reason, Science, Humanism, and Progress*. New York: Viking, 2018.

Russell, Bertrand. *Sceptical Essays*. London: Unwin Hyman, 1977. First published in 1928.

Speckhardt, Roy. *Creating Change Through Humanism*. Washington, DC: Humanist Press, 2015.

Standish, David. "*Playboy* Interview: Kurt Vonnegut, Jr.," *Playboy*, July 1973, 57–74, 214–216. Reprinted in *Wampeters, Foma & Granfalloons* and *Conversations with Kurt Vonnegut*.

Taylor, Frederick. *Dresden: Tuesday, February 13, 1945*. New York: Harper Perennial, 2005.

Vonnegut, Mark. *The Eden Express: A Memoir of Insanity*. New York: Praeger, 1975. From paperback edition by Seven Stories Press, New York, 2002.

_____. *Just Like Someone Without Mental Illness, Only More So: A Memoir*. New York: Delacorte Press, 2010.

Online sources

Kurt Vonnegut Museum and Library, https://www.vonnegutlibrary.org

Kurt Vonnegut Society, http://blogs.cofc.edu/vonnegut/

Kurt Vonneguys podcast, https://soundcloud.com/kurtvonneguys

Copyrights

Archival *Playboy* Magazine material. Copyrighted © 1973 by Playboy. Used with permission. All rights reserved.

Various materials by Kurt Vonnegut. Copyright © 1969 ("Carols for Christmas" poem), 1969, 1977 (introduction to SLAUGHTERHOUSE-FIVE), 1988 ("Light at the End of the Tunnel?"), 1977 ("Kurt Vonnegut: The Art of Fiction No. 64") by Kurt Vonnegut, Jr., used by permission of The Wylie Agency LLC.

Excerpt(s) from PLAYER PIANO by Kurt Vonnegut, copyright © 1952, 1980 by Kurt Vonnegut. Used by permission of Dell Publishing, an imprint of Random House, a division of Penguin Random House LLC. All rights reserved.

Excerpt(s) from THE SIRENS OF TITAN by Kurt Vonnegut, copyright © 1959, copyright renewed 1987 by Kurt Vonnegut, Jr. Used by permission of Dell Publishing, an imprint of Random House, a division of Penguin Random House LLC. All rights reserved.

Excerpt(s) from MOTHER NIGHT by Kurt Vonnegut, copyright © 1961, 1966 by Kurt Vonnegut, Jr. Used by permission of Dell Publishing, an imprint of Random House, a division of Penguin Random House LLC. All rights reserved.

Excerpt(s) and adaptations from CAT'S CRADLE by Kurt Vonnegut, copyright © 1963 by Kurt Vonnegut, Jr. Used by permission of Dell Publishing, an imprint of Random House, a division of Penguin Random House LLC. All rights reserved.

Excerpt(s) from GOD BLESS YOU, MR. ROSEWATER by Kurt Vonnegut, copyright © 1965 by Kurt Vonnegut, Jr. Used by permission of Dell Publishing, an imprint of Random House, a division of Penguin Random House LLC. All rights reserved.

Copyrights

Excerpt(s) from SLAUGHTERHOUSE-FIVE: A NOVEL by Kurt Vonnegut, copyright © 1968, 1969 and copyright renewed 1996, 1997 by Kurt Vonnegut, Jr. Used by permission of Dell Publishing, an imprint of Random House, a division of Penguin Random House LLC. All rights reserved.

Excerpt(s) from HAPPY BIRTHDAY, WANDA JUNE: A PLAY by Kurt Vonnegut, copyright © 1970 by Kurt Vonnegut, Jr. Used by permission of Dell Publishing, an imprint of Random House, a division of Penguin Random House LLC. All rights reserved.

Excerpt(s) from BREAKFAST OF CHAMPIONS by Kurt Vonnegut, copyright © 1973 and copyright renewed 2002 by Kurt Vonnegut, Jr. Used by permission of Dell Publishing, an imprint of Random House, a division of Penguin Random House LLC. All rights reserved.

Excerpt(s) from WAMPETERS FOMA & GRANFALLOONS by Kurt Vonnegut, copyright © 1965 1966, 1967, 1968, 1969, 1970, 1971, 1972, 1973, 1974 by Kurt Vonnegut, Jr. Used by permission of Dell Publishing, an imprint of Random House, a division of Penguin Random House LLC. All rights reserved.

Excerpt(s) from SLAPSTICK OR LONESOME NO MORE!: A NOVEL by Kurt Vonnegut, copyright © 1976 by Kurt Vonnegut. Used by permission of Dell Publishing, an imprint of Random House, a division of Penguin Random House LLC. All rights reserved.

Excerpt(s) from JAILBIRD by Kurt Vonnegut, copyright © 1979 by Kurt Vonnegut. Used by permission of Dell Publishing, an imprint of Random House, a division of Penguin Random House LLC. All rights reserved.

Excerpt(s) from PALM SUNDAY: AN AUTOBIOGRAPHICAL COLLAGE by Kurt Vonnegut, copyright © 1981 by Kurt Vonnegut. Used by permission of Dell Publishing, an imprint of Random House, a division of Penguin Random House LLC. All rights reserved.

Excerpt(s) from DEADEYE DICK by Kurt Vonnegut, copyright © 1982 by The Ramjac Corporation. Used by permission of Dell Publishing, an imprint of Random House, a division of Penguin Random House LLC. All rights reserved.

Excerpt(s) from GALAPAGOS by Kurt Vonnegut, copyright © 1985 by Kurt Vonnegut. Used by permission of Dell Publishing, an imprint of Random House, a division of Penguin Random House LLC. All rights reserved.

Excerpt(s) from BLUEBEARD by Kurt Vonnegut, copyright © 1987 by Kurt Vonnegut. Used by permission of Dell Publishing, an imprint of Random House, a division of Penguin Random House LLC. All rights reserved.

Excerpt(s) from FATES WORSE THAN DEATH by Kurt Vonnegut, copyright © 1991 by Kurt Vonnegut. Used by permission of G. P. Putnam's Sons, an imprint of Penguin Publishing Group, a division of Penguin Random House LLC. All rights reserved.

Excerpt(s) from HOCUS POCUS by Kurt Vonnegut, copyright © 1990 by Kurt Vonnegut. Used by permission of G. P. Putnam's Sons, an imprint of Penguin Publishing Group, a division of Penguin Random House LLC. All rights reserved.

Excerpt(s) from TIMEQUAKE by Kurt Vonnegut, copyright © 1997 by Kurt Vonnegut. Used by permission of G. P. Putnam's Sons, an imprint of Penguin Publishing Group, a division of Penguin Random House LLC. All rights reserved.

Excerpt(s) from BAGOMBO SNUFF BOX: UNCOLLECTED SHORT FICTION by Kurt Vonnegut, copyright © 1999 by Kurt Vonnegut. Used by permission of G. P. Putnam's Sons, an imprint of Penguin Publishing Group, a division of Penguin Random House LLC. All rights reserved.

Excerpt(s) from LOOK AT THE BIRDIE: UNPUBLISHED SHORT FICTION by Kurt Vonnegut, copyright © 2009 by The Kurt Vonnegut, Jr. Trust. Used by permission of Delacorte Press, an imprint of Random House, a division of Penguin Random House LLC. All rights reserved.

Excerpt(s) from ARMAGEDDON IN RETROSPECT by Kurt Vonnegut, copyright © 2008 by The Kurt Vonnegut, Jr. Trust. Used by permission of G. P. Putnam's Sons, an imprint of Penguin Publishing Group, a division of Penguin Random House LLC. All rights reserved.

Excerpt(s) from KURT VONNEGUT: LETTERS by Kurt Vonnegut, edited by Dan Wakefield, copyright © 2012 by The Kurt Vonnegut, Jr. Trust. Used by permission of Delacorte Press, an imprint of Random House, a division of Penguin Random House LLC. All rights reserved.

Acknowledgments

A few paragraphs into *Slaughterhouse-Five,* Kurt Vonnegut complains, "I would hate to tell you what this lousy little book has cost me in money and anxiety and time."

So what has *this* lousy little book cost *me*? Not that much money, actually.

But anxiety? Time?

I would hate to tell you.

But I'd love to tell you whom I thank for helping me get this lousy little book written and published—those without whom it would have been much tougher.

The biggest *without whom,* of course, is Kurt, still gripping my psyche, my writing, and my thinking although dead for fifteen years. So it goes.

Still alive as I write this are several other people who merit attention for their witting and unwitting contributions.

Not counting Vonnegut's own work, I turned most often to four books: *The Vonnegut Encyclopedia* by Marc Leeds (the world's preeminent Vonnegut expert), *Unstuck in Time: A Journey Through Kurt Vonnegut's Life and Novels* by Gregory D. Sumner, *And So It Goes: Kurt Vonnegut, a Life* by Charles J. Shields, and *The Brothers Vonnegut: Science and Fiction in the House of Magic* by Ginger Strand.

I have met two of these authors. I talked to Charles Shields briefly, long enough for him to sign my copy of the biography after he spoke at the Baltimore Science Fiction Society in 2012. Marc Leeds and I had communicated mostly through electronic media, then last year we had a long in-person conversation—inside a funeral home. He signed my copy of the encyclopedia as the body of a mutual friend lay several feet away. So it goes.

Another *without whom*—or rather a *without which*—is the American Humanist Association. In 2016, the AHA posted a call for someone to "curate a thematic biography of Kurt Vonnegut's humanism" that it would publish. As it happens—as it was *supposed* to happen, I hope—I was that someone.

Fred Edwords is the first AHA person I met. When he told me shortly after I was given this project that I could call myself the AHA's resident Vonnegut expert, I felt proud. Fred knew Vonnegut, but I admired him only from afar. An early editor of this book, Luis Granados, offered feedback to drafts of the first few chapters and initial advice about aspects of publishing that, through no fault of Luis, still mystify me.

After Luis retired, no less than the AHA's then-executive director, Roy Speckhardt, took up stewardship. His patience, encouragement, and support helped me persevere through a process that stretched out longer than either of us desired.

Once Roy moved on from the AHA, Deputy Director Nicole Carr and Graphic Design Manager Sharon McGill steered me to the end. Many of the final, tedious production details fell to Sharon. Both helped me feel good about the final product.

They and other dedicated folks at the AHA, by the way, disprove something Vonnegut wrote in *Timequake*: "That we have an organization, a boring business, is to let others know we are numerous. We would prefer to live our lives as Humanists and not talk about it, or think more about it than we think about breathing."

This book is my attempt to think about humanism more than I do about breathing.

Among those who read the manuscript and wrote detailed editing notes for which I am very grateful are Justin Jagoe of the Unitarian Universalist Humanist Association, my good friend Joe Krocheski, and the closest person I have to a mentor, Hugh Taft-Morales, the Leader of Ethical Culture Societies in Baltimore and Philadelphia.

In fact, the Baltimore Ethical Society is another *without which*. Hugh's talks at BES mix with Vonnegut's observations and other influences to form my own take on many matters of morality. There's a more practical connection too: Emil Volcheck, a former president of BES, tipped me off to the AHA's Vonnegut project. If I had not been involved with BES at that time, it's possible I would not have spent the past six years pecking away on a laptop until bleary-eyed many nights and weekends.

Thanks a lot, Emil.

Another way BES helped is by hosting two of my Vonnegut-related presentations. They were crafted in harmony with the preceding chapters and became testing grounds for some of the material.

The same is true of three other presentations I gave elsewhere throughout Greater Baltimore and a segment I contributed to the inaugural joint German/American commemoration of Liberation Day, marking *Germany* being freed when the Nazis were defeated. The May 8, 2021, online event was arranged by Vonnegut enthusiast Jan-Christian Petersen, co-founder of the Humanist Initiative in his hometown Husum, Schleswig-Holstein, Germany.

There might not be a more ardent Vonnegut advocate than Julia Whitehead, founder and CEO of the Kurt Vonnegut Museum and Library in Indianapolis. Julia provided useful advice and contacts along the way, and she has also written a new book, *Breaking Down Vonnegut*, for young adults.

Yes, and the KVML begat Vonnegut Baltimore, the informal name applied to a book club that was created as an extension of the museum. Our reach grew when our meetings converted to online-only during the COVID-19 pandemic. The above-mentioned Jan in Germany became a regular.

I'm reluctant to mention more names from the book club out of concern that I'll leave out someone. However, I must acknowledge John "Dūz" Dusenbury, our chief recruiter and social media communicator, whose devotion to the group seems boundless, and the late Lane Berk (1928–2017), the most remarkable person I ever met. Lane, who also was a BES member, would have relished conversations based on this book's topics and doubtless would have picked apart several of my conclusions. She was generous, driven, and challenging, and I miss her. So it goes.

Vonnegut Baltimore itself would not exist without Jane Wehrle, who with her husband, dear Al Wehrle, founded it in 2010 even before the KVML in Indianapolis opened its doors. Jane stepped away from most of her community activities and turned the club over to me in 2016. That was Al's funeral mentioned above, in July 2021. So it goes.

Wandering into my first Vonnegut Baltimore meeting as it began its second season, fortuitously discussing *Player Piano* (Lane's favorite), rekindled and deepened my reading of Vonnegut. Between the book club about my favorite writer and the humanist focus of BES, the two main elements of this book merged.

Thank you, Jane.

Hers is the second name on the dedication page. The first is second to none in my book and in my life. After I met Jean Paffenback in 2001, I acquired a second set of parents, three siblings despite being an only child, three nieces, and several more good friends. What did I give Jean? Well, multiple drafts of this book to proofread. (Any remaining mistakes are mine, not hers.)

My eternal thanks and love to you, Jean.

About the Author

Wayne Laufert, formerly a reporter/editor for a weekly newspaper, now proofreads material published by the United States government. He has been a member of the humanist Baltimore Ethical Society since 2013. A fan of Kurt Vonnegut since long before that (thanks to a perceptive high school English teacher—where have you gone, Michael McDermott?), Wayne joined the Vonnegut Baltimore book club in 2011, as it began its second season. These days he runs the club with lots of help. This is his first book.

www.ingramcontent.com/pod-product-compliance
Lightning Source LLC
Chambersburg PA
CBHW051041160426
43193CB00010B/1026